PRAISE FOR *THE SCIENTIST AND THE SPY*

"A nuanced look at some of the pawns in the U.S.-China rivalry . . . [T]hrough her reporting in China and the United States, Hvistendahl recounts the case with the vivid details and pace of a spy thriller." —*Foreign Policy*

"A compelling whodunit . . . [A] captivating and well-researched book."
—*The Wall Street Journal*

"Mara Hvistendahl's compelling account of the drama reads in parts like a spy thriller, replete with car chases, phone-tapping and aerial surveillance as agents track the shovel-carrying suspects across America." —*The Economist*

"If there is a subplot that makes this book essential reading, especially for those working in the sciences today, it is Hvistendahl's documentation of the disturbing effects that the too-vigorous pursuit of industrial spies has had on Chinese scientists and engineers in the United States." —*Science*

"[A] fascinating story, which speaks to the larger geopolitical tensions shaping our time." —*Bookpage*

"A true-crime thriller about a Chinese-born scientist's agricultural espionage."
—*Men's Journal*

"[A] compelling tale of industrial espionage . . . This engaging book has something for everyone; it can be read as a spy thriller, an examination of U.S.-China relations, or a case study of agricultural espionage." —*Library Journal*

"[A] fascinating and well-researched study . . . Those looking for insights into the current tensions with China will be rewarded."
—*Publishers Weekly* (starred review)

"Not since Alfred Hitchcock's *North by Northwest* has a cornfield produced so much excitement. . . . Hvistendahl makes industrial espionage both understandable and riveting. . . . This is a complex story, but it's presented clearly and vividly, thanks to Hvistendahl's background as a science journalist here and in China; to her exquisite pacing; and to her narrative skills. . . . Hard to put down and harder to stop thinking about."   —*Booklist* (starred review)

"Before there was a trade war, there was industrial espionage. To understand today's fight between the United States and China, you need to understand the seeds of the conflict, and this book is on the money. A nonfiction thriller for our times."   —Ian Bremmer, author of *Us vs. Them*

"*The Scientist and the Spy* is as compulsively readable as any espionage thriller and as darkly troubling as any morality tale. Told with empathy, insight, and remarkable detail, the book shines a clear light on the increasingly relentless federal investigation, its Chinese targets, and the powerful government and business interests that drive the story to its fascinating conclusion."
                    —Deborah Blum, author of *The Poison Squad*

"Mara Hvistendahl has given us an utterly original, provocative, and revealing tale of the relationship between China and the United States—and what a tale it is. Intrepid, humane, and always tough minded, she writes with the lucid precision of a science writer and the flair of a seasoned spy novelist."
                    —Evan Osnos, author of *Age of Ambition*

"Mara Hvistendahl is the most fluid of writers and the deepest of reporters, so *The Scientist and the Spy* unfurls with the style and pace of a thriller, yet it also illuminates a key American national security concern, which is the scale and scope of Chinese industrial espionage in the United States."
                    —Peter Bergen, author of *Manhunt*

"*The Scientist and the Spy* is a riveting tale for our times. It addresses some of the most important issues of our era, such as the Chinese drive to innovation in technology and industrial espionage, but does so through all-too-human characters with vulnerabilities, flaws, and often agonizing choices to make. If you enjoyed John Carreyrou's *Bad Blood*, you'll find this fascinating."
                    —Rana Mitter, author of *Modern China*

"Hvistendahl gives the corn-stealing caper the full thriller treatment, complete with evocative, cinematic detail."   —*Star Tribune*

"The author doesn't diminish the presence of Chinese spies, who have been exposed in numerous enterprises; she also digs deep into the rather nefarious business of genetic modification, which so tarnished the Monsanto name that the brand name is being retired under new ownership.... A capable work of cat-and-mouse espionage that suggests that industrial spying is just business as usual."
—*Kirkus*

"*The Scientist and the Spy* vividly illustrates that things happening in China today can be stranger and more spellbinding than in a thriller. Mara Hvistendahl's solid research and science background make it such a convincing and thought-provoking book, which is a must read in the context of the present trade war between the United States and China."   —Qui Xiaolong, author of *Death of a Red Heroine*

THE

SCIENTIST

AND THE

SPY

A TRUE STORY OF CHINA, THE FBI,

AND INDUSTRIAL ESPIONAGE

Mara Hvistendahl

RIVERHEAD BOOKS

NEW YORK

RIVERHEAD BOOKS
An imprint of Penguin Random House LLC
penguinrandomhouse.com

Copyright © 2020 by Mara Hvistendahl
Penguin supports copyright. Copyright fuels creativity, encourages
diverse voices, promotes free speech, and creates a vibrant culture. Thank you
for buying an authorized edition of this book and for complying with copyright
laws by not reproducing, scanning, or distributing any part of it in any
form without permission. You are supporting writers and allowing
Penguin to continue to publish books for every reader.

Riverhead and the R colophon are registered trademarks of
Penguin Random House LLC.

The Library of Congress has catalogued the
Riverhead hardcover edition as follows:

Names: Hvistendahl, Mara, author.
Title: The scientist and the spy : a true story of China, the FBI,
and industrial espionage / Mara Hvistendahl.
Description: 1st Edition. | New York : Riverhead, 2020. |
Includes bibliographical references and index.
Identifiers: LCCN 2019037842 (print) | LCCN 2019037843 (ebook) |
ISBN 9780735214286 (hardcover) | ISBN 9780735214309 (ebook)
Subjects: LCSH: United States. Federal Bureau of Investigation. |
Business intelligence—United States. | Confidential business information—
United States. | Spies—China. | Agricultural industries—United States.
Classification: LCC HV7561 .H85 2020 (print) |
LCC HV7561 (ebook) | DDC 364.16/8—dc23
LC record available at https://lccn.loc.gov/2019037842
LC ebook record available at https://lccn.loc.gov/2019037843

First Riverhead hardcover edition: February 2020
First Riverhead trade paperback edition: February 2021
Riverhead trade paperback ISBN: 9780735214293

Printed in the United States of America
1 3 5 7 9 10 8 6 4 2

BOOK DESIGN BY MEIGHAN CAVANAUGH

For Aksel

Once, when all the maize was planted,
Hiawatha, wise and thoughtful,
Spake and said to Minnehaha,
To his wife, the Laughing Water:
"You shall bless to-night the cornfields,
Draw a magic circle round them,
To protect them from destruction,
Blast of mildew, blight of insect,
Wagemin, the thief of cornfields,
Paimosaid, who steals the maize-ear!"

—Henry Wadsworth Longfellow,
    "Part XIII: Blessing the Cornfields,"
    The Song of Hiawatha

CONTENTS

THE
SCIENTIST
AND THE
SPY

ONE

FALL 2011

Deputy Cass Bollman sped toward the farm, the bright morning sun glaring through the window of his patrol car. To the north was the town of Bondurant, Iowa, where newly built houses huddled together on treeless lots, churches dominated street corners, and the marquee outside Dino's Storage read AVOID ALL NEGATIVE TALK. To the south was a Tetris puzzle of cornfields. God-fearing citizens on one side, vast fields on the other, and two-lane 70th Avenue running like a ruler between the two. A few miles east of town, Bollman steered the patrol car toward the corn.

The fields were a few weeks from harvest, and the corn stretched over seven feet tall. Central Iowa had blossomed into the lingering, pleasant days that make its winter hibernation bearable. Just a few minutes earlier, Bollman had been about to take a coffee break at the Git 'n' Go when an alert came over the radio for an incident out by 96th Street. *South of here walking westbound there is an Asian male wearing a suit walking through a farm field. He was dropped off. Nature of incident: suspicious.*

Eighteen years in the Polk County Sheriff's Office had taught Bollman to suspend judgment. Bondurant was a sleepy place. Its dramas centered on grass clippings left in the street and holes dug in lawns by stray farm cats. But still Bollman saw his share of action. The area he patrolled included the outskirts of Des Moines, and in addition to making traffic stops, he had worked murders and negotiated for hostages. Once he pursued a meth-fueled driver in a car chase that ended with the driver's girlfriend being flung to her death in a grisly crash. Best-case scenario, he thought, the man in the field was simply an unusually well-dressed farmworker whom a neighbor had mistaken for an intruder. Worst-case scenario, the man was burying a body.

Bollman slowed the patrol car to a stop in a grassy clearing alongside a drainage ditch. About a hundred yards into the field was a thin, neatly dressed man. In the distance, row upon row of stalks lined up like infantry. The corn between the man and the road had been cleared, allowing Bollman a direct line of sight. To his left was a cheery stucco dwelling with a broad veranda and a white picket fence encircling a pasture for grazing horses. Two other deputies arrived around the same time and were on their way out to talk to the man, so Bollman walked over to the house to chat with the farmer who owned the land.

The farmer worked this land with his brother, planting part of it for their own use and part of it under contract with Monsanto. He told Bollman that he'd been out doing his morning rounds when he spotted the unfamiliar man walking on the Monsanto plot.

The corn the farmer grew for Monsanto was genetically modified inbred seed that the company used to produce commercial hybrids, which were sold at great profit to farmers for the next year's planting and eventually turned into food or fuel: perhaps Doritos, perhaps ethanol. The seeds had been spliced with genes that made them resistant to certain pesticides—most likely the Monsanto weed killer Roundup—allowing the farmers who eventually purchased the commercial offspring to freely spray for weeds or insects without killing their crop. The company considered them valuable intellectual property. Monsanto kept the locations of such contract plots secret and enforced this secrecy through aggressive lawsuits. Unlike the fields where farmers grew commercial corn, which sported small guideposts that doubled as advertisements for seed lines (Pioneer 3394, DeKalb 62–55), the Monsanto plot was unmarked. Even the farmer himself knew little about the seed growing on his land.

For part of the season, that was sufficient protection. Only locals who watched the Monsanto truck arrive to measure growth or spray pesticides knew that certain fields grew proprietary inbred seeds. The inbred seeds were planted in a pattern, with one or two rows of seeds designated as "males" for every four to six rows of "females." Then, in mid-summer, as the commercial corn in the surrounding fields stood tall, Monsanto sent in machines to detassel the female rows of corn, shearing off their yellow, pollen-laden crowns in a mass spaying, leaving only the male plants intact. Soon after, the males fertilized the females, and then the company mowed down the male rows of corn. The field now looked like a buzz cut with lines shaved into it, making it easy for outsiders to identify. And the man looked like an outsider.

It was his face that the farmer had noticed first. The man had angular features, with a broad forehead framed by a receding flop of black hair. But more important was the way those features combined in the farmer's mind to cancel out other details. Bondurant, population 3,860, is 97 percent white. The man was not.

The man walked with his head down, the farmer reported, as if he were scanning the ground. After considering the man's race, the farmer thought about his clothes—khakis, dress shoes, a short-sleeve collared shirt. And he'd been dropped off by a gray SUV, which had then driven away. *Why the hell did the car leave?* The farmer knew that after the detasseling process, a few stray inbred ears—what in the industry were called escapes—often lingered on the ground. Thinking that something suspicious might be at hand, he called his wife, who worked as a police officer one town over, and she called Polk County dispatch, which sent out the alert that blared over Bollman's radio. At some point in this telephone chain, the stranger's business-casual outfit became a suit, and his race became his defining attribute.

As Bollman and the farmer stood outside the farmhouse talking, the gray SUV the farmer had seen dropping the man off zoomed past.

"Well," the farmer said. "There it is."

THE OTHER DEPUTIES were still talking with the man in the field, so Bollman got back behind the wheel of his patrol car and sped off to pursue the SUV. Flicking on his lights, he soon fell in behind the vehicle. He could see the backs of two heads. The lights worked; a quarter mile or so from the house, the SUV pulled over to the side of the road. The two men remained still as Bollman approached the driver's window.

Bollman asked the men for identification. The driver was Robert Mo, a man identified on his license as Hailong Mo. He was forty-two and lived in Boca Raton, Florida. His head was shaved, and he had broad cheeks that tapered to an undefined jaw. His companion was an older man with taut lips that shifted into a nervous grin. He was identified on his Chinese passport as Li Shaoming. The man from the field was named Wang Lei.

Robert Mo did the talking, and he was utterly polite.

He explained that his two companions were visiting from China, where they researched agronomy. The men were driving across the Midwest looking at crops.

That they would come to Iowa made sense. Corn was big business, both for the state and for the world. Corn is in the animal feed that fattens cows and chickens, and in the high-fructose corn syrup that sweetens ketchup, soda, and salad dressing. Over 90 percent of the starch and 56 percent of the sweeteners in the American diet come from corn. Fifty-six is also the percentage of a McDonald's chicken nugget that is corn. For many years the fungus that produces penicillin was grown in a corn by-product, and many cosmetics contain corn. Altogether, the crop covers ninety-three million acres in the United States, a swath nearly the size of California. And Iowa, which produces more corn than any other state, is the center of the industry.

Bollman wondered, though, how much could you actually learn by just looking at a field? To Robert Mo he said, "Have you been up to Iowa State and talked to them at the university?"

It was a fair question. Iowa State was a big land grant university with a strong agriculture program, a sort of mecca for the study of corn. At football games in Ames, it was not unusual to see a man in a corncob costume leading cheers. It also received millions of dollars in grants from Monsanto for endowed professorships, large-scale research projects, and graduate student fellowships, so for people looking to learn about Monsanto seed, it was not a bad choice.

But Mo's answer was vague.

Soon Bollman's colleagues showed up with Wang Lei in the back of their patrol car. Bollman returned to his vehicle to run a basic background check. It came up clean on all three men.

He let the men off with a warning. "If you're going to be on somebody's property, you need to let them know," he said.

Before the men sped off, one of the other deputies recommended speaking with some local farmers with extensive crop knowledge. Maybe one of them could help the Chinese visitors with their agronomy research, he suggested. In Iowa, people were nice almost to a fault, especially when it came to an interest in corn.

After the men left, Bollman turned to the friendly deputy. "You know, you don't necessarily need to be telling him that," he said. "About farms to visit."

"Oh, these guys are OK," his colleague replied.

"Something doesn't seem right here," Bollman insisted. "Why haven't they gone up to Iowa State?"

Later that day, the memory of the incident began to bug him. He filed a report, just in case. He filled in the lines at the top of the form, leaving other identifiers blank:

```
Type of Suspicious Activity: TRESPASSING IN FARM FIELD
Name: HAILONG MO
Race: ASIAN
```

TWO

FALL 2011

R obert Mo gripped the wheel of the SUV as it barreled away
from Bondurant. Wang Lei and Dr. Li were subdued. A run-in
with sheriff's deputies was not what they needed right now.
Robert was calm under pressure, and he played the part of a curious
professor well. He once *was* a professor, after all. The Iowa deputy
who had stopped his rental car near the field did not seem overly
concerned. Robert had even asked, *Did we do anything wrong?* And
the officer had said no: nothing serious.

But although Robert had so far emerged from such incidents
unscathed, he'd had some close calls. A few months before the Monsanto field encounter, a farmer had spotted him and Wang Lei near
a field planted with inbred seed belonging to the company DuPont
Pioneer. Wang Lei, who had been digging in the field, had bounded
into the car, red-faced and heart pumping, as Robert sped away
through a ditch, his foot heavy on the gas. Who knew how long his
luck would last?

When Robert took a job with the Beijing agricultural company

Dabeinong (DBN) five years earlier, it had seemed like a safe move. As a low-level researcher living in Miami with two unmarketable PhDs, he had struggled to support his growing family. After becoming the company's international business manager, he pulled in more than $100,000 a year. DBN was then mainly a broker of animal feed, and tasked with pursuing the company's legitimate business interests in the United States, Robert helped source feed additives, talked to experts in pork transportation, and worked hard on a bid to acquire a feed company in the Netherlands.

But then his safe job spiraled out of control into something he barely recognized. His duties grew to include tasks that were illegal in the United States, if tacitly encouraged in China. For some time now Robert had complained to Dr. Li that the seed mission was risky.

Robert's kids were U.S. citizens who were more Floridian than Chinese, and he couldn't just flee with his family to China if things got bad. And today he had almost been caught.

ROBERT MO WAS BORN on February 20, 1969, in south central China's Sichuan province. The second of four children, he grew up in a tiny mountain village called Daichi that was about a day's journey from the provincial capital of Chengdu. Daichi might as well have been at the edge of the Earth, and as the Cultural Revolution wrenched through China in his toddler years, that was mostly an asset. Even as dueling factions of Red Guards commandeered tanks from munitions factories and waged bloody battles in city streets, life in the village for Robert and his siblings was peaceful, its rhythm dictated by the seasons and the harvest.

Robert's father, Mo Shifang, was a survey engineer in a coal mine who inhabited a world of jagged walls and brackish water. His mother, He Fangxun, was a rural doctor who tended to the miners, treating the maladies caused by the black dust lining their lungs. His parents' careers exposed them to suffering and death, but at home they were loving and playful with their children. One of Robert's earliest memories involved the birth of his sister, Mo Yun, when he was three years old. As his mother tended to the baby, his father watched Robert and his two other siblings. Mo Shifang had been a gymnast at the university, and he delighted the kids by flipping into a handstand and walking upside down. His sister's entrance into the world carried for Robert an aura of magic.

Cooking oil, rice, and meat were rationed, but living as they did in a fertile swath of the countryside, the family never went hungry. They raised chickens and rabbits and fished in a river, and Robert shot down sparrows with a slingshot and delivered them to a neighbor, who fed the birds to her cats and gave him apples in exchange. On fishing outings he helped his father reel in the catch, which his mother turned into a fragrant stew.

The relative lack of political strife in Daichi left Robert and his siblings plenty of time to play. As Mo Yun grew into a playmate, Robert fashioned toys out of scraps of metal and wood. Over hours on the school track he mastered the long jump, and in his spare time he played ping-pong and read. He studied Chinese classics and the patriotic "red" literature sanctioned by the state, but he had a special affection for detective books.

Despite their modest circumstances, Robert was proud of his parents. Near the fields in Daichi was a deep manure pit that the villagers used for fertilizing crops. One day Robert was with his mother when a young boy fell into the pit and started flailing about in the potent stew of rotting compost, feces, and rainwater. Robert

watched as she dived into the pit to yank the boy out, then pressed
her hands on his trunk, forcing black-green water out of his mouth.
Another time, an engineer who worked under Robert's father's su-
pervision rode his new bicycle to the vegetable market. While the
engineer wasn't looking, a thief swiped it. His father asked around
until he located the thief, then triumphantly retrieved the bicycle.
Robert thought with pride that his father was a true crime-busting
detective, just like in the spy fiction he read. His parents' willingness to help others impressed him and, he felt, shaped his own personality. As his mother and father went, so would he.

ROBERT'S LOVE FOR HIS PARENTS did not extend to the name they
gave him at birth: Mo Tian, 莫天. "Tian" was a nice enough word,
meaning "heaven" or "sky," but his well-meaning parents had not
thought about how it could be distorted by cruel children when
combined with "Mo," which can mean "nothing" or "none." His
classmates christened him Mo Tian Mo Di, 末天末地—No Heaven
No Earth. That sometimes morphed into Wu Fa Wu Tian, which
translates as Without Law or Heaven. By age seven, Robert was sick
of being branded an outlaw, so he changed his name.

He chose Hailong, which means "sea dragon." Mythical sea
dragons, he knew, could swim like fish and fly like birds. They were
transient, mobile. Gliding on water and soaring through the air,
they could propel themselves up and away from whatever challenges
life threw their way. They did not disobey the law. They were simply above it.

The name proved fitting, because in the years that followed,
Robert and rules did not always agree. At Southwest University in
Chongqing, where he studied heat power engineering, he became

enamored with American-style democracy. It was a heady time for science in China, when many researchers advocated political reform. The liberal ideas of physicist Fang Lizhi helped inspire student activism, and as students occupied Beijing's Tiananmen Square in the spring of 1989, similar protests sprang up around China. Robert joined a march to the mayor's office in Chongqing. In his version of events, administrators removed him from the school's honor roll in retaliation. (Fang, meanwhile, took refuge in the U.S. embassy in Beijing and was eventually shuttled out of China to the United Kingdom.)

After college Robert moved eastward to earn a master's degree, and then in 1993 he started his first PhD, at the Chinese Academy of Sciences' Institute of Engineering Thermophysics in Beijing. He specialized in the mechanics of boiling, spending his days happily observing the formation of bubbles in liquids, watching as tiny globules of air spread over the surface of water.

In his free time, Robert met friends for dinner, laughing over steaming vats of Mongolian hot pot, or slapped down tiles in raucous rounds of mahjong. One day at a friend's wedding he was drawn to a woman who was finishing her graduate degree. Her name was Li Ping. They fell in love and married in 1998. Soon after, Li Ping rechristened herself Carolyn, and they moved to America so that Robert could pursue a second PhD at Kansas State University.

Manhattan, Kansas, turned out to bear little resemblance to the island in New York City for which it was named. Robert marveled at how locals heeded stop signs even when no one was around. Nonetheless, puffed up with democratic ideals, Robert was full of hope for his prospects in the land of opportunity. As the number of American-born children studying science and engineering had slumped, the United States depended on a steady influx of researchers and students from other countries to power its labs. The man who knew the darkness of the mines and the voodoo of rural medicine was determined to achieve a comfortable life in America.

Robert arrived in the United States as the Chinese Communist Party was redoubling efforts to influence ethnic Chinese researchers living overseas. Many of these scholars had, like Robert, supported the Tiananmen protests from afar, by providing safe havens and funding for dissidents back in China. That worried party leaders, who expanded the organization that kept tabs on overseas scholars. But Robert was mostly unaffected by this shift. In the end, it was the academic job market that deflated his ideals.

In 2003, after finishing his PhD, he took an untenured research position in a thermodynamics lab at Florida International University in Miami. Any enjoyment he felt in practicing the skills he spent years acquiring was offset by his salary: around $40,000 a year. He and Carolyn scraped by for a while, renting a small apartment near campus. Then Carolyn got pregnant, and the apartment seemed even smaller. Their arguments turned bitter, at one point inviting a visit from the police. Around the time that Carolyn gave birth to a daughter—a small person forever linking them to the United States—the center that Robert worked for was reorganized, and he found himself out of a job.

Robert wanted a paycheck that could cover a mortgage on a real family home, and he knew that it would be hard to find another research position in thermodynamics. When he confided his troubles to his sister, Mo Yun, back in Beijing, she lined up the position at DBN. Robert knew next to nothing about agriculture, but Mo Yun's connections overrode other concerns. Her husband was DBN's CEO—a billionaire named Shao Genhuo whose business interests had earned him a spot on the Forbes China rich list.

By the time Carolyn had a second child, a son, Robert had transformed himself into the family's stable breadwinner. In 2009, three years after he started at DBN, Robert had enough for a down payment on a five-bedroom house in a nice part of Boca Raton, Florida.

The new house had blush-colored paint and a neat tiled roof, and it looked out on a cul-de-sac dotted with basketball hoops and palm trees. He and Carolyn joined a local Chinese Christian church and settled into a rhythm with their children. Carolyn became a U.S. citizen. Robert never bothered to apply. Giving up his Chinese passport would have made travel to Beijing more complicated.

Their house was walking distance from two golf courses and a country club, and the elegant office building where he rented a suite on behalf of DBN offered a view of a second country club. Working for a large agricultural corporation, he had the whole package: nice house, supportive community, and, when he wasn't traveling around the Midwest, plenty of free time for tennis, chess matches, and gardening.

Determined to prove his worth at work and show that he deserved the job he had won through nepotism, Robert happily learned about the pork industry and the business of sourcing animal feed. He worked closely with Mo Yun, who had a PhD in veterinary science and oversaw DBN's research and technology division. At first, his only regret was not joining DBN sooner. But that didn't last.

THE RISKY TRIPS that Robert and other DBN employees made to Midwestern fields had their origins in a single problem: China didn't produce enough grain to feed its people. Like other Chinese agricultural companies, DBN depended on a steady flow of imported corn and soy for its animal feed business. That made its executives, and Chinese leaders more generally, vulnerable to the whims of foreign suppliers. An increase in U.S. corn prices could have a direct impact on Chinese food security—and on DBN's profits.

Shao Genhuo, Robert's brother-in-law, had founded DBN in a Beijing apartment in 1993 with less than three thousand dollars in capital. As China grew wealthier and people ate more meat—braised pork belly, Peking duck, cumin-spiced beef—demand for grain-based animal feed surged. The Chinese central government helped out with its campaign to "modernize" people's diets with meat produced on large industrial farms, and Shao, who was the son of farmers, became wealthy. That had been enough for a while. Then the farmer's son watched as others' riches accumulated at a rate far faster than his. The company's margins could be even higher, Shao saw, if the company went into business growing corn itself.

In 2001, he created a subsidiary to focus on seed breeding. In Chinese the company was called Jinse Nonghua, which loosely translates to "golden agriculture." Kings Nower was an awkward anglicization of that name, and in choosing it, Shao and other executives evidently did not consider whether it had cachet for a Western ear. The goal was not to reach U.S. farmers, though. It was to dominate developing world markets—starting with China.

Despite the Chinese government's best efforts to give local companies an advantage, farmers still tended to favor international players like Monsanto and DuPont Pioneer. A few breakthrough seed lines might allow DBN and Kings Nower to edge out the foreign competition in China. And yet success was far from guaranteed. There were thousands of Chinese seed companies—by one count 8,700—and none of them had successfully managed to create seed lines that rivaled those of the international seed outfits. Developing an elite seed line required a good supply of inbred seed lines, which most Chinese companies didn't have, and the process took years and demanded both talent and money.

Kings Nower shared an office with its parent company in Beijing, and the two companies' operations were mostly indistinguishable. Dr. Li was put in charge of the seed subsidiary. Robert's boss had a peasant's face, with a prominent mole on his right cheek, and a peasant's coarse humor. He was prone to rash ideas, and not long after Robert started working at DBN, he dreamed up a shortcut that avoided years of research. With Robert's help, Kings Nower would swipe top-notch seeds from American seed companies and then reverse engineer the seed lines.

Robert knew that this was illegal under U.S. law, and he made his discomfort clear early on. When he and his sister began talking of targeting American seed lines, Robert wrote Mo Yun that he needed to be careful in order to "drive to somewhere unseen." She agreed. It was, of course, her family's safety that was on the line— not just that of her brother but that of her husband as well. But then Mo Yun cut back on her work with DBN to spend more time with her children. That left Dr. Li fully in charge of the seed operation. Wang Lei, Kings Nower's vice president, mostly deferred to him on business decisions.

Dr. Li sought the components for one hundred seed lines. In some cases, he wanted as many as five thousand samples of a single strain of corn. Robert pleaded with him that a hundred varieties were too many. Although reverse engineering the seeds was theoretically quicker than developing them from scratch, the process of re-creating even one seed line still could take years. But Dr. Li didn't listen. So Robert shipped thousands of seeds back to China, then lived in fear that they would be seized en route by customs officials. He flew from Florida to Iowa and back, wasting time he could have spent with his children or tending the mango and avocado trees in his backyard. Dr. Li always wanted more samples. Robert could send two thousand seeds from a particular seed line to China and still it wouldn't be enough.

In service of the scheme, Robert logged long days driving across the Midwest, burning through tanks of gas, sneaking nervously into fields. Robert worried that someone would notice and report him for suspicious behavior. And what could he do in the face of all of that wide-open land, the roads that shot straight through to the horizon? Cornfields may be where the Midwest hides its secrets—illicit affairs, crop circle hoaxes, covertly seeded marijuana plants—but to Robert, the cover that was provided by seven-foot-tall crops was scant reassurance.

During periods of intensive activity, like planting time, Dr. Li thanked Robert for his hard work. But at other moments his boss could be overly critical, even dismissive. Robert heard that he went around the office in Beijing saying that Robert was afraid of being escorted back to China as a business spy.

Dr. Li would have known that the risk of this happening was very real. He had, no doubt, heard of the case of former Boeing engineer Greg Chung, which was followed by the Chinese press. After the FBI found hundreds of thousands of pages of sensitive documents stashed in a crawl space beneath Chung's house, he was charged with stealing secrets connected to the Delta IV booster rocket and the U.S. space shuttle. In 2010, at the age of seventy-four, Chung was sentenced to fifteen years in federal prison.

But Dr. Li was unsympathetic to the dangers that Robert faced. If Robert was in fact deported as a business spy, Dr. Li had joked, at least the company would save money on flights.

When a colleague in Beijing relayed this anecdote to Robert in an online chat one day, Robert's response was bold. *Let Dr. Li come to the United States*, he told his co-worker. Let him face the guards patrolling the seed companies' parking lots. Let him see the ominous DO NOT ENTER signs. Let him read all the news in America about people being shot by a trigger-happy vigilante. See if he'd be scared.

Now Dr. Li was here in the rental car, his smug grin for once wiped off his face by their run-in with the authorities in Iowa. And yet he still wanted to continue with the plan.

THREE

2014

When I first came across the story of Robert Mo, I was working as a journalist in Shanghai. I researched and wrote articles from a home office on the seventh story of an apartment tower. From my desk I could hear the drone of traffic below and watch as tiny figures on motor scooters zoomed between cars, tempting fate. One afternoon, an article on my screen captured my attention and made it hard to look away. DESIGNER SEED THOUGHT TO BE LATEST TARGET BY CHINESE read the headline in *The New York Times*. The story described a man found in a cornfield in Iowa, in what the article called "an unusual and brazen scheme to undercut expensive, time-consuming research."

By then I had lived in Shanghai for two stints totaling eight years. Before I became a foreigner in a city of twenty-three million, I spent my childhood in the wide-open country of southern Minnesota and central Iowa. In the Midwest, corn and not people were the backdrop. As a child I ran through corn mazes, visited roadside monstrosities constructed from corncobs, and sat on the porch during barbecues, shucking husks into paper bags. As a teenager I sneaked off to cornfields to party. I knew that corn's role in American society is more complex than is often portrayed—that high-fructose corn syrup contributes to the high rate of obesity in the United States, for example—but nonetheless the case of the man in the field awakened some latent nostalgia in me. I was fascinated by how it spanned my country of residence and the place of my birth, and by the fact that it purportedly combined mundane corn seed with the cloak-and-dagger drama of espionage.

I worked for the journal *Science*, which meant that I spent my days interviewing Chinese researchers and contemplating China's technological rise. Tales of industrial espionage had always lurked in the background. I had heard Western businesspeople try to outdo one another at dinner. *You know the American company whose Chinese supplier set up an identical factory right across the street? The joint venture partner who made off with the technical plans six months into the partnership? The guy who comes around with auto parts that fell off the truck from factories in Taiwan?* Usually these stories were laced with cynicism. I never heard anyone suggest a solution to this technological drain. But now, suddenly, industrial espionage was one of the top priorities of the Federal Bureau of Investigation. I watched from afar as federal prosecutors charged a string of scientists, engineers, and entrepreneurs. Some of the technologies at issue had military applications, but others were more prosaic. Working closely with corporations, U.S. attorneys brought cases involving wind turbines, pharmaceuticals, the whitener used to brighten the creme in Oreo cookies—dozens of cases in all, with prison terms extending to more than ten years. The United States government had declared war on Chinese trade secrets theft.

For decades, countries all over the globe had relied on professional intelligence agencies to glean nuggets of critical importance. Compared with this more conventional spying, industrial espionage was a free-for-all. To succeed, it wasn't necessary to be trained as a spy. Trade secrets theft could be perpetrated by defense agencies, private companies, and profit-minded individuals alike. Pundits alleged that the United States and China were locked in a new cold war, and that technology and research was its major battleground. Stealing the color white was a national security threat, they contended, because it was an assault on American innovation and jobs. America, it was said, faced a new kind of spy.

I came to wonder: Were criminal prosecutions really the best way to safeguard American ingenuity? Could arresting researchers from the country responsible for much of America's scientific talent backfire? And what did this crackdown mean for relations between my home country and the one where I had lived most of my adult life?

The answers to these questions only grew more complex as I delved into the story of the stolen seeds and the Chinese scientist at its center.

I MOVED TO SHANGHAI IN 2004, at the age of twenty-four. I arrived as China was in the throes of a remarkable scientific rise. The economic reforms that had transformed a stagnant state-owned economy into a vibrant consumer market were closely linked to funding for science and technology. The first major boost to research had come back in 1986. That was the year China adopted the 863 Program, which allocated funding for spaceflight and information technology at a time when for many families in the Chinese countryside a refrigerator was a luxury. In the decades that followed, spending on research and development shot up. Between 1991 and 2016, it grew by a factor of almost thirty.

In 2006, China overtook Japan to become number two in the world for spending on research and development, behind only the United States. China tends to dominate metrics because its population is so large, but there is no doubt that the country has become a center of high-quality research. As Chinese researchers publish in English and reach a broader audience, citations in international journals have skyrocketed. Today China ranks first in the world in the number of science and engineering papers published in international journals and second in international patent filings. It claims several of the world's fastest supercomputers, as well as the world's first quantum communications satellite. An institute in Beijing has proposed building the world's largest supercollider, a project that if approved could lead to significant breakthroughs in physics.

As a reporter, I saw this transformation up close. Science journalists in the United States typically specialize in one area. They might cover infectious diseases or particle physics or climate change. China was developing so quickly, and the hunger for Chinese stories was so great, that I had to cover it all at once. I visited biosafety facilities where virologists studied highly pathogenic flu, tissue engineering labs where scientists saved lives by building artificial organs for transplant, and construction sites where archaeologists rushed to collect artifacts before they met the wrecking ball. (A building boom can be a godsend for researchers whose careers depend on digging.) At one point, I traveled to Guizhou province, one of the poorest regions of China, to tour the planned site of the largest radio dish telescope in the world. When I arrived, my astronomer host drove me to a ridge overlooking a verdant valley, where we looked out at a scene straight out of a classical Chinese painting. On

the other side of the depression, mist obscured the peaks of lime-
stone karst cliffs. The plan, he explained, was to build a dish covering an area the size of thirty football fields into the valley, where it
would be cradled by the surrounding ridge. The telescope was completed in 2016, and since then astronomers have used it to discover
eighty-four new pulsars.

Much of the progress I witnessed in my job with *Science* was due
to the efforts of earnest, well-meaning scientists. Many of the researchers I interviewed were accomplished scholars who had studied in the United States, Europe, or Japan. An unspoken urgency
marked their work. No one kept to normal business hours. Sources
would frequently call me on the weekend, or at eleven on a week-
night. On reporting trips, my hosts would often plan programs that
lasted well into the evening. Once, I sat in a yurt in Inner Mongolia
with a paleobotanist who was wooing the local officials he depended
on for permits, watching as waiters slow-roasted an entire lamb. For
the most part, I enjoyed these assignments. At a time when much of
Chinese society was obsessed with making money, nerdy scientists
made for refreshing company. On the same trip where the lamb was
roasted, the paleobotanist discovered a new fossil. He generously
named it after me: *Aphlebia hvistendahliae.*

But that wasn't the whole story. Lucrative incentives and readily
available grant money bred corruption as well as excellence. As
money for science increased, a portion was wasted on luxury cars,
bribes, and mistresses. In the city of Foshan, Guangdong, science
administrators reportedly pocketed 30 percent of the funds that
they handled. While six months pregnant, I spent a few days reporting on biomedical research in a city outside Shanghai. As I
climbed into the van that would take me back to Shanghai, the

Chinese Communist Party secretary from the university gave me an envelope filled with cash. When I refused and handed it back to him, he threw it through the open window of the van, where it landed on my belly, and instructed the driver to pull away. I later concocted an excuse to meet the official so that I could return the money. At that meeting, he tried to give me a second bribe.

China's central government places a high priority on strategic breakthroughs, no matter how they are achieved. Science and technology plans are treated as critical directives, and Chinese universities pay bonuses to researchers who publish in top journals. No wonder, then, that some companies hire hackers to tunnel into the servers of their American competitors and swipe designs for their latest product, or that some researchers are tempted to steal work from elsewhere, particularly if it has commercial potential. Real research takes time. Theft is expedient—especially if there is little chance of getting caught.

Chinese leaders are open about their interest in developing technologies in strategic sectors by any means possible. Party leaders have long charted a goal of "indigenous innovation," or assimilating and adapting imported technologies in order to edge out foreign companies in the Chinese consumer market. A U.S. Chamber of Commerce report called one Chinese state document on indigenous innovation "a blueprint for technology theft on a scale the world has never seen before." Finding technologies and know-how that can be brought back to China is also a major goal of the United Front Work Department, an arm of the Chinese Communist Party that focuses on expanding the country's influence and neutralizing potential opposition forces.

At first, the seed story seemed to combine both of these themes:

the frenzied drive toward success and the willingness to take short-cuts. Robert Mo was an internationally trained scientist, a man who spent his twenties buried in arcane research only to be tempted toward vice later in life. But as I learned more, I realized that the story was not just about the theft of corn seed and how it served China, but also about the way that the United States reacted to that theft. If China is shaped by the dueling forces of copying and innovation, America is locked in its own internal struggle, between openness and security. And if China is an environment where intellectual property can be freely stolen, the United States is one where it is aggressively guarded by ever-larger corporations. In the case of the corn heist, the effort to protect an American product would cast two of the world's most powerful agriculture companies in the role of victims.

FOR U.S. COMPANIES that are deeply invested in China, intellectual property theft presents a thorny challenge. An array of policies limits non-Chinese companies' market access while encouraging them to transfer technologies. Some foreign companies have been pressured into setting up local research and development centers. Others are in awkward embraces with joint venture partners that threaten to drive them out of business.

Among foreign businesspeople working in the country, it was a widely held belief that China had reneged on the commitments to free trade it made when it joined the World Trade Organization in 2001. Incidents of industrial espionage merely added to their complaints. Randal Phillips, the former chief representative for the CIA in China, became a consultant with the Mintz Group in Beijing after retiring from intelligence. "I don't think we've ever seen anything like it," he told me, referring to China's technology transfer efforts. "It's brilliantly mercantilistic."

Before the FBI got involved, enforcing intellectual property rights in China entailed a great deal of creativity. Pioneer executives, for example, tried to deal with the situation by developing a seed line called Pioneer 335 exclusively for the Chinese market. Agricultural supply stores promptly filled with counterfeits. Duped farmers complained that seeds marketed as Pioneer 335 sometimes yielded putrid, black ears of corn. Western companies faced with counterfeiting issues often hired private detectives or risk consultants to identify the culprits and strong-arm them into compliance. The detectives would lean on the Chinese police to raid factories, but it could take multiple busts before they saw any results. Alex Theil, head of the investigative agency Harvest Moon, said that his basic strategy was to "push and push until it's too much trouble to battle my company."

Theil mentioned the cautionary tale of the Chery QQ, a cute, compact hatchback produced by Chinese auto manufacturer Chery. When it debuted in May 2003, General Motors' management balked. The vehicle was nearly indistinguishable from GM-Daewoo's Matiz, which is marketed in China as the Chevy Spark. It wasn't just that the Chinese auto company's name, Chery, resembles Chevy. The doors of the two cars were interchangeable. GM sued in Chinese court, and the case ended in a settlement. At the time, Theil was director of Asia-Pacific investigations for General Motors. He said he knew the man who stole the designs, but taking further action against him was nearly impossible. "The difficulty in pursuing it is, where are you going to get the evidence? The car fits on a thumb drive."

In the end, there was no surefire way for companies to escape technological theft. This was underscored by a conversation I had with a Hong Kong lawyer named Joe Simone, who prefers the moniker "Mr. IP." Simone runs a small consultancy called SIPS that advises businesses on protecting trade secrets in China. He told me that American start-ups that raised money on Kickstarter for product launches often found their ideas swiped by a Chinese rival even before the money from backers had paid out.

But concern about industrial espionage also obscured a broader truth. While executives at multinationals have not gotten as rich as they would have liked in China, over the past few decades many have turned considerable profits. KFC has nearly six thousand outlets in China. Starbucks has more than three thousand, and at one point it was opening a new store in the country every fifteen *hours*. Even with regulations restricting its market access in China, at the time that I read the *New York Times* article about Robert Mo, Pioneer claimed 12 percent of the country's highly fragmented corn seed market. Despite the theft of its designs for the Matiz, General Motors sells more cars in China than it does in the United States. Pretty much the only people who have not made money on China's rise are American wage workers and farmers, starting with the Iowans who grow inbred seed. Nor would they be helped by efforts to find the Chinese man accused of swiping corn.

FOUR

SUMMER-FALL 2011

Two months before Deputy Bollman stopped the SUV near a Monsanto contract field, FBI Special Agent Mark Betten drove out to DuPont Pioneer's headquarters with two other agents. It was a blistering hot Thursday just before the Fourth of July, the sort of day when no one wants to be in a hot car on the interstate. But the agents had work to do, so Mark steered the group to Johnston, a town ten miles north of Des Moines that revolves around Pioneer, eventually arriving at a low-slung brick building crowned by gigantic images of corn. Pioneer was the first commercial hybrid seed outfit in the United States. Even though it had been bought by the chemical conglomerate DuPont in 1999, it still clung to lore about feeding America.

Mark had the tanned skin of the Marlboro Man, a close-cropped haircut left over from years in the Air Force, and a gravelly voice. His team's appearance at Pioneer was supposed to be what the FBI calls a routine liaison visit—a chance to swap ideas with corporate security. The bureau's leadership saw these visits as a crucial part of the effort to fight economic espionage. The FBI's Office of Private Sector cultivates close relationships with U.S. corporations, and at companies under the DuPont umbrella the relationship is particularly cozy. DuPont often hires former federal agents as security, and by 2011, the U.S. Justice Department had brought at least four federal trade secrets theft cases on behalf of DuPont subsidiaries and affiliates. As the meeting with Pioneer got under way, Mark explained the bureau's efforts to combat industrial espionage and tackle cybersecurity threats. Afterward, he asked if the seed company's security officers had any concerns.

One officer mentioned that in the spring, a Pioneer contract farmer in remote Tama County, Iowa, had found a Chinese national crouched on his knees in a cornfield. The man was digging up seeds as another man waited nearby in a parked car. When the contract farmer asked what he was doing, the kneeling man grew flushed and stammered out an excuse. He said he worked for the University of Iowa, and that he and his friend were on their way to an agricultural conference. Then the farmer's cell phone rang, and the man seized the opportunity to bolt for the car and jump in the passenger seat. The driver sped away, veering through a ditch. The farmer notified Pioneer security, and security officers used the license plate number to trace the car back to a rental company at the Kansas City airport. It was registered to a man with a Florida driver's license named Hailong Mo. He went by Robert.

After the meeting, Mark drove back to the FBI field office in Des Moines and made a few calls. There were no records of a Hailong Mo or Robert Mo teaching at the University of Iowa. But that only confirmed that the encounter in the Tama County field was suspicious. He still had no idea who the man was.

An analyst suggested that they contact another seed company in the area, Stine, to see if its executives had any useful information. Stine was a boutique breeding outfit that sold research on corn and soy seeds to Monsanto and Pioneer. A string of high-performing seeds had turned the company's septuagenarian founder, Harry Stine, into one of the richest men in Iowa. Harry Stine had visited China in 1976, as it was just beginning to open up to the West, and he had kept up his ping-pong game ever since. Now he saw opportunity in the country's growing demand for grain.

At Stine's headquarters in Adel, twenty minutes outside Des Moines, executives told Mark that they had just been to China, where they had met with several businesspeople from Chinese seed companies. Mark asked to see the business cards they received on the trip. Reviewing the list of contacts back at his office, his eyes alighted on one name: Hailong Mo. The card described Mo as an international business manager for DBN, an agricultural company in Beijing.

Surely that can't be the same guy, Mark thought. *What are the chances?*

He called the Miami field office and asked agents there to hunt down a copy of Robert's driver's license. When the license arrived, Mark showed the photo to people at Stine and asked them if the man looked familiar. They confirmed he was the man they'd met in Beijing.

Mark marveled at the implications. One of the men found near the Pioneer field was high-level management at a Chinese seed company that competed with Monsanto and Pioneer.

IN SEPTEMBER, MARK STOOD IN the FBI's Des Moines field office, chatting about this revelation with a colleague. The office occupied a suite in a T-shaped building in a suburb just west of Des Moines.

The outpost was overseen by the bureau's Omaha Division, and with the management mostly elsewhere, it was small and collegial. As Mark talked with his colleague, cars zoomed by on the parkway beyond on their way to Home Depot or the Olive Garden.

He explained what he knew about the Pioneer field incident, recounting the uncanny discovery that one of the men from that encounter had met with Stine in Beijing. Just then a detective with the Polk County Sheriff's Office who worked with the bureau's Joint Terrorism Task Force happened to walk by and overhear. The detective was struck by the similarity to another encounter he'd heard about.

"Hey," he said to Mark. "One of our deputies was recently tipped off to a report of some Asian males acting suspiciously near a cornfield."

Asian males near a cornfield. When Mark got back to his desk, he tracked down the report that Deputy Bollman had filed. There it was again:

```
Name: HAILONG MO
```

His heart raced. The Chinese seed outfit appeared to be targeting not one but two major U.S. agriculture companies.

A few years earlier, an attempt to swipe hybrid corn seed might have been a shaky premise for an investigation. But now that China was charting a bold economic and scientific rise, helped on in some areas by technological theft, the FBI had taken up the cause. The bureau's economic espionage cases were increasing by 50 percent year on year, cropping up across the country—in states like Missouri and Wisconsin as well as California and New York. The vast majority of them involved China. The corn matter had the markers of a possible economic espionage operation. That it centered on genetically modified corn only made it the perfect case for Des Moines agents to take on.

INDUSTRIAL ESPIONAGE IS AS OLD as industry itself. The oldest known recognition of intellectual property rights came thousands of years ago, in the ancient Greek city of Sybaris, when chefs presiding over extravagant feasts complained of scheming rivals stealing their recipes. The solution city leaders devised was to grant cooks exclusive rights to their concoctions for one year. Back then the target was literally the secret sauce. In the intervening centuries, as our choicest products progressed from gravy to engines to supercomputers, the metaphor remained.

The Byzantine Empire, imperial China, the Ottomans, Great Britain, America: Theft of one nation's technologies by another marked the transfer of power from one empire to the next almost as routinely as bloodshed. For most of history, industrial espionage was regarded as something that nations just did, much like spying for political or military secrets. The victor was the one who stole the spoils, while the act of theft was typically forgotten. History remembers the East India Company and its vast colonial tea plantations, but not the British botanist who journeyed to China's Fujian province improbably disguised as Qing nobility, his head shaved except for one long braid, to purloin the technique for processing tea leaves. It remembers delicate French white and blue ceramics, but not the Jesuit priest who traveled to China's imperial kilns to filch the technique for making hard-paste porcelain. And it remembers the industrialist Francis Cabot Lowell, father of Lowell, Massachusetts, but not his 1810 trip to England and Scotland, where he spent weeks touring factories and memorizing the blueprints that would allow him to "invent" the power loom on the western side of the Atlantic.

In most parts of the world until the mid-1990s, companies dealt with trade secrets theft through civil lawsuits. No international treaty or agreement explicitly tackled industrial espionage. In the United States just one federal statute did, and it only covered theft by a government employee. Then, a year before Mark Betten started his career at the FBI, President Clinton signed into law the Economic Espionage Act, which made trade secrets theft a federal crime. The 1996 law represented a seismic shift: It was the first time in American history that attacks on American business were branded as a national security threat.

The act was born in the wake of the Cold War, as intelligence leaders cast about for a new mission. In some ways industrial espionage was a logical choice. Technologies of all sorts were rapidly increasing in value, making them attractive to spies. The dawn of the internet and breakthroughs in global communications, meanwhile, provided more weak points than ever before for siphoning off information.

At the time, policy makers were particularly concerned about France, whose secret service chief had been blunt about his interest in obtaining American economic secrets. But critics suspected that the drive to designate industrial espionage as a federal crime was also about the intelligence agencies' interest in self-preservation. The fall of the Iron Curtain had made the mandate of the FBI and CIA unclear. Newspapers were running headlines like COLD WAR'S END BRINGS ENEMY GAP and CIA—COSTLY, INEPT, ANACHRONISTIC. After he was sworn in as CIA director in 1991, Robert Gates had promptly

written on a notepad, "New world out there. Adjust or die." Gates
became a staunch advocate of the Economic Espionage Act.

Legal scholars pointed out that state law was deemed sufficient
for a range of high-stakes crimes, including many types of murder.
Why did trade secrets theft deserve different treatment? Senator
Bill Bradley worried that economic espionage could become "a pre-
text for a new program of counterintelligence surveillance by the
FBI of either foreigners or Americans." Others simply thought that
the threat was inflated. "The law gives the FBI not only a cold war
reason for being but a reason for using once again the formidable
methods of the cold war," journalist Robert Dreyfuss wrote in *The
New Republic*.

Whatever the reality, a consensus built in Washington that technical information was so dangerous a weapon when in the hands of
a foreign company or government that America needed tougher
tools to deal with it. The 1990s was an era of intense globalization
and consolidation, and multinational corporations were advancing
into new markets where they faced foreign competitors. Stiffer pen-
alties provided a way to hobble those competitors in court, or at
least bog them down in costly litigation. And because economic espionage was a federal crime, corporate lawyers could step back and
let federal prosecutors bring charges on their companies' behalf.
Large corporations were among the law's biggest backers. Some
even felt that the United States should go further, by actively spying
on other countries' firms—a proposal that was rejected mainly because it was impractical, not because of strong moral objections.

In the years following the Economic Espionage Act's passage,
the Justice Department brought cases involving cancer drugs, software programs, and razors. Then, on September 11, 2001, terrorists

associated with al-Qaeda hijacked four commercial airplanes and steered two of them into the World Trade Center. As the United States waged an assault on terrorism, economic espionage faded from view.

In the late 2000s, when trade secrets theft investigations picked up again, the focus shifted to China. Western elites agreed that while other countries, including nineteenth-century America, had relied on industrial spying to advance technologically, China took it to a new level. "In a manner of speaking, the United States stole books; China steals libraries," quipped James A. Lewis, an expert on industrial espionage at the Center for Strategic and International Studies. It helped that China's rise as a global economic power had coincided with a democratization of spy tools. The 160-kilobyte floppy disk, just small enough to slip into a purse, was replaced by the 128-gigabyte flash drive, with nearly 1 million times more storage compressed into a gadget as slim as a pinky. Clunky recording devices gave way to sophisticated spyware that allowed for commandeering the microphone and camera of a user's smartphone. Unsophisticated cyberattacks could expose whole company servers to plundering. In 2009, as Mark Betten moved into his second decade at the FBI, the bureau created a dedicated Economic Espionage Unit.

On May 2, 2011, President Obama announced that Osama bin Laden had been killed in an American military operation in Pakistan. The menace of terrorism, it appeared, had subsided. The emergence of Islamic State militants would later shake this sense of security, but in the meantime the national security establishment moved on to a different threat: economic espionage. The day after Obama announced bin Laden's death, the Pioneer contract farmer spotted a Chinese man in a cornfield in Tama County, Iowa.

THE SCIENTIST AND THE SPY

· · ·

MARK KNEW THAT it wasn't just computer chips and aeronautic secrets that Chinese companies coveted. In 2010, the Justice Department had charged Kexue Huang, a researcher with Dow AgroSciences, with stealing secrets related to organic pesticide production. Accused of using Dow secrets to build up pesticide manufacturing facilities in China, Huang was sentenced to seven years in prison. It followed that seed breeding might be targeted as well. With the FBI on high alert for incidents of technological theft involving China, corn theft could be a high point in Mark's career.

But in taking on the case, the special agent was treading into a minefield. Analysts disagreed on how Chinese intelligence was organized and whether individuals found stealing secrets from American companies were necessarily emissaries of the Chinese government. A case involving an ethnic Chinese man was also apt to trigger accusations of racial profiling. FBI leaders often maintained that they were simply following Beijing's lead—that Chinese intelligence agencies and companies were the ones who targeted Chinese nationals, and the bureau was obligated to respond. But when cases fell apart entirely, as sometimes happened, it was harder to defend this strategy. And even the most well-meaning agent could trip up on a case involving complex science.

FIVE

FALL 2011

K evin Montgomery sat in a booth at the Texas Roadhouse, in
Forsyth, Illinois, with the three men from China. This was
one of the stranger job interviews he had ever experienced. It
was not what he had had in mind five years earlier when, out of a job
at the age of fifty, he had launched a seed consulting business. In
Kevin's experience, clients either asked direct questions about his
background—*Tell me about your breeding work*—or posed hypotheti-
cal questions: *What will you do if you run into trouble licensing a strain?*
The men from DBN were doing neither.

Robert Mo, Kevin's principal contact, sat across from him in the
booth and seemed the most at ease of the three. Years in Florida
had worn the hard edges off his Chinese accent, and despite his lack
of standing at DBN—he was the least senior of the three—he did
all the talking. But his questions struck Kevin as oddly broad, as if
he were conducting a survey about the state of the American seed
industry rather than hiring someone to perform a specific task.

"What are the top ten seed companies in the country?" he asked Kevin. "And who are the top ten breeders?" Robert wanted an actual list.

Next to Robert sat Dr. Li Shaoming, the man Kevin figured had the real hiring power. Dr. Li wore a coat and tie and spoke halting English, though he seemed to understand most of what was said. Every once in a while he flashed a taut grin. Next to Kevin, facing Dr. Li, was Wang Lei, Kings Nower's mousy vice president. Wang Lei had a receding hairline and, like Robert, was dressed more casually.

Outside, drivers turning off Route 51 cruised by the steakhouse on their way to the Hickory Point Mall. Kevin had suggested the restaurant because in his experience Chinese guests liked places where animal protein—Kevin was the sort who said "animal protein" in place of meat—was the main event. The Roadhouse satisfied that requirement and then some. Rough wooden siding lined the walls, giving the restaurant the appearance of a gargantuan log cabin. Just inside the entrance, next to an enormous portrait of some appropriated Native American chief, was a long glass display case of steaks. The place was packed with families eating rolls by the basketful and washing down one-pound cuts of corn-fed beef with bottomless sodas. Now that they were here, though, Kevin was annoyed by the twangy country music blaring on the jukebox, which made it hard for him to hear the conversation. And there was no denying that the Chinese men looked out of place.

From a distance Kevin could be mistaken for a typical Midwestern farmer: a face of indeterminate northern European heritage, ample waistline housed in loose-fit jeans. But a closer look would reveal a pen and a notebook neatly tucked into his breast pocket.

Kevin approached most situations in life as the scientist he was: with cautious deliberation. He prided himself on what he described as his photographic memory.

It was this exactitude that explained Kevin's confusion over Robert's top-ten questions. Kevin worried that whatever answers he did give would provide no insight into his capacity as a consultant. He blocked out the music and the diners brushing past on their way to the bathroom and parsed Robert's queries for hidden meaning. Was Robert trying to ascertain if there was a mismatch between the best companies and the best breeders? Or did he have a preconceived notion of the best companies and want to see if Kevin's answer matched up? Did he mean top ten by size of research staff? Sales volume? And why did he want names of other breeders? Did Robert want Kevin to lead him to another candidate, meaning that a careless answer could put him out of a job?

"I'll need to think about it," Kevin said finally.

He had been corresponding with Robert for months, and he still had no idea exactly what Robert saw in him or what his duties would be if he was hired. Kevin was interested in China and had worked with a number of Chinese seed breeders over the years, but he knew little about DBN. The Taiwanese friend who had referred him for the position knew the company by reputation only. When Robert explained in his initial approach that DBN was interested in licensing innovative hybrids from the United States, it struck Kevin as a good idea. He knew that while Chinese science on the whole was rapidly developing, China remained a few decades behind in plant breeding. Because it had little arable land, the country needed corn that could be planted in dense rows. North American varieties fit the bill, and smaller American seed companies were often happy to license their hybrids for a share of revenue from sales. It seemed perfectly plausible that DBN would try to secure a few licensing deals. Such deals took time to broker, so for Kevin the project would bring in a steady flow of work at $55 an hour.

Before he was laid off from the seed company Golden Harvest, Kevin spent decades working as a seed breeder. He grew up on a farm near Forsyth, living and breathing corn. For entertainment as a child, he sketched out baseball diamonds on his family's pasture and took turns with friends hitting the ball into the cornfields beyond. By age nine, he was driving a tractor solo in the summer heat perched on the edge of the seat so that his feet could reach the brakes. In his spare time, he read his father's discarded copies of *Successful Farming* and *Prairie Farmer.* That was a different era of American farming, when small family farms dotted the plains and farmers sold their crops to local grain elevators. Kevin wanted nothing more than to be a part of it.

In high school, he snagged his first breeding job. He spent the summer of 1973 walking cornfields wearing an apron heavy with tools, transferring pollen from the tassel of one corn plant to the ear of another. Kevin went on to major in agronomy at the University of Illinois Champaign-Urbana. Finally, he earned a PhD from Iowa State, the mecca for corn.

Seed breeding was his job and his passion. Kevin loved seeds the way some people loved quilting or woodworking. Being both brutally honest and unconcerned with social niceties, though, he wasn't a great fit for the corporate world. When people didn't grasp something that was obvious to him, he would say that enlightening them was like trying to teach calculus to horses. At the series of seed companies where he worked, this directness sometimes undercut his talent for research. His friend Craig Davis, another seed breeder, had once sent him a quote from the philosopher Bertrand Russell:

"I don't know how anyone can advocate an unpopular cause unless one is either irritating or ineffective." The quote, Davis thought, summed up Kevin's troubles at work; he was an effective advocate of unpopular views, and as a result he was sometimes irritating.

Then there were the larger shifts in the seed industry that were out of his control. Kevin's career coincided with a period of rapid consolidation in food and agriculture, when grocery store sales and meat production came to be dominated by just a handful of companies. Even in a sector where consolidation was the norm, the seed industry stood out. Concentration in seed was more rapid than in any other area of food production.

The FBI would later maintain that the big seed companies represented the best that American ingenuity had to offer, but for Kevin the industry shifts ran counter to the spirit of innovation that had attracted him to the discipline. The larger the companies got, the more ideas were generated from the top down, and the less willing management was to experiment. Instead, Kevin felt, huge sums were wasted on ill-advised projects, simply because no one had the courage to point out exactly how bad they were.

Throughout the 2000s, as agricultural companies grew into leviathans and their revenue increased, the percentage of sales that they spent on research and development dropped. That trend had a direct impact on breeders like Kevin. He lost his job with Golden Harvest in 2005, after the company was acquired by the Swiss seed giant Syngenta.

Cash poor but flush with spare time, he tried to make the best of his situation. Devoting himself to his dream of backyard breeding, he began creating his own seed lines on a section of the family farm that he'd inherited from his parents. As industrial agriculture

THE SCIENTIST AND THE SPY

became a question of squeezing the maximum yield out of vast tracts of land, Kevin focused his efforts in a space of five acres. He was happiest when out in the fields, a dirty Chicago Cubs cap perched on his head. But still he needed money.

A few days before the meeting at the Roadhouse, thousands of people had gathered in Zuccotti Park in New York City to protest high unemployment and bank bailouts, spawning the Occupy Wall Street movement. The U.S. economy appeared on the brink of recession, and farmers in particular were suffering. As agribusiness companies consolidated, they also integrated vertically, buying outfits up and down the supply chain, a process that squeezed the farmers at the bottom. Antitrust scholars Diana Moss and C. Robert Taylor called this consolidation "likely one of the most troubling phases in U.S. agricultural history." Farmers like Kevin now had to pay more than twice what they had paid for commercial corn seed just a decade ago. The seed yielded more crop, but not enough to make up the difference. To generate income, the meeting at Texas Roadhouse was crucial. Kevin had to convince Robert Mo to hire him.

Small talk didn't come naturally to Kevin, but as a waiter took their orders, he remembered something he had heard in a career counseling course. *Ask about other people's interests.* Kevin knew from the friend who introduced him that Robert's sister was married to DBN's billionaire CEO, and that Robert had gotten his position because of his family connections. He knew little else about him, though. "Robert, I'd like to hear about your background," Kevin said.

"I'm in engineering and fluid dynamics."

For most people, this phrase was a conversational dead end. For

Kevin, whose Facebook page was littered with Richard Feynman's lectures and a post titled "20 Jokes That Only Intellectuals Will Understand," it lit a spark of interest. "Tell me about that," he said, leaning in.

Robert alluded to having a PhD and to having worked at a university in Florida. He talked about solving a certain problem in dynamic flow, a field dealing with the behavior of fluids.

Kevin perked up. "You solved the Navier-Stokes equations?" he asked. Although the equations were commonly used in fluid mechanics, the underlying theory stumped mathematicians. The equations worked, but no one knew exactly why they worked under broad conditions. The theory was so elusive that one mathematics institute had offered a million-dollar prize to the first person who could explain the mathematics involved.

Robert stared at Kevin in silence, as if surprised that he even understood the reference. Later Kevin would say that this was one of the few times he saw Robert speechless. "How do you know about the Navier-Stokes equations?" Robert asked.

"Well, one of the things I do for recreational reading is math problems," Kevin said. It sounded like a boast, but no one who knew him doubted that in his free time he actually did sit around working through equations.

"I solved one tiny little piece of them," Robert said. In fluid mechanics, it was common to solve the equations for specific problems bounded by clear conditions. Kevin was nonetheless impressed. He thought he glimpsed a kindred spirit. For both Kevin and Robert, life had not worked out as planned. They were two overeducated men in middle age whom fate had propelled toward unexpected work. Years of studying thermodynamics had ill equipped Robert to deal in corn, just as years of researching corn had little prepared Kevin for the business side of seed breeding. Charmed to find himself facing a potential intellectual equal, Kevin let his doubts about the job slide. When Robert later wrote him to invite him to visit DBN's office in Beijing, he happily accepted.

SIX

FALL 2011

At the FBI's Des Moines field office in the weeks that followed
Robert's run-in with the Polk County deputies, Mark Betten
devoted himself to the budding investigation. Out the window
of the brick building, he could see a vast expanse of pristine grass,
with only a handful of pedestrians in sight. In many parts of Iowa,
hogs outnumbered people. The question for Mark was whether Robert would take a chance on all that open land again.

The fall harvest for commercial corn was still a few weeks
away, and for a short while longer, sensitive research fields would
remain conspicuously cleared, unlike the commercial fields around
them, making them easy to identify. That meant that Robert and
crew could freely gather inbred ears—the so-called escapes—off
the ground, with the towering stalks of nearby fields providing some
cover.

Mark worried that Robert had already managed to cover significant ground on his trips to Iowa. The Monsanto field outside Bondurant where Bollman encountered him driving the getaway car

was seventy miles southwest of the Tama County field where a Pioneer contract farmer had found a Chinese man digging on his knees a few months earlier.

As he started the investigation, the FBI agent had only the vaguest notion of what corn breeding involved. His own state of Nebraska was home to the Cornhuskers football team, but his calling was not in agriculture. The Air Force had taken him as a young man to a base in Germany, and the various roles he assumed before joining the FBI—prison guard, military lawyer—had only led him further from the farm. Like most Americans, he could not explain the difference between inbred and hybrid seed. But in his research he soon learned more. Behind hybrid corn seed was a fascinating origin story—and one that closely tracked with the rise of industrial agriculture.

IN THE BEGINNING, corn—*Zea mays*—was a uniquely New World plant, cultivated and in some cases worshipped for thousands of years by societies throughout the Americas. The Aztecs believed that the world was created five times. In the first four rounds, humans ate nuts and seeds, and the Earth was destroyed by a mixture of natural disasters and divine intervention. Then, in the final round, the gods gave man corn, and humanity endured.

When Christopher Columbus came across the remarkable New World grain, he, too, was in awe. Corn could be consumed without being threshed, milled, or kneaded, which counted for a lot in the centuries before processed foods. In 1493, Columbus wrote with excitement to Queen Isabella's court about ears as thick as a man's arm, with kernels "affixed by nature in a wondrous manner and in form and size like garden peas, white when young." The settlers who followed brought wheat and apples and notions of vanquishing what came before them. But it was corn that ended up saving them from starvation. A botanical curiosity and culinary wonder, corn spread around the world nearly as rapidly as syphilis, another New World introduction.

Among grains, corn has the unusual feature of being monoecious, meaning that it has male and female sex organs housed separately on the same plant. In a young corn plant, the male is contained in the yellow tassel that crowns the stalk, and the female halfway down the stalk in the ear shoot, a nub covered with tiny ovules and soft silk. In the absence of human involvement, corn sex is a straightforward affair. When the time is right, the tassel sheds millions of grains of pollen, which are carried by the wind onto the ear shoot's silk. The silk transports the pollen to the ovules, which in time grow into kernels.

For centuries, farmers simply left corn plants to wind pollinate and then harvested the results. Sometimes the pollen from the male tassel would drift to the silk of a neighboring plant. Other times it would fall downward to the female silk of the plant that spawned it, resulting in the corn equivalent of kissing cousins, or what's called an inbred. Then, in 1926, in a Des Moines basement, Henry A. Wallace founded the Hi-Bred Corn Company, which would become Pioneer Hi-Bred and finally DuPont Pioneer. Researchers had by then shown that by crossing two inbreds, or pollinating the female part of one inbred with the male part of another, they could produce a crop that was both predictable and robust. It was these crosses that Wallace brought to market as hybrid corn—and versions of these crosses that were being bred in the Pioneer and Monsanto fields where Robert was found.

Traditionally, farmers had saved seed at harvest to replant the next year, a practice known as brown bagging. Sophisticated hybrids produced quality corn for only one season, so there was no use in keeping seed from one season to the next. But farmers might pay for it year after year, Wallace figured, if it improved their yields. There was precedent in the mule, a sterile animal that is nonetheless hardy and extremely useful.

Hybrid corn seed proved incredibly lucrative, at least for the executives who sat at the top of seed companies. As the Dust Bowl swept through America in the 1930s, the new hybrid varieties were more resistant to drought, and they produced a uniform height that made them much kinder on modern farm machines. Enthusiasts compared corn to a "self-building food-factory" that was "governed by advanced business methods." Hybrid corn became one of the first true industrial foods. Wallace, meanwhile, became secretary of agriculture and later vice president under Franklin Delano Roosevelt, in an early example of the revolving door between government and agribusiness. Reflecting on the changes he set in motion, Wallace later wrote, "No plant has changed so fast in so short a time as has corn in the hands of the white man."

But more change was on the horizon. In the 1970s, scientists began experimenting with inserting small amounts of DNA from other organisms into seeds, producing varieties that could withstand certain weed killers or fight off pests. For DuPont and Monsanto, which were then primarily chemical companies, the new seeds were a potential gold mine. DuPont marketed a popular insecticide called Lannate, and Monsanto sold the weed killer Roundup. In 1997, DuPont purchased a 20 percent stake in Pioneer Hi-Bred, and two years later it bought the remainder for $7.7 billion. Around the same time,

Monsanto acquired the seed company DeKalb. The companies soon controlled both the sale of genetically modified seeds and the products used to treat them.

In the years that followed, DuPont and Monsanto bought up so many small seed companies that people in the industry began passing around a bubble diagram in which the megafirms were represented by two large red circles, with spokes linking them to dozens of tiny acquisitions. Often the new owners kept the small seed companies' names, so that many farmers did not even realize that their preferred brand had been acquired. Because the conglomerates also produced the pesticides that were sprayed on transgenic seeds, they had powerful incentive to insert genes into more and more seed lines. Soon nearly 90 percent of hybrid corn grown in the United States was genetically modified. Transgenic seeds might have been the product of American ingenuity, but they also became a symbol of corporate consolidation in agriculture. At the time of Mark's meeting with DuPont Pioneer, the big four seed companies—Monsanto, Pioneer, Dow AgroSciences, and Syngenta—controlled 80 percent of the lucrative global seed market.

Monsanto was particularly aggressive. The company patented the gene that ensured resistance to Roundup, or glyphosate. Glyphosate kills a broad spectrum of plants, and the gene ensured that the corn survived while the weeds withered. Any competitors that wanted to use the gene to make so-called Roundup Ready seed lines needed to license it from Monsanto. Observers sometimes likened this to Microsoft's licensing Windows to other PC manufacturers; Monsanto profited both from its own seed lines and from selling a gene widely used by its competitors. The tactic was so successful that by 2009 Monsanto genes, or traits, were inserted into 80 percent of all corn

THE SCIENTIST AND THE SPY

grown in the United States—a fact that enabled the company to raise prices at will.

That same year, the Justice Department's Antitrust Division launched a probe into Monsanto's practices. Previous administrations had been too lax, declared chief antitrust enforcer Christine Varney, and "the ultimate result is that consumers are harmed through higher prices, reduced product variety, and slower innovation." She added, "We must change course." The investigation followed on independent probes of the St. Louis–based corporation by several state attorneys general, including Iowa's. While the Antitrust Division began other investigations around the same time, the Monsanto inquiry inspired special excitement. "Of all the new scrutiny by Justice, the Monsanto investigation might have the highest stakes, dealing as it does with the food supply and one of the nation's largest agricultural firms," noted *The Washington Post*.

In 2010, the Justice Department and U.S. Department of Agriculture convened a workshop on competition in agriculture in Ankeny, Iowa. The town housed a Monsanto research facility, but that did not soften attitudes of farmers who showed up to complain of high prices and a lack of choice in seed selection. "When I started farming thirty-four years ago, there were fifty seed companies," said Minnesota farmer Fred Bower, who worked as a seed dealer on the side. "At the present time there are four." As a result, he added, people were made to pay "through the nose for seed." Another lamented, "I agree we need GMO technology, but the products the companies are bringing to the marketplace are not the products needed to feed the world. They are all about company profits."

Intellectual property protections are ostensibly about promoting innovation, but in taking on the Monsanto probe, the Antitrust

Division signaled that such protections could also be used to drive out competition. Opponents of genetically modified seeds and environmental activists had long abhorred Monsanto. Now the company came under fire for its business practices as well.

But Monsanto's cooperation was critical to another arm of the Justice Department: the National Security Division, which worked closely with the FBI as it developed economic espionage investigations. The FBI's goal with such cases was to nail people who stole intellectual property, not expose extortionist business practices. And even if Monsanto bullied farmers and rival seed producers, when it came to Robert Mo, the company was the victim—if one unlikely to win sympathy from many farmers.

TO SUCCEED AT DERIVING Monsanto's and Pioneer's seed lines, Mark learned, DBN would need to obtain both inbred parents for each seed line it targeted—the male and the female. To get the female, DBN could use a reverse-engineering technique called chasing the self. This depends on the fact that a small amount of female inbred seed makes it into each bag of commercial hybrid seed. To chase the self, a rival company could purchase a bag of seed, plant it out, and then scrutinize the crop for differences in growth. The stalks produced by rogue female inbreds are noticeably shorter. If the rival company could also find a way to obtain the male inbred, the seeds from the female inbreds could then be used to re-create the hybrid. If seed breeding is a code, chasing the self is a step toward cracking it.

But procuring male inbred seed is difficult, because there is no obvious way to do it discreetly. An aspiring industrial spy could either dig it out of the soil, as the DBN employees had been caught doing at the Pioneer field in the spring, or wait until harvest and roam mowed-down test fields looking for full-grown ears lying on the ground, as Wang Lei had apparently done at the Monsanto plot outside Bondurant.

Whatever method the men used, it was clear that they were busy collecting seed. In late September, after Mark had been investigating him for a few weeks, Robert hauled fifteen packages into a local UPS store and addressed them to his home in Boca Raton. The boxes weighed in at 341 pounds, and the shipping costs came to $1,152.97. He labeled the contents CORN SAMPLES.

SEVEN

FALL 2011

As the autumn days grew shorter and the nights longer, Robert drove Dr. Li and Wang Lei across the Midwest through forgotten towns with clapboard main streets. They passed diners that served sandwiches smothered in Thousand Island dressing, drinking establishments with neon signs in their windows that said simply BAR, and corn paraphernalia of all kinds. Iowa claimed the cornfield from the film *Field of Dreams*, the world's second-largest popcorn ball, and a ten-foot-tall rotating sculpture modeled after an ear of corn. Normally Robert enjoyed Midwestern kitsch. On one slow day in Iowa he had taken a break to tour the bridges of Madison County, the second-rate tourist destination made famous by the 1990s novel and subsequent movie. He was no longer easily cheered, though.

His companions frustrated him. Somehow Dr. Li and Wang Lei knew everything back in China, and yet they were clueless once they set foot in America. Robert found himself easily losing patience.

And driving through farm country, it was hard not to notice the creative renditions of American flags everywhere—painted on the sides of businesses, adorning old packing crates, embroidered on denim jackets. They were part of the landscape, just like the billboards arguing that abortion was murder and that guns were a civil right. At one point, he drove near the town of Pekin, so named because its founders imagined that if they dug straight through the Earth they would get to China. Until 1980, Pekin High School's teams were called the Chinks. Fans cheered to the sound of a clashing gong.

Robert was proud of his capacity to go anywhere and get along with anyone. He did not feel that his interactions with the people he met in Iowa and Illinois were marred by racism or xenophobia. But as tensions with China rose, ethnic Chinese living in the United States increasingly faced questions about their loyalty. Robert sensed that for some Americans, the people of China were inseparable from leaders in Beijing, and that when these Americans looked at him, they saw a stuffy Communist apparatchik rather than a suburban dad. At one point, a farmer asked Robert if he was working for the Chinese government.

Robert was offended. Although he had not bothered to get U.S. citizenship, he had two children who were U.S. citizens, and in some ways he felt fully American. And while DBN and Kings Nower enjoyed a close relationship with the Chinese government, on paper at least they were privately held businesses. His work for DBN was simply a job, he maintained.

And yet Robert admitted that his was a job with increasingly strange duties. As time passed, he grew superstitious about the forays into cornfields to collect corn. "If God wants you to go into the field, He will not put a man there," Robert told Wang Lei one day.

"If He doesn't want you to go into the field, He will put a man there." And now God had put a man there. Twice.

OF ALL THE SPY FICTION Robert read as a child, his favorite stories were the ones starring Sherlock Holmes. Back then he knew the detective only as Xialuoke Fu'ermosi, which was a phonetic approximation of Holmes's name in Mandarin. Sir Arthur Conan Doyle's tales first came to China in 1896, when four of his stories were translated into Chinese and published in a popular newspaper. After the Communist Revolution, they were mostly spared from censorship by a Maoist reinterpretation: Holmes fought the evils spawned by rapacious foreign capitalists. As a result, translations of Doyle's works were available even in remote villages like Daichi. Robert devoured the tales of the private detective using logic and forensic science to ingeniously solve crimes.

He dreamed of applying a similar empiricism to life, of perhaps one day becoming a scientist. To achieve that end, he spent long hours observing rabbits and studying flowers. He collected cement bags and copper debris and tied them to a Forever bicycle that was too large for his child's body, then pedaled to the local recycling station to sell his haul. In the process, he learned about the properties of various metals.

Now here he was again, collecting specimens in the field, replaying scenes from his youth on a different continent. In a way, he had become Xialuoke Fu'ermosi: Robert versus the rapacious foreign capitalists.

In China, Pioneer and Monsanto were often the object of public ire. Not long after genetically modified crops were first unveiled in the United States, the Chinese government set aside funding for research, seeing the new grains as a possible answer to China's food supply problems. By the 2010s, though, sentiment had shifted. A series of food safety scandals made consumers reluctant to accept genetically modified foods. Conspiracy theories about Monsanto and Pioneer lived large. Some believed the agribusiness companies' seeds were biological weapons that the United States aimed to use against China. Others saw transgenic crops as a Pentagon-led effort to control the global food supply and jeopardize China's food security. In 2010, a newspaper owned by the state news agency Xinhua alleged that Pioneer 335, the conventional seed the company had developed for the Chinese market, was in fact a genetically modified product that was killing rats and pigs. Because such misinformation bred suspicion of foreign companies, the Chinese government mostly allowed it to fester uncensored. Greenpeace, an anti-GMO organization that might otherwise have had a difficult time operating in China, set up a Beijing office and staged radical stunts that included stealing seed from research fields. The Chinese government had initially banned the sale of genetically modified seeds as a protectionist move, allowing the import from the United States and elsewhere of only a few select seed lines. But when disputes about foreign imports or market access arose, anti-GMO sentiment became a convenient crutch.

Many observers of the Chinese seed industry expected the ban to eventually be lifted, but no one knew exactly when. Food issues were so cloaked in secrecy in China that even the size of grain stockpiles was considered a state secret. In the meantime, Robert knew that the country's dependence on imported grains was deeply troubling to Chinese leaders. China had close to the same number of acres of corn in production as the United States, but those acres yielded far less crop per acre, and its population was much larger. As a result, China was the world's top importer of corn and soy, with much of its supply coming from the United States.

Leaders worried that as Chinese people grew wealthier, eating more meat and triggering demand for still more corn, the country would need to lean on imports even more. If tensions with the United States ever rose, American politicians could simply cut off China's supply of grain. There were other countries that supplied corn, like Ukraine and Chile, but an American exit would drive up global prices.

The Chinese government also had urgent concerns about other technologies. Leaders did not want the United States controlling the 5G mobile communications network or the semiconductor industry. But anxiety about the grain supply was an existential concern that even the most geriatric member of China's ruling Politburo could grasp. Economic growth in China had led to a yawning income gap that could spark rural unrest. Improving crop quality was critical to raising farmers' incomes. Like the FBI, leaders in Beijing equated food security with national security.

For them, hope lay in China's $16 billion domestic seed industry. If the country's thousands of companies could be whittled down to a few industry leaders, and those outfits could rapidly improve their seed lines, perhaps they could compete with the likes of Pioneer and Monsanto—and the Chinese government could legalize genetically modified crops without handing over the market to foreign firms. In an effort to speed up the process, the agriculture ministry began encouraging mergers and acquisitions and favoring some companies over others.

Among the anointed leaders was DBN. Both DBN and Kings Nower received tax breaks, access to low-interest loans, and direct financial support from the Chinese government. They were known as dragon head enterprises—a notion taken from the dragon dance performed at the lunar new year, where one performer stands tall, wearing the head, while a row of others trails behind him, hunched down to play the body. Chinese companies are often rewarded for nationalism, and DBN's clunky slogan read like it had been crafted with government interests in mind: SERVE THE COUNTRY TO HELP AGRICULTURE FLOURISH, STRIVE FOR NUMBER ONE, DEVELOP TO-GETHER. Dr. Li talked about the need for a "national hero," and he and other employees were open about their end goal: to use the foreigners' technology to beat them at their own game. That DBN targeted genetically modified American seed lines meant that its executives foresaw a change in policy, and even that they might have inside information on when it could happen.

PARTWAY THROUGH THEIR TOUR of the Midwest, Robert, Dr. Li, and Wang Lei stopped in Illinois to meet an American agronomist whom Robert hoped to hire to help with the U.S. seed project. Then Robert flew back to Florida. He wanted to spend more time with his family. Having known little beyond life in America, his children experienced few of the language and cultural stresses that he faced. But his daughter was entering adolescence, and his son was in elementary school, and they needed him around. His break was brief, though. Shortly after he arrived home, he was on the road again. He needed to take a quick trip to Beijing.

EIGHT

FALL 2011

Kevin exited the plane with a gaggle of other passengers and made his way through the Beijing airport to the security exit, where an assistant from DBN greeted him. She was tall, with skin that looked like it did not see much sun. Her name was Mao Li. She introduced herself as Molly in excellent English.

Mao Li led Kevin to a company car in a nearby lot, where a driver took his luggage. The journey into the city center followed a six-lane highway, and it lasted a small eternity. The thick haze that normally shrouded Beijing had lifted that day, but even so the city lacked a clear skyline and seemed to go on forever, a decentralized blob. Beijing's roads are laid out like concentric rings on a target: first ring, second ring, third ring, fourth ring, all the way out to the eighth ring. The airport was just inside the sixth ring road. They had a ways to go.

This trip to DBN's headquarters was an afterthought. Kevin had been invited to China by Jilin Academy of Agricultural Sciences in

Changchun, a city in the northeast. His flight returned through Beijing, and after the awkward dinner at the Roadhouse, he figured that stopping in at DBN might improve his chances of getting hired. When Robert learned about Kevin's trip and extended the invitation, Kevin set aside a day for the meeting. Compared with Changchun, the capital felt fast-paced. The highway was clogged with swerving, honking cars. On the surrounding streets, small dramas unfolded as tempers flared and then died out. The air had a sickening aftertaste, of secondhand smoke mixed with cough syrup and car exhaust. Then there was the odor: metallic and acrid at the same time.

They eventually cut west toward Zhongguancun, the area sometimes called China's Silicon Valley. Kevin eyed office buildings of varying vintage, a few of them emblazoned with names like Lenovo and Baidu, but the neighborhood was no Palo Alto. The structures were caked with a layer of dust.

When the car finally pulled into a U-shaped drive and stopped beneath a bizarre-looking high-rise, Kevin craned his neck to look up. It was as if a rectangular prism had been plopped on top of a futuristic Buddhist temple. At the very top of the building, mounted to the roof, were four dingy Chinese characters that he couldn't read. Beneath them were block letters, originally white but now gray from smog: HUBEI HOTEL.

Mao Li ushered him inside. In the center of the lobby, cordoned off with a red velvet rope, was a six-foot-tall chunk of carved lacquered wood. Scattered around the space were stiff armchairs in which the stuffing looked like an afterthought. Mao Li helped him check in, explaining that DBN would pick up the tab. He was pleased. Because he hadn't yet signed a contract, he had expected to pay for his own lodging. This seemed like a good sign.

His room was spare but clean. There were two double beds with crisp white sheets, and underneath the bedside table were two pairs of white disposable slippers. Facing the beds was a heavy desk and a counter that held heavy lidded mugs and bags of green tea. Kevin found a placard on the back of the door advertising a daily room rate of what worked out to be around $120. He considered this sum and decided that he must be at the Beijing equivalent of downtown Chicago's Hyatt Regency, the hotel that hosted the American Seed Trade Association's annual Seed Expo. He felt good. Robert had not flinched when Kevin quoted his rate. If all worked out, the gig would help him pay the bills, and then some. In the back of his mind, he harbored a more ambitious hope—that he could convince DBN to license some of the hybrids that he bred in his backyard.

He left his bags in his room, and Mao Li took him to lunch. Being in China felt right to Kevin. Decades earlier, his father had been stationed on a minesweeper in Shanghai during World War II, and Kevin had always been curious about that period of his life. Partway through Bill Montgomery's tour of the Pacific, he had planned to travel with his shipmates to Beijing to see the Forbidden City. The night before they left, the Communists captured a key railway line, rendering the journey impossible and dashing the American sailors' plans. Now, Kevin hoped, he could complete the trip on his father's behalf.

After lunch, he asked to be driven to the imperial palace complex. As he passed street vendors selling trinkets and walked through the entrance gate to the Forbidden City, he took satisfaction in taking the steps that so many years ago his father could not. Once inside the complex, he marveled at a tilted stone sundial that told the time throughout the year, with the hours in winter signaled through a shadow cast on its underside. He reflected that life could be like that. How a situation looked could depend on where you stood. He wondered whether a new angle would give him insight into his relationship to DBN—whether now that he was in China he might finally understand what it was that Robert wanted him to do.

AFTER BREAKFAST THE NEXT MORNING, Mao Li picked Kevin up in the DBN car and escorted him to the company's headquarters. He looked out the window as the driver pulled in next to a rundown hospital. Zhongguan Tower was an aging office building with a curved façade covered by mirrored windows. DBN and Kings Nower shared an office on the fourteenth floor. For the base of a large agricultural company, the headquarters was unimpressive. Later, Kevin would learn that fourteen, *yao si*, was a homophone in Mandarin for "going to die." Often, the fourteenth floors of Chinese buildings rent at a heavily discounted rate. At DBN, apparently, the bottom line trumped superstition.

Someone showed him to the conference room. Kevin had prepared a short presentation on his breeding work, and he was setting up his laptop, struggling to plug it into an adapter that worked with Chinese outlets, when Robert appeared and greeted him warmly. Here was his ally, Kevin thought.

After Kevin got done presenting, Robert explained how seed breeding fit into DBN's larger business operations, boasting that in just a decade Kings Nower had become one of the largest seed companies in China. Kevin glanced at the seed catalog he'd been handed. It was thick and glossy, like the seed books published by American companies. Clearly a great deal of energy went into marketing DBN's products.

They spent the morning in the conference room as an assortment of people came and went. At one point Kevin recognized Dr. Li from the Texas Roadhouse. But Robert did most of the talking. By now Kevin was getting the sense that Robert liked to talk.

At noon they broke for lunch. The group shuttled into an elevator and down to a restaurant on a lower floor of the building, where a waiter seated them around a large table in the corner. A gas fireplace was set into a nearby wall. Kevin got the impression that it was DBN's regular spot. He took a seat between Robert and Mao Li. Across the table from him, with his back toward the fireplace, was a man with a square jaw and rectangular rimless glasses who seemed to command respect despite saying little. Someone introduced him as Shao Genhuo, DBN's CEO.

The group mostly talked in Chinese, and as the wait staff brought out dish after dish, Kevin caught only a few phrases in English. But it was clear that Shao was the center of attention. Even Robert seemed humbled by the presence of his brother-in-law.

Kevin noted, with some disappointment, that the lunch was not about plant breeding. Most of the people at the table seemed to work in sales and marketing. He grew more hopeful that afternoon when he got in a car with Robert and a Kings Nower breeder and rode to DBN's biotechnology facility, where the company's experimental work on genetically modified seeds was done. The breeder mentioned that he had spent time in Iowa working for Pioneer. Kevin deduced that the man knew a lot about seed breeding, and he saw a potential ally. When they arrived at a brick building on the city's outskirts, Robert escorted Kevin inside and said to the breeder pointedly in English, "Let him see whatever he wants." Then he left.

Kevin was confused. He was accustomed to seed companies maintaining a veil of secrecy over their operations. Secrecy, in fact, is critical to the intellectual property protection strategies of most American corporations. In order to claim that something is a trade secret, companies have to treat it as confidential. If they take out a patent, or give out blueprints to any employee who asks, the information in question is no longer protected. Companies sometimes wield trade secrets as weapons against competitors, but secrecy was seen as the best way to protect sensitive information, especially at the experimental stage.

Kevin had a sense that the intellectual property situation in China was different—that the rapid scientific development on display in Zhongguancun had a dark side. Back in the 1980s, when a few fledging computer companies spun off from the Chinese Academy of Sciences and opened up shop along Zhongguancun's Electronics Street, or *Dianzi Jie*, pirated software was so abundant that some preferred the moniker *Pianzi Jie*, or Crook Street.

Years earlier, as a seed breeder at the Iowa company Garst, Kevin remembered fielding requests for proprietary inbreds from visiting delegations of Chinese seed scientists. The first time it happened, he was shocked that the breeders openly asked for information that people in the industry knew was closely held. By the time the third group arrived, he had come to expect the request. He always said no, but he suspected that the breeders found other ways to obtain proprietary seeds. But Robert had worked at U.S. universities, and the breeder who was escorting Kevin had worked for Pioneer. They should have understood these sensitivities better than anyone. What could DBN possibly gain from granting an American consultant unfettered access to its facilities?

The lab was long and rectangular, the windows facing south to let in sunlight. Inside Kevin saw dozens of young people seated at long benches. Whether they were students or newly minted scientists he couldn't discern. He immediately recognized the tasks they were performing, though: placing seeds in the germinator, putting plantlets into the growing medium, slicing off pieces of leaves. Lining the south end of the room were stainless-steel cabinets about the size of industrial walk-in refrigerators. Each growth chamber was calibrated to a specific humidity or temperature or light regime. As his host opened the doors to one, the lights inside cast an eerie glow. Kevin glimpsed small corn seedlings, lined up in neat rows.

At the time, the setup seemed perfectly normal. Later Kevin would wonder if it had all been for show. But then he would remember the mortar and pestle for grinding up seed parts, the dissecting microscopes for examining seedlings, the polyacrylamide gels for running DNA sequences, the chemical storage cabinets, the centrifuges, the homogenizers. Kevin knew that China's restrictions on selling genetically modified corn were expected to be lifted, and yet DBN seemed to be preparing for more than just selling transgenic corn in China. The researchers he talked with were also developing resistance to pesticides that killed insects found only outside Asia, suggesting that DBN had international ambitions. When he asked more about this aspect of their work, though, his host interjected in Mandarin. An awkward silence followed. So much for his new friend showing him everything.

The next day, his last in China, Kevin visited the Great Wall. In the centuries since it was completed, the wall had come to stand as much for cultural segregation as for defense planning. The local seed industry had always struck him as similarly isolated. Weaving through the throngs of other tourists, he wondered if his meeting the day before meant that the sector was now opening up to the rest of the world. Or did DBN have some larger plan?

NINE

2015–2018

In 2015, I moved with my husband and kids to Minneapolis, and we settled into a life strangely close to the one I'd had growing up. We traded out the sautéed meat and vegetable dishes we had eaten in China for chili and cornbread and attended barbecues where we ate corn on the cob. One of the first gifts my mother gave us for our new house was a set of corn skewers crowned with polka-dotted flip-flops.

Now, I knew, I could chase the seed theft story in earnest. From information about the FBI investigation that had surfaced in court proceedings, I had the names of people who had interacted with Robert Mo at various points in his travels across the Midwest. I drove to Iowa and knocked on their doors. Like our new lifestyle, this reporting was weirdly familiar. My grandfather had been a journalism professor at Iowa State, and for a while my father was an agricultural reporter at a small-town newspaper in southern Minnesota. Traveling around the rural Midwest, I recognized scenes from my youth: brightly lit truck stops, county fairs staffed by carnies with faded tattoos, motels with ancient televisions and contemporary roaches. The small towns I visited seemed hollower and more decayed than I remembered. Adjusting for inflation, farm income in America had plummeted in the past three decades, and in many towns that shift was palpable. "There's a feeling that we're going into a farm crisis everywhere," the food activist and farmer's daughter Ash Bruxvoort told me over coffee in Des Moines.

I was finally home, though. Like villagers in rural China, Midwesterners were warm and hospitable, but the difference was that they read me as one of them. When I knocked on doors, the farmers who opened them would often tell me they had nothing to say and then proceed to spend twenty minutes chatting. It was only when talk turned to China, or to ethnicity more generally, that the conversation sometimes grew strained.

One day while I was retracing Robert's steps in rural Iowa, a retired farmer invited me into his home and offered me a seat at his kitchen table. He told me he had gotten out of the farming business because he had trouble making a living as crop prices fell. He rented out his fields to his neighbors and spent the harvest holed up inside watching television, occasionally venturing out to check on the litter of kittens in his barn. I had a few names of people I wanted to contact, and he helpfully pulled out a dusty phone book and began paging through it in search of their details. Then before I left, he leaned in and told me that Hillary Clinton and Barack Obama had staged the Black Lives Matter protests as part of an effort to institute martial law. I blinked stupidly, bewildered that he could be so welcoming and so mistrustful at the same time. I mumbled an excuse and got up to leave.

Many farmers rightly felt excluded from the economic gains brought by globalization, some of which had been made possible by their labor. They were hostage both to the whims of U.S. commodities traders and to orders from China—as was underscored in 2013, when the Chinese government rejected millions of tons of Syngenta corn at port because they contained an unapproved genetically modified variety. The move cost U.S. farmers billions of dollars, prompting them to bring a class-action suit against Syngenta. Sometimes, I wondered if this discontent was channeled into something more visceral. When I asked people who had run into Robert or other DBN employees to describe them, they often looked at me quizzically, as if it were unfathomable that the men might possess traits besides their ethnicity. "Well, he looked like a Chinese man," one farmer said of Robert. Others immediately went to epithets.

After my visit with the retired farmer, I drove into town. The tallest building for miles was a towering grain elevator belonging to the Heartland Co-op. Kernels of corn spilled out the bottom of the structure, blanketing the surrounding parking lot in yellow dots.

When I walked into the co-op's office, a manager told me flat out that he had never seen the man I was tracking. He would remember if he had, he said, taking a sip of coffee from a Styrofoam cup. "A Chinaman in Redfield, Iowa, would stick out like a sore thumb."

BEING BORN A WHITE AMERICAN means being insulated from having to think much about either race or nationality. Until I moved to China at the age of twenty-four, I hadn't grappled with either in a meaningful way. My eight years in China were my education. It was an incomplete one—white people occupy a position of privilege in China, and I did not live in the shadow of a long-standing history of discrimination and systemic inequality, as people of color do in the United States. But I learned how it felt to have my race and nationality overwhelm other aspects of who I am, and to be confused with other white people who looked nothing like me. As the years passed and I grew comfortable in my surroundings, I would often forget that I didn't belong. Then I would run out to buy milk and notice a shopkeeper's face screw up in confusion before I opened my mouth.

My line of work didn't help. Western journalists enjoyed freedoms that were rarely afforded to our Chinese counterparts, but we were nonetheless viewed with wariness. Local officials were often hypercontrolling, even with stories that had a positive spin. At moments, average citizens could also be suspicious. A friend's mother in Shanghai once cautioned him that I could be a spy. I found that sentiment funny when I was a twenty-five-year-old freelancer with a degree in literature; who would possibly want me as a secret agent? I wondered. But as time went on and I strove to be taken seriously as a journalist, it bothered me. My articles probably took on a more negative tone because of this. Being treated with suspicion, I came to realize, could breed animosity where there had been none.

As I learned more about the case of Robert Mo, I realized that I needed to understand how race and ethnicity had shaped FBI investigations involving Chinese scientists over the decades. I spoke with former FBI agents and with Asian-American activists who advocated for people accused of crimes. It was clear from the start that there was a lot of bad intelligence on China. During the Cold War, the United States was almost singularly focused on the Soviet Union. After 9/11, radical Islamist terrorism became the hot area to study. China analysis, by comparison, was meager. But piecing together how that analysis had evolved over time was tricky. The FBI gave one story. Its critics gave another. Then one day an email arrived in my inbox from a woman named Ling Woo Liu.

Liu had worked for an advocacy group called Advancing Justice—Asian Law Caucus in San Francisco. An article I'd written had reminded her of something that happened to a close family friend, a Chinese-American engineer who worked for defense contractors. The friend, she wrote, "was fired from his job and effectively blacklisted from his industry after visiting his family in Jiangsu province in the early 1970s. For years, he tried to find an answer regarding his wrongful termination. He was not successful."

I set up a call with Liu. In 1973, she told me, Harry Sheng was working as a mechanical engineer for Sparton Corporation, a defense contractor in Jackson, Michigan, when his mother got sick back in Jiangsu. Richard Nixon had just made the historic visit to China that led to normalized relations with the United States, so Sheng took advantage of the thaw to travel to the mainland to visit her. When he returned to Michigan, his company mysteriously transferred him to a drafting position, and he was separately interviewed by agents from the FBI, the CIA, and the Department of Defense. In 1975, Sheng was laid off from his job at Sparton and two offers he had received from other defense firms were suddenly rescinded. He never worked in his field again.

Sheng and his wife scraped by. His wife began nannying for Liu and her sisters—a job that lasted fifteen years. The girls did not learn why Sheng had stopped working at age fifty until decades later, after his death. Then, while sorting through his belongings, the sisters found a packet of papers containing six years' worth of letters from Sheng to Michigan lawmakers seeking answers about why he was fired. "I contributed my best knowledge to the U.S. defense work," Sheng wrote in a 1975 letter to his U.S. representative, Milton Robert Carr. "I will continue to fight until the truth comes out." As far as Liu knows, that never happened. She learned the truth only after obtaining her uncle's FBI file and other documents through Freedom of Information Act (FOIA) requests: Her uncle had been investigated for vaguely delineated ties to China.

Liu sent me the files. It was hard to know what to make of them, because the FBI had redacted large sections of text. I could see why she was concerned, though. The parts that were legible didn't appear to suggest any wrongdoing. "SHENG stated he loves America and the freedom provided by this country for its citizens and that he considers himself to be a loyal, patriotic American," read the report of an FBI agent who interviewed him outside his home in 1972. "SHENG displayed a friendly, cooperative attitude during the interview. . . . Review of the files regarding subject . . . reveals no significant data ███████████ or security risk on the part of the subject which would justify his being interviewed a third time." And the top of each document bore a curious label: "IS-CH: Chinese Communist Contacts with Scientists in the U.S."

"Have you heard of this program?" Liu asked me. I hadn't. She wanted to know who else had been monitored or investigated under it. I filed my own FOIA request for any documents connected to the program, then moved on to other work.

Two years passed. After I had all but given up on the request, the FBI released a partial batch of documents. The picture painted by the documents was incomplete and, like Sheng's file, marred by redactions. But the documents did prove the existence of a classified program, begun in the late 1960s under FBI director J. Edgar Hoover and lasting into at least the mid-1970s, to track Chinese scientists working in the United States.

. . .

THE STORY OF THE FBI'S Chinese scientist program dates to the 1950s Red Scare, when the FBI investigated Chinese-born rocket scientist Tsien Hsue-Shen (later known as Qian Xuesen) for being an alleged member of the U.S. Communist Party. Tsien was a talented researcher at the California Institute of Technology in Pasadena, where he worked with Hungarian-American mathematician Theodore von Kármán on classified government projects. At Caltech, he helped found the Jet Propulsion Laboratory, and he befriended several left wing scholars who were members of the U.S. Communist Party. New research suggests that for a time Tsien himself was a member of the party, though apparently not as active as some of his friends. His ethnicity—he was described in his FBI file as "yellow"—might have heightened investigators' suspicions. In 1950, the year after Mao rose to power in China, FBI agents questioned Tsien, and the U.S. military revoked his security clearance.

With his loyalty to America under scrutiny and his job prospects diminished, Tsien tried to leave for China with his family. The new government in Beijing had begun openly courting overseas scientists, in some cases putting pressure on their relatives to invite them back to contribute to the motherland, and Tsien, who was a U.S. permanent resident, knew he would be welcomed there. But U.S. immigration agents prevented him from returning to China after one of the movers he had hired told investigators that his possessions included documents labeled SECRET and CONFIDENTIAL. After inspecting the papers, investigators disagreed on whether they contained critical secrets. But they knew that Tsien had valuable information in his mind. They ordered his arrest.

The next five years were tumultuous. Tsien was released and allowed to return to teaching at Caltech, but he remained under near-constant FBI surveillance. In September 1955, after a Chinese diplomat raised Tsien's case in high-level talks in Switzerland, the United States allowed him to leave for China in exchange for the Chinese government returning Americans captured during the Korean War. In Beijing, leaders greeted him as a hero and put him to work on critical weapons and space research. In 1966, with Tsien's assistance, China stunned the world by testing a nuclear-tipped missile.

I was once taken to see Tsien's apartment in Beijing. It was in a low-rise concrete building in a leafy courtyard—a setup that looks humble now, but that back in the 1960s was reserved for only the most esteemed experts. Inside, Tsien's son, Qian Yonggang, gestured to a living room decorated with blond-wood accents. "Many Chinese leaders have sat here," he told me in Mandarin. He showed me the chipped paint on the walls, and his father's small study, and the twin bed where Tsien had spent his final days, emphasizing that his father was a simple man to the end. The apartment had only one bedroom, so I asked Qian Yonggang where he and his sister had slept growing up. He mumbled that the family had been given a second apartment in the building—a marker of their privilege at the time.

Back in the United States, Tsien's first cousin, Tsien Hsue-Chu, cautiously instructed his children to act as American as possible. "I grew up speaking not a lick of Chinese and eating hot dogs at baseball games," his granddaughter, Sarah Tsien Zetterli, told me. Within national security circles, meanwhile, Tsien's case became proof that overzealous investigations could seriously backfire. Dan Kimball, who was secretary of the Navy in the early 1950s, said of the decision to allow Tsien to leave the United States, "It was the stupidest thing we ever did." But to J. Edgar Hoover, China's nuclear ambitions justified further investigations of Chinese scientists in the United States. Hoover penned an article in *Nation's Business* titled "How Red China Spies." He wrote of the danger posed by "persons who have strong ties to the Orient," particularly "students and scientists with living relatives behind the Bamboo Curtain."

The documents that I received through my Freedom of Information Act request showed that in 1967, after the test of China's nuclear-tipped missile, the FBI launched an internal effort aimed at surveilling Chinese scientists and students. On June 28 of that year, the director's office dashed off a memorandum to FBI field offices directing them to closely monitor researchers of Chinese descent. "While it is known that numerous Western-trained scientists, particularly Chinese from U.S., have returned to China and have the training and ability to accomplish a nuclear program," the memo read, "the Chicoms must keep up to date on technological advances in the West in order to create the finished product. We have long suspected that Chicom collection of needed information is accomplished through contacts with ethnic Chinese scientists and technicians in this country." A later memo ordered agents to cull names of ethnically Chinese researchers including, implicitly, U.S. citizens from the membership records of scientific organizations. The name of each target was to be written on a card, and the cards then assembled into an index—a Rolodex of an estimated four thousand ethnically Chinese scientists under surveillance. The first memo bore the same code that appeared in Harry Sheng's file: IS-CH.

In fact, many ethnic Chinese students at U.S. universities at the time had come from Taiwan and Hong Kong, meaning that they were likely not die-hard socialists. Nonetheless, the New York field office soon opened an estimated two hundred files on ethnic Chinese students in technical fields. San Francisco opened as many as seventy-five files. Cincinnati and Seattle responded as well. In their haste to follow orders, some offices pursued shaky leads. The Cincinnati field office worked off the membership list of a Chinese scientific organization from seventeen years earlier. The special agent in charge of the New York office noted in a response to the director's office that there were some two thousand ethnic Chinese students in his region, but that their institutions might not cooperate on such "a sensitive area of inquiry." He suggested contacting defense contractors and asking security officers to compile lists of ethnically Chinese employees—which may explain why Harry Sheng was singled out in Michigan. The file of Tsien Hsue-Shen was reopened, even though he was now in China. The FBI tracked people with even a tenuous connection to Tsien, including relatives of his friends.

After China and the United States restored ties in 1972, the FBI's surveillance of Chinese scientists and students persisted. As Chinese-American scientists like Harry Sheng returned to visit long-lost friends and relatives, the bureau kept close tabs on them.

Interviewing scientists following their trips to China was logical. United States leaders were so desperate for insight into what was happening in China that travelers were a natural source of information. But the interviews might have ended up alienating potential allies at a time when they were being actively courted by the Chinese government. Chen Ning Yang, a Nobel-winning physicist who visited his ailing father in 1971 and was unexpectedly invited to dine with Premier Zhou Enlai, told reporters that he was questioned by the FBI with "some hostility" upon his return to the United States. Several decades later, Yang did relocate to China, where he became honorary director of Tsinghua University in Beijing and renounced his American citizenship. Whether the FBI had reason to question his loyalty, or whether the questioning instead pushed him toward China, is unclear.

The FBI file of Chih-Kung Jen, a physicist at Johns Hopkins Applied Physics Laboratory who traveled to China in the early 1970s, includes several references to efforts to ascertain his "loyalty" to the United States. The bureau monitored the phone numbers that he called and the duration of those conversations. In his memoir, Jen recalled that FBI and NSA agents tried to persuade him to spy on friends back in China, at one point cutting him a blank check in an apparent effort to buy his cooperation. (Jen never cashed it.)

Other scientists were tracked as they went about their lives in America. In an attempt to dig up dirt on Chang-Lin Tien, a professor of mechanical engineering at the University of California, Berkeley who later became the university's chancellor, the FBI followed him to art openings, combed credit bureau records and university directories across the country, and called hotels he had booked to make sure he checked in.

During the Cold War era, the FBI also ran overzealous investigations of scientists suspected of having Soviet sympathies. But these were broader inquiries that encompassed non-Russians, like the theoretical physicist and Manhattan Project contributor Richard Feynman. In the case of the Chinese scientist program, subjects came under suspicion primarily because of their ethnicity. The FBI's targets included subjects who were ethnically Chinese but had only loose ties to the mainland. One person monitored under the program was an MIT professor from Indonesia.

The program continued into at least the late 1970s. Not everybody took the questioning in stride. Tien's file included a note that read: "He expressed his belief that the FBI was continuing to harass Chinese academicians like himself just as was done during the 1950s."

Reading these files, I wondered to what extent misguided investigations had persisted. Answering that question would involve unraveling decades of espionage theories.

TEN

FALL 2011

Within a few months of the Polk County sheriff's deputy stopping Robert Mo near the Monsanto field, the FBI's investigation grew to include field offices in Miami and Chicago. The effort was code-named Purple Maze, and Mark Betten oversaw it from Des Moines, with help from Economic Espionage Unit management in D.C. The case had taken on new urgency. In November 2011, the Office of the National Counterintelligence Executive, which advises the president on intelligence matters related to national security, published a report to Congress calling out Chinese actors as "the world's most active and persistent perpetrators of economic espionage."

To FBI investigators, Robert became Muddy Hooves—a name selected by the Miami field office that preserved his initials while also evoking an image of a creature digging in the dirt. Mark formed an impression of him as competent and serious. The Chinese scientist's primary weakness, the issue that propelled him to work for DBN, was his desire to support his wife and two kids.

Much of the time he lived the life of a suburban dad. He played tennis, made frequent trips to Walmart and Costco, and fished, using the skills he had picked up as a boy in the mountains of Sichuan. FBI agents dutifully followed him as he stocked up on groceries and cast his fishing line into placid waters. But then, when on assignment for DBN in the Midwest, Robert was diligent, often working fifteen- or sixteen-hour days.

It was those marathon days that most concerned Mark. The appearance of Robert in two Iowa fields raised the question: Of all the cornfields in America, how did the DBN employees know where to look for inbred corn? Both the Monsanto plot where Deputy Bollman had stopped the men and the Pioneer plot where the men were found digging were unmarked. And they had trespassed onto the Pioneer field in the spring, before the corn had germinated, when inbred and commercial hybrid fields were nearly identical. The Monsanto field was in the middle of nowhere, miles from a major road. It wasn't as if Robert Mo had taken a quick detour while cruising along Interstate 35. Someone must have told him where to find it.

One clue involved Stine, the small seed company outside Des Moines whose executives had recently traveled to China. A young, Chinese-born former employee named Lily Cheng* had set up the trip and arranged the meeting with DBN. A source told Mark that she and Robert appeared to know each other well.

While no longer on staff at Stine, Cheng worked as a consultant for the company, a position from which she led the company's China strategy. She had emigrated from China in her twenties, and she had a cherubic smile, along with an assured confidence that had

---

*This is a pseudonym.

earned her a profile in a local magazine as an up-and-coming business leader.

Like Robert, Cheng was not a polished political operative. Just five years before Mark came across her name, she had been a bright-eyed foreign student in Europe, overwhelmed at the experience of being unexpectedly bumped up to business class on a flight from Hong Kong. "After I sat down, I started to study the strange buttons, but when I pressed them they did not react," she wrote on an online forum for Chinese students. "I was dying of shame. I was too embarrassed to call a flight attendant and reveal that it was my first time sitting in business class." But by the time Mark looked into her, Cheng had matured. She was married to a successful American businessman, and she sat on the boards of several Des Moines organizations.

Mark learned that Cheng kept in touch with Robert after the trip to China. Not long after they were found in the field outside Bondurant, Robert Mo, Wang Lei, and Dr. Li drove to Stine's headquarters in Adel to meet with her. Mark tailed the group as Cheng showed them around and then took them out for lunch at a nearby Shanghainese restaurant. At least superficially, the relationship was legal. Cheng consulted for both American and Chinese clients, and she was in the process of brokering an agreement for DBN and Kings Nower to license some of Stine's hybrids for export to China. But Mark believed that as an insider with a deep connection to Stine, she might have access to some of the experimental inbreds that the company had under development.

In the FBI's view, employees were a common vector through which trade secrets leaked out to China. The bureau regularly briefed corporate security officers on how to detect "insider threats" in their companies, and the criteria provided were quite broad. Some purported warning signs were obvious, like employees who unnecessarily copied proprietary information or seemed overly interested in spy work—what the FBI calls James Bond Wannabes. But other behaviors potentially meant nothing. Corporate security officers were told to look out for employees who had marital problems and money issues, and were vulnerable to flattery. Viewed in this light, the smug guy at the water cooler who was going through a divorce suddenly became a potential industrial spy—especially if he was from China.

In a number of cases, the insider threat approach panned out, and a Chinese or Chinese-American employee of the victim company had ended up convicted of an offense. Greg Chung, the Boeing engineer who was sentenced to fifteen years in federal prison for stealing space shuttle secrets, was an insider. So was Xiang Dong Yu, a product engineer at Ford who got nearly six years in prison for trying to transport four thousand sensitive documents to China, and Ye Fei and Zhong Ming, software engineers who were arrested at San Francisco International Airport while attempting to leave the country with microprocessor design trade secrets belonging to several of their former employers, including Sun Microsystems. But there were other cases in which the investigation of an insider suspect was seriously botched. Was Lily Cheng an accomplice in a federal crime? Was she a person who had gotten unwittingly mixed up in illegal activity and who might be turned into a potential informant? Or was she what she purported to be: a consultant who was helping DBN license seeds?

In the months that followed, the FBI subpoenaed Stine for an image of Cheng's company-issued computer and secured a court order to get subscriber information and subject line headings from her Google, Hotmail, and MSN accounts. In an affidavit attached to one warrant application, Mark mentioned in support of probable cause the fact that Robert and Cheng spoke Mandarin together— an unremarkable detail that, because of the focus on Operation Purple Maze, morphed into a marker of guilt.

ELEVEN

WINTER 2011–2012

After a winter spent with his family in Florida, Robert traveled to Iowa to join a Chinese agricultural delegation led by Xi Jinping. Wang Lei flew in from Beijing to join him. The timing was fortuitous for DBN and Kings Nower. As China's vice president, Xi was widely expected to be tapped to be the country's next top leader. He had gotten his start as a deputy party secretary in Hebei, a rural county in eastern China that happened to be Iowa's sister province, and he had long-standing ties to the state. On his first trip to Iowa in 1985, Xi had stayed with a couple in a small farming town, sleeping in their son's bedroom beneath football-themed wallpaper. As he toured agricultural sites on that early visit, he met a young governor named Terry Branstad. Now, after stints in finance and education, Branstad was again governor, and Iowa's economy relied on the export of vast quantities of pork, corn, and soybeans to China. State officials spared no expense in welcoming Xi on his return visit. That meant that any businesspeople who accompanied the anointed leader would get prime access to Iowa's agricultural facilities.

Robert tagged along as the delegation toured a Pioneer research facility, using the name tag of another man in the group, Wu Hougang. In Robert's somewhat dubious account of this event, tour organizers handed out name tags as participants filed off the bus, paying no attention to who got what name. Whatever the story, the real Wu was chairman of a fishery company in northeastern China. As a prominent businessman, his image could easily be found online. He had jolly features, with round cheeks, a broad nose, and the sort of waistline that in China is called *laoban du*, or "boss belly." Even in rural Iowa, where locals often had trouble telling East Asian people apart, it was easy to ascertain that he looked nothing like the small-framed, professorial Robert. But it did not occur to Robert that anyone would actually check.

THE NEXT DAY, while Wang Lei was elsewhere, Robert slipped into the cornerstone event of Xi's visit: a symposium at the World Food Prize Hall of Laureates, held in the stately former Des Moines Public Library on the bank of the Des Moines River. A relic from an era when government buildings were adorned with lavish touches rather than furnished for perfunctory use, the library had recently been given a $30 million overhaul, thanks in part to funding from Monsanto.

Robert strode through heavy mahogany doors into an atrium decorated with gold-leafed molding. Above the marble staircase was an engraving that read FOOD IS THE MORAL RIGHT OF ALL WHO ARE BORN INTO THIS WORLD. Every October, researchers from around the world gathered in the hall for the awarding of the $250,000 World Food Prize. The brainchild of Norman Borlaug, the father of the Green Revolution, the prize was intended to recognize those who made outstanding contributions to food security. In recent years, though, the World Food Prize Foundation had cultivated close ties with both industry and China. The previous October, Monsanto CEO and president Hugh Grant and DuPont executive vice president James Borel were featured speakers at the conference accompanying the prize. They were joined by executives from Walmart and Kraft. The foundation now treated Xi with similar reverence. Staff were preparing to memorialize his visit by hanging a large bronze plaque in the hall's ballroom. In the years since Borlaug had envisaged the prize, food security had become big business.

Robert took a seat in the ballroom. Elsewhere in the audience were the U.S. agriculture secretary, the Chinese agriculture minister, and Governor Terry Branstad. Eventually Xi stepped up to the podium. He talked of deepening cooperation between the United States and China by jointly conducting research and working together to improve food security. Afterward the Chinese side agreed to buy $4.3 billion worth of U.S. soybeans—an agreement that a USDA official called a "momentous one for U.S.-China agricultural relations."

Although the talk that day was all of cooperation, the truth was more complicated. In his State of the Union address a few weeks earlier, President Obama had signaled a desire to get tough on China for intellectual property theft. "I will not stand by when our competitors don't play by the rules," he said. And yet the United States and China were locked in an awkward embrace from which neither side could easily extricate itself. It wasn't just China's purchase of vast amounts of corn and soy, which helped the American economy. The United States also depended on Chinese manufacturers, who made everything from iPhones to auto parts; on a steady flow of Chinese students, who often paid full tuition and helped keep U.S. universities afloat; and on Chinese scientists, who staffed American labs. For each of these relationships, in turn, there was a flip side in China. American grains fed China cheaply and had done so since the early 1970s, when one of the first products that Nixon arranged to be exported to China was corn. The students trained by American universities returned to China better equipped to contribute to economic growth there. And while many of the overseas Chinese working in American labs preferred a Western working environment, a portion could be lured back to lead labs in China. If the two countries were on the brink of a technological cold war, it was a conflict with no clear winner. The United States and China had become, in essence, frenemies.

As Robert listened in the ballroom, wearing another man's name tag, his fate was starting to shift. He felt at ease in America, and that ease, he thought, made him good at his job, even when what was asked of him was illegal. On the phone one day, the Stine consultant Lily Cheng complimented him on his ability to understand both sides—both the United States and China. His family connections might have gotten him hired, but he had proved his worth, no matter what Dr. Li said.

And yet his confidence was rapidly fading. Understanding both sides meant that there were times when he was suspended between them. His sister and parents were in one country and his wife, kids, and social life in another. His livelihood in one, his life in another.

Without Law or Heaven, the cruel nickname assigned to him by his childhood classmates, was becoming strangely apt. For a while he still had heaven on his side, thanks to his church. But other aspects of his existence had become more complicated. At U.S. airports on his trips to and from China, he noticed that he was often pulled aside for searches. It was unclear how much longer he could continue to outrun the law.

TWELVE

SPRING 2012

Kevin stood in a field on DBN's new farm, surveying the land. The sky above him was cloudless, and the air smelled of peat, yet the scene was not entirely pastoral. Realtors called the area around Monee Far South, meaning south of Chicago. The property sat at the junction of suburban comfort and crumpled-up beer cans, in a stretch of homes in varying states of disrepair.

Kevin was excited about being officially hired to work with DBN and eager to help, so when Robert told him that DBN was looking to buy a farm in Illinois, he had offered to help scout out land. Robert responded that he had it under control. These forty acres were the result. The land had poor soil and inadequate drainage. The house was not much to speak of, either. A squat tan brick dwelling with small windows, it stood atop a small hill, to the right of a clearing just large enough for turning around a pickup. Three run-down outbuildings encircled the left side of the clearing, looking like they might be easily toppled in a storm.

Robert had asked Kevin to plant strips of test corn on the land, with the goal of comparing how the varieties performed. Robert said he wanted everything aboveboard and by the book. He had instructed Kevin to find publicly available hybrids developed by small seed companies. If the trials went well, he explained, DBN would license the seeds, send them on to a winter nursery in South America, and eventually export them to China. The seeds had to be conventional, with no genetic modifications, so that they could be sold commercially in China.

That this was a grand fiction was difficult for Kevin to discern; the plan actually struck him as a good idea. It was the sort of project that Robert claimed to be doing with Stine—and the sort of cooperation that U.S. scientific organizations encouraged.

Kevin did question the choice of location, though. He doubted whether the soil on the test plot was consistent enough to give meaningful results. A few weeks earlier, he had asked Robert: Why here? Did Monee approximate agricultural conditions in China? No, Robert said. The plot was near O'Hare International Airport. Representatives from DBN frequently flew in on direct flights from Beijing to Chicago. Monee was convenient. The logic baffled Kevin. It was as if Robert had selected a car based entirely on how close the dealership was to his house.

The agronomist heard the roar of a tractor as Brian Schubbe approached on his John Deere machine, pulling a sixteen-row planter behind him. Robert had hired Schubbe, a local farmer, to plant commercial crops elsewhere on the farm, and as part of the deal Schubbe had agreed to help with the research plot.

Kevin opened a bag, hoisted it upside down, and dumped five pounds of seed into one of the receptacles attached to the planter. The seed rattled as it settled in the bin. Schubbe did the same with another strip test bag, and the two men made their way down the length of the machine, pouring a different bag of test seed into each box.

In an era of massive industry consolidation, finding small seed companies that were interested in collaborating with DBN was difficult. But through his networks of contacts, Kevin managed to find two partners who agreed to provide small amounts of seed for the trial. Money would change hands once DBN selected seeds for export.

The other hybrids he planted in Monee came from his sister, Lynette, who like Kevin was a hobby breeder, and from Kevin himself. He saw in the test plot the possibility of finally getting one of his backyard seed lines commercialized. He knew the odds were long, especially with the land as poor as it was, but it was worth a try. As benchmarks against which to track the growth of the test seeds, Kevin also planted a handful of "check hybrids," most of them well-known varieties belonging to Pioneer and Monsanto.

DBN's plan to license American hybrids made sense to Kevin because he knew that Chinese companies had trouble breeding topnotch seeds on their own. Agronomists speak of "races" of corn, and those races subdivide into groups. Like animal breeders, agronomists in the United States strive for a pure lineage, working with inbreds that have been kept separate, or bred within a certain group and race, for generations. China did not have well-maintained groups, Kevin knew. Corn breeding was a long-term game, and it was impossible to catch up in a generation. So Chinese companies had to import seeds—legally, or so Kevin believed—and then use the preferential market access they were given in China to turn a profit.

After they had poured all the seed into the planter, Schubbe fired up his tractor. As he hauled the planter down the length of the field, sixteen pairs of blades angled toward one another in V shapes, carving sixteen furrows into the soil. The seed dropped into these furrows, and then a second row of blades pushed soil over the newly planted seed. Kevin trailed behind on foot, checking the depth and spacing of the seeds. Decades of fastidious engineering and experimentation had turned the planter into a machine that for Kevin had the precision and beauty of a symphony. When it came to American innovation, he thought of this, not the huge conglomerates that had taken over the seed industry.

A few months earlier, as part of New York's Occupy Wall Street movement, farmers from around the country had traveled to Zuccotti Park to protest corporate control of food and agriculture. "Farmers are hanging on by their fingertips," one explained. They blamed commodities speculation and greed. Tenet number four in the Declaration of the Occupation of New York City asserted of the corporate overlords: "They have poisoned the food supply through negligence, and undermined the farming system through monopolization." Kevin saw genetically modified seed as a breakthrough innovation and didn't share more radical farmers' concerns about poisoning the food supply. But he, too, worried about corporate consolidation.

For Kevin, the effects of consolidation were most apparent in the impact on the land. When Monsanto first began marketing genetically modified seeds, Kevin recalled, company representatives had promised that the company would consider the health of farmland by rotating pesticides out of production after a number of years. As time passed and Monsanto could not come up with a competitive new pesticide, the company began inserting Roundup Ready traits in seemingly everything, leading to the development of Roundup-resistant weeds.

The solution was to "stack" traits onto seeds by tweaking additional genes, creating the seed equivalent of broad-spectrum antibiotics. But just as broad-spectrum antibiotics gave rise to superbugs that were resistant to multiple drugs, stacked traits led to hyper-resistant superweeds. Critics believed that resistance was one reason that companies like Monsanto were so interested in China. Developing-world markets were virgin territory. Because China had not yet commercialized genetically modified seeds, it didn't yet have superweeds. Once government policy changed, the company's seed could be wildly successful there.

In bringing an antitrust suit against Monsanto, Justice Department officials had promised to finally do something about these issues. In the meantime, Kevin was focused on broadening his potential sources of income. He hoped that the DBN gig would lead to more work in China, bringing him closer to his goal of retracing his father's footsteps. He had started studying Mandarin by collecting fortune cookies from Chinese buffet restaurants and logging the words printed on the slips of paper into an Excel spreadsheet. *Understand, success, corn.* He now signed off his emails to Mao Li, DBN's assistant in Beijing, with *Zuihao de wenhou,* a translation he had found online for *Best regards.* He was becoming an international scientist, he thought. He had counterparts in China, people who easily moved between the two countries and whose allegiance was mainly to research.

But Kevin was starting to suspect that Robert was not one of them. The bond he had once felt with the DBN employee had given way to strained communications. It didn't help that Robert could be tactless. At one point he mentioned to Kevin that the agronomist was not DBN's first choice for the consulting gig. Kevin could not imagine why he had been told this, but now that he knew, he had trouble forgetting it.

And yet if someone had told Kevin that the Monee tests were a ruse, that they were somehow an elaborate cover for illicit activity targeting two American seed companies, he would have been shocked—not by the fact of the crime but by the thought that anyone would be stupid enough to mess with Monsanto and Pioneer.

THIRTEEN

SPRING 2012

When the Chinese agriculture delegation led by Xi Jinping arrived in Iowa, Mark Betten received a tip that Robert Mo and Wang Lei would fly in for the occasion. He didn't know what the men hoped to gain from the experience or exactly how it connected to efforts to reverse engineer seed, but he figured it would be worthwhile to surveil them nonetheless. At the Des Moines airport, Mark tailed Wang Lei as he filed out of the arrivals hall and boarded a bus to a hotel. His team didn't manage to locate Robert, so he told Pioneer security to be on the lookout. Sure enough, Robert surfaced the next day at Pioneer's research facility. Corporate security confirmed that he had checked in for a tour using the name Wu Hougang.

Within the FBI, foreign delegations were seen as a common feature of economic espionage cases. The *Intelligence Threat Handbook*, a publication used by the Interagency OPSEC Support Staff to train U.S. government organizations on national security threats, included a passage that could have described Robert's surreptitious tour of Pioneer. "Visitors are an obvious vector for loss of critical information," it read. "[One] situation involves foreign visitors accompanied by a diplomat who attempts to conceal the visitors' identities or official positions during the visit." In this case, the diplomat whom Robert had accompanied happened to be the future leader of China. Mark's team worked every angle of Xi Jinping's visit. Agents dug through the trash in Wu Hougang's hotel room, hopeful his castoffs might yield insight into DBN's plans. They tailed Robert to a meeting at a sports bar. The next day, Mark watched from outside the World Food Prize Hall as Robert showed up for Xi's speech.

In the weeks that followed, the surveillance continued. Much of it was fairly standard. An agent in Florida obtained a warrant to slap a magnetic GPS device under the chassis of Robert's silver Honda CR-V, then tracked him as he drove around Boca Raton, taking note of his frequent visits to Walmart and Costco. Other agents kept tabs on the location of Robert's cell phone, reviewed his bank records, and watched footage from a camera installed outside of his home.

Then, on April 20, an agent in Miami informed Mark that the tracking device on the CR-V showed it parked in the long-term parking lot at the Fort Lauderdale airport. Three days later, the car was still there, and Robert was nowhere to be found. Mark knew that soon fields across the Midwest would be planted with inbred seed. At exactly the wrong moment, he had lost his suspect.

At the time, the FBI could determine the rough location of a cell phone without a warrant, by using a device that identified the cell phone towers pinged by the person's phone. But in the rural Midwest such towers were often ten or more miles apart. Mark rushed to secure a warrant that would allow him to access so-called Phase II data developed as part of America's Enhanced 911 system.

This would enable him to access GPS data from T-Mobile that could pinpoint Robert's cell phone to within a few hundred yards, ensuring that the team didn't lose their suspect again. In the application, Mark laid out the bureau's operating theory for the case. "[T]here is probable cause to believe that Mo has developed a network of 'insider' contacts at bio-engineered seed companies, e.g. Pioneer Hi-Bred, Monsanto, etc., that provide him and his associates 'insider' information where the victim company's most sensitive bio-engineered seed is being grown in test plots," he wrote. The FBI, he continued, wanted to "witness first hand Mo's theft of the seed." The judge signed the warrant the same day. It was not the last time that surveillance in the case would escalate.

SOON AFTER, MARK CAUGHT UP with Robert in the Midwest, and they began a protracted cat-and-mouse chase through the Corn Belt. Even though the FBI could now easily track Robert's location using GPS, Mark still wanted someone physically following him in case he made an interesting pit stop. Sometimes he directed bureau surveillance teams from his desk in Des Moines. At other moments, Mark tailed Robert himself.

Robert spent whole days driving slowly through rural Illinois and Indiana. Often there were no other cars for miles. Cruising through farm country, Mark sometimes thought of passages he had read in the journals kept by explorers Meriwether Lewis and William Clark. As Lewis and Clark's expedition ventured west of the Mississippi, the men were amazed at how far they could see in any direction. "The Surrounding Plains is open void of Timber and leavel to a great extent: hence the wind from whatever quarter may blow, drives with unusial force over the naked Plains and against this hill," Clark wrote. "[T]he Plain to North N. W & N E extends without interruption as far as Can be Seen." When it came to visibility, not much had changed in the intervening two hundred years.

It was tricky enough for Mark to keep cover on asphalt roads, but even trickier on country routes while stirring up clouds of dust. To add to the challenge, Robert seemed to be trying to foil efforts to follow him. On the interstate, he would drive slowly for periods and then suddenly speed up. On smaller roads, he would head in one direction, then abruptly turn around.

Mark was close behind, though, when Robert walked into the seed dealer Crossroads Ag in Dallas County, Iowa. The dealership stood at the intersection of two rural roads, where it was housed in a hangar-like building covered with green and white aluminum siding. Adirondack chairs emblazoned with the University of Iowa Hawkeyes logo flanked the front door. Inside, a small shop adjoined a cavernous warehouse where the seed was kept. Late April was boom time for Crossroads Ag. In the warehouse, workers were loading trucks with dozens of bags of Pioneer seed at a time.

On that particular day a colleague of Mark's had what agents called "the eye" on Robert, which meant the most direct view of the suspect. Mark was a block or two away as Robert walked into the warehouse and approached Crossroads Ag's owner, Joel Thomas. Later, Thomas filled him in on the encounter.

Inside the warehouse, Robert asked for six bags of Pioneer seed, all different varieties. The request signaled to Thomas that he wasn't an experienced farmer. Most farmers stuck to a single type of seed so that all of their corn would be ready to harvest at once.

Thomas was also struck by Robert's ethnicity and the fact that he was not a native speaker. The farmers Thomas knew didn't look or talk like him. But he remembered Robert stopping in around planting season the year before, saying that he owned a farm nearby. He figured he might be a hobby farmer from the city.

Like other major seed companies, Pioneer required all customers buying seed to sign a document, called a tech agreement, stating that they understood the seed they were purchasing was DuPont intellectual property. The document forbade farmers from reusing or distributing the seed. Critics saw these contracts as overly restrictive. In a case then winding its way through the courts, Monsanto had used a tech agreement to sue an Indiana farmer for planting soybean seeds he bought from a grain elevator. The seeds contained Monsanto traits and were intended to be sold as commodities, not planted in fields. Thomas could lose his dealer's license if he didn't insist on a signed agreement before someone made a purchase. At the moment Robert came into the shop, though, he was too busy to think straight. Deciding that Robert must have signed an agreement on his previous visit, Thomas loaded six bags of seed into the trunk of Robert's rental car and sent him into the shop, which featured shelves stocked with pet food and garden gnomes. The total came to $1,533.72. Robert paid cash.

The next day, Mark directed an FBI surveillance team from Omaha to follow Robert as he got in the rental car and headed south. He drove for two hours. Finally, he reached a seed store in Pattonsburg, Missouri, where he bought six more bags of seed, again paying cash. Then he drove back to Iowa, the FBI surveillance team following close behind.

A short distance from Crossroads Ag, in the town of Adel, Robert stopped at A&M Mini Storage. Three long sheds, subdivided into small units, stretched across a desolate asphalt lot. The place projected an aura of decay. A sign posted on one shed was missing letters. PICK OUT YOUR UNI, it read. FIND RENTAL FORM AND RE D V R. The manager later said that many of the sheds were transitional garages for the evicted and jilted, for the man who had been kicked out but who could not bear to part with his gas grill.

Robert had more focused intentions, though. The Omaha surveillance team watched from a safe distance as he opened the padlock to unit 48 and unloaded several bags of seed from his trunk. Then he secured the padlock and took off.

FOURTEEN

2016-2017

As time went on, I came to see Robert's case as a lens that refracted growing hostility between the United States and China. At first, people who used the term "new cold war" were accused of hyperbole. Then the term was everywhere. Scholars and businesspeople of Chinese descent worried about being caught in the middle. Every week brought a new battlefront. Industrial espionage cases were often swept up in this larger fight, and Robert Mo's case was no exception.

One trope in particular cropped up again and again. This was the idea that China commanded an army of amateur intelligence collectors of which Robert was just one part—or, as *Newsweek* columnist Jeff Stein put it, that Robert was among the "locusts in a swarm, feasting on American technological secrets." This swarm of amateurs extended from Chinese scientists to Chinese students studying at U.S. universities, Stein wrote. Many of these students were "sleeper cells," he added, who would "lie low for years before they're called into action, usually after they've gained employment in high-tech firms."

I knew many Chinese scientists and students who were not locusts, and I wanted to figure out where this notion originated. I interviewed experts and dug up old papers. Eventually, I traced the idea to the 1990s, as U.S. intelligence agencies struggled to understand China in the wake of the Cold War. At an intelligence conference in 1996, the year before Mark Betten began working at the FBI, an FBI China analyst named Paul Moore presented what came to be called the thousand grains of sand theory. Essentially, his idea gave the surveillance of Chinese scientists theoretical backing.

In his presentation, Moore explained China's approach to spying in opposition to the James Bond–like tactics of the United States and Russia. If intelligence collection by the world's most powerful nations were aimed at determining the composition of the sand on a beach, he said, the Russians would station a submarine in deep waters. Then, in the middle of the night, a commando team would paddle a raft to shore, scoop up a few buckets of sand, and retreat to the submarine. The United States would use sophisticated technology, flying satellites over the beach and scanning the sand with infrared and spectrographic scanners. China, on the other hand, would rely not on technology or covert operations but on its large population. The question of beach composition could be solved by sending ten thousand people—students, scientists, and entrepreneurs—to spend a day in the sun. At the end of the day, this mass of people would head home and shake out their towels. China would end up with a lot of sand.

This has also been called the vacuum cleaner approach: China sucks up small bits of information, as if they are dust, then assembles these seemingly useless bits into a complete whole. Both meta-phors owe a debt to yellow peril, the trope of nameless hordes over-whelming U.S. borders, which dates to the nineteenth century but never really vanished from the American discourse. After 1949, the Chinese Communist Revolution lent blatant racism a veneer of ide-ological heft, and journalists and politicians began referring to the Chinese as "blue ants," a reference to the blue Mao suits worn by many people. Moore's version focused on espionage, but the gist was roughly the same. Instead of professional agents, China relies on a dispersed network of nontraditional collectors: a "human wave" of students, scientists, and engineers, or beachgoers, who gather in-telligence ad hoc.

To come up with this theory, Moore drew on his understanding of *guanxi*. This is a notion that is familiar to anyone who has read an introductory business guide to China: A network of favors and obligations governs social relations in the country. It was as if China were to develop a theory of how the CIA functioned based on American individualism.

Chinese intelligence agencies, he proposed, reach out to people of Chinese descent for help with small tasks, appealing not to a love of money or vice but to a presumed allegiance to the motherland. In his view, other nations typically look for people with weaknesses who might be turned into professional spies. The Chinese govern-ment, meanwhile, seeks good people—people who are diligent and active in their communities and good at their jobs—who might be persuaded to do a little moonlighting.

A CIA agent might pass a message to a source by leaving it in a secret location, called a dead drop. China's virtuous spies, Moore argued, would use nontraditional methods, like attending presenta-tions and events that are open to the public, to pursue small pieces of information. The information they gathered would then be sent back to China and somehow collated and redistributed. Exactly how was never explained.

Moore's theory made little distinction between China's national security spying—the kind of spying that all nations do—and industrial espionage. Taken to its natural conclusion, the theory meant that the Chinese government commanded a network of amateur spies and that all incidents of trade secrets theft, whether of widgets or weapons, traced back to the Chinese Communist Party. It also suggested that investigations could start and stop with ethnic Chinese suspects. "The reason that it is always ethnic Chinese who seem to be involved in Chinese intelligence matters is that they typically are the only ones China asks for assistance," Moore wrote in the *Los Angeles Times* in 1999. "It's just that simple."

When I called Paul Moore years later, he stressed that his theory wasn't a prescription for targeting a specific ethnic group. "The important thing you have to realize about racial profiling in Chinese cases is that it does not work," he told me. "If you say, 'Let's go into this company, and we'll investigate all of the Chinese employees there, and that will be where we start our investigation,' you immediately run into a situation where you have an awful lot of Chinese and you're going to burn through your resources before you get to the end of the problem. So as a shortcut it's not useful." He also noted that many of the people who were targeted as spies by China refused to help—that the frustrating thing about dealing with Chinese intelligence operatives was that they "dirtied the nest" by reaching out to people who turned out to be innocent.

He was right that Chinese Communist Party officials viewed ethnic Chinese as critical to China's rise. "Although overseas Chinese scholars and ethnic Chinese specialists are living abroad, their hearts belong to their families and country," two science policy experts wrote in a Chinese journal in 2001. The goal, as one Ministry of Personnel official put it, was to "borrow brains" by luring overseas Chinese to help with the project of China's ascendance. Moore was also correct that many people refused to help. But I thought he was oblivious to how easily his idea could be misused.

For officials and journalists struggling to understand China, the beach metaphor was colorful and easy to grasp. The notion that the country operated in a fundamentally different way from the United States or Russia fit in with stereotypes about Chinese leaders being bumbling and inscrutable. It was a narrative that flattered U.S. interests: Our foe was unsophisticated.

Soon after Moore introduced the thousand grains of sand theory, it was put to the test in the case against Wen Ho Lee, a Taiwanese-born scientist in Los Alamos, New Mexico, who in 1999 was accused of stealing secrets connected to the U.S. nuclear arsenal.

The case against Lee had its genesis in the rapid advancement of China's nuclear weapons program throughout the 1990s. Some in Washington suspected that the only possible explanation was that China had stolen weapons secrets from the United States. Then, in 1995, a defector claiming to have worked on China's weapons program turned up at the offices of Taiwan's internal security service. The man carried with him documents indicating China had some knowledge of the United States' W88 warhead. Deciding that the leak must have come from Los Alamos National Laboratory, Department of Energy investigators went in search of a suspect. The FBI was enlisted to help. The investigation was code-named Kindred Spirit, after China's assumed tendency to target ethnic Chinese. In an echo of Hoover's 1967 directive, early plans called for the investigation of all ethnic Chinese researchers who worked in any way on the development of the W88. Investigators soon settled on Lee, a longtime Los Alamos scientist, as their suspect.

Lee had come onto the FBI's radar before. In the 1980s, he cold-called a Taiwan-born scientist who was under surveillance, offering his help. He also failed to report contact he had with Chinese science officials, and he had downloaded restricted information off a Los Alamos computer. But the claim that he had stolen secrets connected to the W88 was tenuous. Nonetheless, the investigation soon spun out of control in a series of blunders. To justify searching Lee's home, the FBI submitted an affidavit noting that "People's Republic of China intelligence operations virtually always target overseas ethnic Chinese with access to intelligence information sought by the PRC." The U.S. government also subpoenaed UCLA, where Lee's daughter was enrolled, seeking the names of all students from Taiwan and China.

Before Lee could be formally charged, someone leaked his name to *The New York Times*, which published an article fingering him as a suspect in March 1999. Republican leaders in Washington had criticized the Clinton administration for being soft on China, and the Lee case appeared to offer a way for officials to prove that they were tough. The mood in Washington reached a fevered pitch. Then, in May, U.S. Air Force pilots working for the North Atlantic Treaty Organization dropped bombs on the Chinese embassy in Belgrade.

I visited China with my father a few weeks later. I was nineteen and a beginning student of Chinese. United States officials said that the bombing was an accident, but that didn't deter the angry protesters who attacked McDonald's and set fire to the home of the U.S. consul general in Chengdu. I remember my father sewing Canadian maple leaf patches on our backpacks. The experience underscored for me the degree to which espionage charges against a single person could inflame tensions between the two countries.

Lee was arrested in December 1999. For the better part of a year, he was held in solitary confinement twenty-three hours a day in a New Mexico jail. Asian-American advocacy groups mobilized. A few called on researchers to boycott the national laboratories by rejecting any job offers. The activists' cause was strengthened when the case against Lee swiftly unraveled. In September 2000, Lee was acquitted of fifty-eight of the fifty-nine charges against him. He pleaded guilty to a single felony count of mishandling classified information.

After ordering his release, Judge James A. Parker chastised the Justice Department and the FBI for leading him astray and apologized to Lee for the harsh conditions of his detention. Later, Lee sued the federal government for leaking his name before he was formally charged. In 2006 he received a $1.6 million settlement, which was paid in part by *The New York Times*. In an essay for *Slate*, Lowen Liu called Lee "the Patient Zero of the unnerving present and uncertain future of being Chinese in America."

Despite the bungling of the Wen Ho Lee investigation, the thousand grains of sand framework was soon enshrined in the *Intelligence Threat Handbook*, a U.S. government publication made available to intelligence agency staff. The Chinese Ministry of State Security (MSS), the manual claimed, focused 98 percent of its recruitment efforts in the United States on Chinese Americans and overseas Chinese. The Russians, by contrast, supposedly focused no more than a quarter of their recruitment efforts on people of Russian descent. The handbook also asserted that MSS operatives spent time culling *People* magazine for dirt on important Americans. (It did not explain whether accounts of celebrities' weight gains and affairs actually resulted in any useful intelligence.)

In the years that followed, the theory drove assessments like Stein's that many Chinese students in the United States were aspiring spies and that American companies founded by ethnic Chinese—all of them—were primarily fronts. A 2010 report from the private intelligence firm Stratfor stated, for example, that "China has the largest population in the world, at 1.3 billion, which means that it has a vast pool of people from which to recruit for any kind of national endeavor, from domestic road-building projects to international espionage." In a follow-up report, Stratfor explained, "The Chinese intelligence services rely on ethnic Chinese agents because the services do not generally trust outsiders." But at the time, there was already abundant evidence that this was false.

Around the time that Mark began investigating Robert Mo, a former CIA analyst named Peter Mattis published a series of articles debunking the thousand grains of sand theory. In reality, he noted, China has a collection of sophisticated intelligence agencies, not an army of centrally commanded amateurs. The Ministry of State Security, the Ministry of Public Security, the People's Liberation Army, and a host of smaller provincial offshoots all conduct their own operations. A case of national security spying typically originates with one of these agencies. Nor do Chinese intelligence agencies necessarily seek out good people, as Paul Moore proposed. For decades, these agencies have run sources in a textbook manner, by playing on the same vulnerabilities that other intelligence services exploit—enticing them with money and sex and using clandestine tradecraft. In the end, China spies much the way the United States and Russia do.

With industrial espionage, meanwhile, state direction isn't nearly so clear-cut. An instance of technological theft could come from a state-owned enterprise that is deeply entwined with the Chinese government, or from a private company like DBN with murkier government ties but plenty of other incentives to steal. Then there are hustlers who simply spot an opportunity to make money and move forward without any overt government direction. In a number of Chinese industrial espionage cases, the perpetrators have tried to find buyers for trade secrets only after they stole them.

This distinction was not as subtle as it might seem. When it comes to crafting remedies to technological theft, it matters greatly whether Beijing is directly involved.

More important for people like Wen Ho Lee, Mattis pointed out that neither Chinese intelligence services nor Chinese companies necessarily prefer to rely on intelligence collectors of Chinese ethnicity. Doing so makes sense in some cases, like when the Ministry of State Security keeps tabs on dissidents living overseas. But in others it severely limits the types of information that can be collected.

In fact, non-Chinese defendants have surfaced in both national security spying and industrial espionage cases. In 2009, University of Tennessee professor John Reece Roth was sentenced to four years in prison for violating export control laws by transporting sensitive information about a U.S. Air Force project to China. The next year, a jury found Clark Roberts and Sean Howley guilty of economic espionage after they surreptitiously photographed Goodyear's tire designs. Wyko Tire, their employer, had a contract with a Chinese manufacturer to make tires for mining and earth-moving equipment. Not long afterward, a court in Austria convicted Dejan Karabasevic, a Serbian engineer at Wisconsin-based American Superconductor

Corporation, for helping the Chinese firm Sinovel steal source code for operating wind turbines from his American employer. Karabasevic was a colorful character and in many ways a classic spy, driven by sex and wealth—not by the patriotism or virtue that Moore claimed motivated Chinese operatives. "All girls need money. I need girls. Sinovel needs me," Karabasevic wrote in one email that surfaced in court.

I met Mattis for coffee one day in central Washington, D.C. We sat outside, in a pedestrian passageway, and between the sirens whirring past and the fact that Mattis had lost his voice, I had to strain to hear him. The conversation felt appropriately clandestine.

The persistence within the FBI of incorrect and blatantly racist theories can damage U.S. intelligence interests, he told me. "Chinese investigations in the bureau have basically skipped over what Chinese intelligence is doing, because they've been dealing with a false view of what is Chinese intelligence," Mattis said.

His alternative portrait of Chinese spying—of a mixture of highly professional intelligence agencies, companies, and profit-minded hustlers—is sometimes called the multilayered theory of espionage. But unlike the thousand grains of sand theory, it doesn't fit into a pat metaphor. The old thinking has persisted within the intelligence agencies, raising the possibility that counterintelligence agents could overlook perpetrators because they don't fit the notion of what a Chinese industrial spy should look like, and that they might miss organized Chinese intelligence efforts that pose a more direct national security threat.

A month before our meeting, the news had leaked that Chinese security services had breached the CIA's network. From 2011 to 2012, as the FBI was chasing Robert across corn country, Chinese operatives had taken out sources across China, imprisoning some and killing others in broad daylight. In one case, a source was shot in a government courtyard as his colleagues looked on in shock. Chinese security services were believed to have penetrated the CIA's covert communications channel. "We didn't see that coming," Mattis told me.

Another failure was the 2014 Office of Personnel Management data breach, when Ministry of State Security hackers stole records for 21.5 million Americans, many of them government employees. The records included Social Security numbers, addresses, dates and places of births, and in some cases fingerprints—making it impossible for secret agents to continue in their work, because they couldn't change their prints. In essence, the emphasis on students and scientists working as freelance spies was leading U.S. intelligence agencies astray. The focus on amateur intelligence collectors also alienated the very community that the intelligence agencies needed most: the Chinese and Chinese-American scientists and engineers who might be critical to discovering breaches. But ideas rooted in thousand grains of sand theory would continue to pervade FBI thinking on China—and come to shape the fate of Robert Mo.

FIFTEEN

SPRING 2012

Kevin returned to the Monee farm every ten days or so to check on the hybrids. As the seeds germinated and sent up stalks, he evaluated weed pressure and scrutinized the leaves for signs of disease. No one lived in the farmhouse, and most days he was alone. He now communicated with Robert mostly by email.

Robert had neglected to provide him with a critical piece of information about the test seeds: at what density they would be planted in China. Kevin had asked five or six different ways but had not gotten a straight answer. Robert's evasiveness merely added to a string of other frustrations. Kevin still had no contact with DBN's breeders in China. Why, he wondered, had he been invited out to lunch with the company's CEO and asked to present his work, only to be kept from communicating with the very people who could help bring his idea to fruition? But the information on seed density was particularly crucial. Without that detail, it was impossible to know if the seeds that survived in Monee would survive in China.

Then one day while at the Monee farm, Kevin was caught in the rain. He hurried up the long gravel drive in search of shelter. Two long parallel depressions, rapidly turning to mud, marked the place where tires had ground the gravel into dirt. He did not have a key to the house, so when he reached the clearing at the end of the drive he took refuge in one of the outbuildings.

The structure had the quality of an archaeological site. It was frozen in midcentury disarray, as if a family had fled the farm in 1956 and no one had occupied it since. In one corner pink and yellow fiberglass insulation had fallen from the walls and ceilings, creating a carpet of cotton candy. Elsewhere a plastic watering can levitated, lodged in a coil of chicken wire. In the middle of the space, surrounded by saplings, weeds, and half-eaten corncobs, was a mossy utility sink. The scene gave the farm a spooky aspect. As rain pounded in through a gaping hole in the roof, it dawned on Kevin that something was not right with DBN's North America operation.

Early in his career, Kevin had heard tales of "flashlight breeding," or scientists slinking through fields at night to steal parent varieties out of the ground. In the late 1970s, it was widely believed that several seed lines produced by Holden Foundation Seeds, a company headquartered in Williamsburg, Iowa, were the product of flashlight breeding in Pioneer fields. Despite the rumors, LH38, LH39, and LH40 came to be considered three of the industry's choicest inbreds, and Holden licensed the seed to companies across the industry—including Garst, where Kevin then worked. He was expected to use the inbreds in his breeding experiments.

In 1981, Pioneer sued. Back then, such disputes were still mainly handled through civil lawsuits, one company versus the other. The lawsuit dragged on for more than a decade, going all the way to the U.S. Court of Appeals.

It turned out that Pioneer had a powerful new weapon in its case against Holden: a test that could prove the parentage of a seed line by determining the presence of certain enzymes in the seed, like a paternity test for corn. Called an isozyme electrophoresis test, it involved zapping seed enzymes with an electric current, causing them to separate. When the results came back, they suggested Pioneer stock. The test made flashlight breeding a foolish undertaking. After a fourteen-week trial, Pioneer won $46.7 million in damages.

The companies that had used the three suspicious inbreds, meanwhile, had to scramble to comply with a court order halting the use of any seed lines that had been derived from them. Kevin remembered his supervisor calling him after the case.

"How many LH38 and LH39 crosses do you have?" the supervisor asked.

"Three," Kevin said. For breeders who made upwards of 150 crosses in a year, this was a remarkably low number. The court decision, he felt, justified his stubbornness.

As the industry consolidated, lawsuits became more common. Kevin remembered a near mutiny at one company where he'd worked after a supervisor tried to introduce new seeds into the company's product line. The seeds were bred from Pioneer inbreds that had been reverse engineered through chasing the self.

Monsanto and Pioneer might have been archrivals, but Kevin knew they were united in one goal: the protection of their intellectual property. The new tests helped them along in that effort. The procedures reminded Kevin of *Barnaby Jones*, a detective show from his youth in which a milk-guzzling private investigator solved murders in the lab using forensic evidence and deduction. "The spectrophotometer doesn't lie," Barnaby Jones used to say, like a 1970s Sherlock Holmes.

Monsanto, in particular, became notoriously litigious. It sued farmers for growing unlicensed Roundup Ready seed. Then, when one of these farmers went on the speaking circuit to rail against the company, Monsanto published a smear page on its website about him. This sort of legal aggression lay at the heart of the Justice Department's antitrust investigation of the company. But even as it stamped out competition, Monsanto's sheer power meant that the company could also wield intellectual property law to its advantage. The Economic Espionage Act strengthened the company's position by turning trade secrets theft into a federal crime.

Even as Kevin understood that the intellectual property situation in China was different, he would have had trouble imagining that DBN would be so brash as to target the two giants' inbreds on U.S. soil. And yet, taking shelter in the dilapidated outbuilding, he reflected that something about the Chinese company's plans seemed off.

How could the company afford to spend so much on GM seeds when the technology hadn't yet been approved for sale in China? he wondered. Did the research facility that he was taken to see in Beijing even belong to DBN? He remembered now that he had seen nothing that identified the place as a DBN or Kings Nower facility. None of the equipment was labeled as company property. No one in the lab wore a DBN cap or shirt. Kevin began to suspect that perhaps DBN did have big aspirations—just not ones that involved robust seed science.

SIXTEEN

SPRING 2012

After days of tracking Robert as he drove across the Midwest that spring, Mark Betten got a call from an FBI surveillance team in Illinois, alerting him to the fact that Robert had picked up three new companions, all of them different from the men who had accompanied him when he was stopped near the Monsanto field in Iowa seven months earlier. Two were in their thirties, and one was older and balding. Mark consulted with an agent in the Chicago field office, and together they devised a way to figure out who the men were without revealing the existence of the FBI's investigation: enlist two Chicago Police Department officers to help.

Detectives Angel Lorenzo and Alex Reina took on the assignment. At around 5:00 P.M. one Friday, Lorenzo maneuvered an unmarked car through rush-hour traffic near O'Hare Airport. As Reina sat in the passenger seat on the phone, coordinating plans with FBI agents also on the trail, Lorenzo fell in behind Robert's rental car, being careful to stay two or three cars back. Watch for a traffic violation, ID the men, and send them on their way—that was the plan. Lorenzo was a twenty-two-year veteran of the Chicago Police Department and a member of the FBI's Joint Terrorism Task Force, and he was occasionally asked to make traffic stops of this sort. If there was no violation, he knew, he and Reina were to do nothing. But everyone went home frustrated when that happened.

Robert steered his GMC Yukon due south on North Cumberland Avenue, a four-lane road with good visibility. Alongside the road, businesses of assorted cultural origin rubbed shoulders in strip malls: Lin's Mandarin, Annetti's Pizzeria, Havana Hookah Lounge. Robert drove past a Weight Watchers and a barbershop and a few tanning salons, Lorenzo following one or two cars behind. Then the strip malls gave way to St. Joseph the Betrothed Ukrainian Church, an ornate monstrosity decked out with gold-leafed towers.

It was right around the church that Robert ran a red light. The violation was borderline. The light changed ten or so feet before the Yukon reached the crosswalk. But Lorenzo decided it would do. He turned on his lights, exposing his car as a police vehicle, and sped up to catch his target.

Robert pulled over just south of West Montrose Avenue. The road had no shoulder, and the two cars jutted out into traffic, making the evening commute even less bearable for the Chicagoans who happened to be stuck behind them. Diagonal across the intersection was a supermarket with a sign in the window proclaiming HUGE PRICE CUTS. To the right of the cars lay a forest preserve, a refuge of green in the bleak commercial stretch.

As departures from O'Hare rumbled overhead, Reina took the passenger side, and Lorenzo approached Robert in the driver's seat. Robert protested that the light was yellow when he started to cross the intersection. The officers played along, agreeing to let him off without a citation—but not before they took down the names of the passengers so they could pass them to the FBI.

The first new suspect in the car was Lin Yong, thirty-six years old. He had meek eyes and a teardrop-shaped birthmark on his forehead. Next was Ye Jian, a thirty-year-old man with a chubby build and flared nostrils. Third, and most curious, was the bald man: Michael Yao,* a fifty-something real estate agent in the Chicago area.

The FBI soon identified Lin Yong and Ye Jian as research managers for Kings Nower. Michael Yao's role was harder to parse. The portrait posted on his realty page suggested little interest in selling. The picture was out of focus, shot against the backdrop of a door half ajar, and oddly elongated. Yao appeared unsmiling in the center of the frame, his irises gray from a red-eye correction tool. He and his wife also operated a rundown-looking mortgage brokerage that was housed next to a vasectomy clinic, in a string of brown buildings resembling sad ski lodges. But Yao's role became clearer when the FBI tailed Robert to Monee and discovered that Kings Nower had purchased a forty-acre farm—a plot of land large enough to hold vast cornfields. The address listed on the deed was the office unit next to Yao's mortgage brokerage.

PROPERTY RECORDS INDICATED that Kings Nower had purchased the property from a man named Bill Rab. When Bill and his wife, Ann, got the news that someone was finally interested in his parents' farm, they had been vacationing in Las Vegas at the pyramid-shaped Luxor Hotel, which Ann Rab called "the pointy place." The

---

*This is a pseudonym.

mysterious buyers offered $600,000. For days the Rabs had watched as slot machines doled out winnings to others, and now they felt like they'd hit the jackpot.

Because it was close to Chicago, Monee attracted a fair number of urbanites interested in living out their days golfing and organic gardening. But the house had been on the market for four years, and it needed serious work. City folk tended to reconsider when they got their first whiff of pig manure. "Take the money and run, honey," Ann urged Bill. "Take the money and RUN." They scrambled to sign the paperwork that the men faxed to the Luxor.

Later, back in Illinois, the Rabs sat down at a table with Robert Mo and a lawyer. Robert wrote a check for the entire $600,000, and the property deed was transferred to Kings Nower North America Co., Inc.

Learning of these developments at the Des Moines field office, Mark wondered whether DBN might own other farms. He had his team query land purchases in farm states across the Midwest. He soon discovered that Robert owned a plot of land on a forgotten gravel road forty minutes west of Des Moines, a short drive from the seed shop Crossroads Ag and from the storage space where he had been observed stashing corn.

Mark consulted with prosecutors and seed breeding experts. He theorized that perhaps DBN planned to use the two farms to chase the self, or isolate the female inbred parent from the Monsanto and DuPont seed lines he had purchased from seed dealers. This was a fairly efficient way of reverse engineering seed. Instead of shipping whole bags of seed back to China, DBN's scientists could simply plant them in the Midwest, wait a few months for harvest, and identify any rogue female inbreds by their shorter height, then send the seed from the plants to China. The Iowa farm lacked a house or outbuildings, so it made sense that Robert would need a storage locker nearby.

But the harvest was a long way off, and Robert was still shipping corn seed to Asia. A week after the Chicago traffic stop, Robert, Ye Jian, and Lin Yong pulled into a suburban strip mall, parking near a store called Happiness Is Pets. They hauled five boxes into the FedEx next door and paid for their shipment. After they left, an FBI agent intercepted the packages.

This time the FBI had a warrant to search the packages, which together weighed in at 250 pounds. An inspection revealed that the boxes contained a total of forty-two Ziploc bags of seed, each labeled with a unique four-digit code. The recipient address was a logistics company in Hong Kong.

Mark didn't want to let potentially stolen seed leave the country, so he devised a novel solution: replace it with outdated seed that looked identical. Seed companies' products have distinctive shapes and colors. Pioneer seed is typically dull red and almost round. Other seeds might be purple or yellow and more flat. To make sure the switch was believable, the FBI had to get the replacement seed from Pioneer. After speaking with prosecutors in the U.S. attorney's office and with company representatives, Mark settled on using a ten-year-old Pioneer product. He just had to figure out how to transport it from Pioneer's headquarters in Iowa to the FedEx outside Chicago in time to make the shipment's deadline.

The FBI operates a fleet of low-flying, single-engine aircraft, registered under fake company names, and Mark enlisted one of the bureau pilots to help. As the pilot flew to the Des Moines airport, preparing to jet the seed to Chicago, Mark drove to Pioneer's headquarters in Johnston to fetch the decoy seed. On his way back, as he headed toward the Des Moines airport, Mark got word that the pilot could spend only a few minutes on the ground because he was close to reaching his flight hours for the day. If the pilot lingered, he would be grounded and the replacement seed would have to fly the next day—which would mean delaying the arrival of the FedEx shipment in Hong Kong and possibly arousing suspicion among employees at DBN.

Mark looked at the time and realized he had ten minutes to make a journey that normally takes around half an hour. Flicking on his lights and siren, he raced down Interstate 35, arriving at the airport just in time. He passed the seed to the pilot, who rushed the package to Chicago. On the other end, agents meticulously filled forty-two Ziploc bags with old Pioneer product and laid the bags in the FedEx boxes, taking care to arrange them exactly as they had been found. Soon the decoy seed was soaring over the Pacific on its way to Hong Kong. The shipment arrived on schedule.

As THE INVESTIGATION EXPANDED, Mark's team began relying on FBI aircraft for another purpose: surveilling Robert and others from the air. The FBI's planes are equipped with high-tech cameras and in select instances with cell phone tracking technology, and they sometimes circle locations for hours, keeping a suspect in view. The aircraft took the pressure off Mark and other agents on the ground as they tried to evade detection in corn country. Whenever a pilot was involved, Mark knew he could drop back and watch Robert from afar. But the increased surveillance also jacked up the cost of the investigation—and raised the stakes for Mark if the government failed to apprehend the targets.

The FBI also began collecting evidence using a secret warrant authorized by the Foreign Intelligence Surveillance Act. FISA warrants were designed for targeting terrorists and foreign government spies, and they permit broad electronic and physical surveillance, including covert "sneak and peek" searches—meaning agents could search Robert's house or property without his knowledge and intercept entire cell phone calls. This is likely how the FBI went from tracking the location of Robert's cell phone and the numbers that he called to capturing entire phone conversations.

One day in May 2012, the FBI intercepted a phone conversation between Robert and Lily Cheng. Mark had continued to track the insiders whom Robert was believed to be cultivating at seed companies. The relationship between Robert and Cheng was often ambiguous.

In this particular conversation, Robert told her about the arrival of Ye Jian and Lin Yong in America. "They came, uh, to map the roads in the U.S., so to speak," Robert said in the FBI's translation, clearing his throat. He complained about the time he had to spend training the men, without elaborating on exactly what he was training them to do.

Then he explained that Chinese leaders had placed a lot of emphasis on developing the seed industry, mentioning that the vice minister of agriculture had recently visited DBN's facilities. "I told Dr. Li, when I had a discussion with him—I said, 'The leader didn't come without a purpose. He wasn't here to have fun. He was here to point out the direction for you.'" That direction included the development of genetically modified seeds, he added.

"Oh," Cheng said.

"'He was there to point out the direction for you,'" Robert repeated. "Don't think that he was there to waste time—to just chit-chat with you."

"Right. Right."

"All the leaders have their purpose."

"Mm." As Robert went on about the company's government connections, Cheng mostly just listened. Their talk eventually turned to DBN's legal partnership with Stine, and about how lucrative the swine industry could be.

A thousand grains of sand framework would suggest that Cheng was a tentacle of the Chinese state and that because of her ethnicity she should be looked at with more suspicion. And yet if Cheng was deeply involved in a plot to steal corn, the conversation didn't prove it. Robert may have simply been making the case that DBN had influence in China, which was not an unusual thing to argue to a business partner. Mark didn't speak Chinese, and while the FBI had Chinese-speaking analysts on the case, there were quirks in the bureau's translations.

Then one day at the Monee farm, FBI agents noticed a white man—a man in a Cubs hat and jeans, with a pen tucked neatly into his breast pocket.

SEVENTEEN

SUMMER 2012

Kevin trudged from the cornfield to his farmhouse, dripping with sweat. Behind him the horizon stretched emptily, fields of soy and corn extending as far as the eye could see. He had spent the morning slipping paper bags over ear shoots on his corn, preparing the plants for pollination. These were basically corn condoms, designed to protect the females from being fertilized by unwanted pollen. He wore a plaid shirt with the sleeves ripped off, a mesh apron heavy with tools, and cutoff shorts. The job brought the risk of leaf scratches, so to protect his cheeks Kevin had let his stubble grow, taking as his inspiration Don Johnson's white-suited, slick-haired character on *Miami Vice*.

The day was on track to be the hottest of the year, and already at 10:00 A.M. the temperature soared. Kevin was parched. He walked into the house, letting the screen door thud behind him, and opened the fridge to pour a glass of lemonade. He drank it standing in the kitchen in his dirty clothes. He debated whether to go back to the fields to start in on weed control or take a nap. The nap was tempting.

"Kevin!" his wife, Kathy, called from the adjoining great room. "Are you expecting visitors?"

"No."

"There's a black SUV coming up the driveway."

The car thundering over the drive had tinted windows. Kevin puzzled this over. People in the area didn't go out in heat like this unless they had to. And the farmhouse was on an isolated road some distance from town. He typically directed people there by giving them the GPS coordinates and parking his blue Buick LeSabre to indicate where to turn.

The SUV slowed to a stop, and two men wearing dark sunglasses and navy blue sport coats got out. Kevin opened the screen door.

"Are you Kevin T. Montgomery?" one of the men asked.

"Yes—?" Kevin said. He marveled at the inclusion of his middle initial.

"We're from the FBI." The man flashed his badge. "We understand that you went to China in October 2011. We want to know everywhere you went, everyone you talked to, and what you talked about."

The men were white and in their early thirties, clean-shaven and physically fit. They looked like something straight out of the movies. In the movies, though, the FBI was out to catch bad guys. In the real-life version playing out on his farmhouse deck, he had done nothing wrong. He had his qualms about DBN, but he hardly suspected that anyone there had committed a crime meriting investigation by the FBI.

"OK," Kevin said, confused. He considered whether to call his cousin, who was a lawyer. He concluded that involving him would be interpreted as a sign that he was guilty. Whatever the visit was about, he figured, cooperating could only work to his advantage.

The house was a mess, and there was no air-conditioning, so he led the men to a table on the deck. They sat in the meager shade provided by a hackberry tree—Kevin in his cutoff shorts, his face smudged with dirt, and the men from the FBI in their stiff jackets.

China, Kevin thought, as a farm cat rubbed up against his bare sweaty legs. "What do you want to know?"

The men gave him little direction, so Kevin started by talking about the friend who had introduced him to researchers at the agricultural institute in Changchun that was his principal host. Then, in excruciating detail, he went through the details of his China trip, beginning with his departure from O'Hare Airport. By the time he got to his arrival in Changchun, he was thirsty again.

"Can I offer you a cold drink?" Kevin asked the agents. "Water or lemonade?"

The lead agent said they could only accept drinks if the container was unopened, so Kevin walked to the kitchen and poured a glass of lemonade for himself.

He returned to the deck and resumed his story. He talked about the salted duck eggs that were served for breakfast his first morning in Changchun, about the people he met there and the laboratories he toured. He explained that a friend from Iowa State had joined him for the trip. He recounted how on that first afternoon, as they fought off jet lag, their hosts took the two men to a museum devoted to the Japanese occupation of Manchuria. While browsing the exhibits, the visitors figured out that their fathers had served in similar divisions during World War II.

The agents appeared uninterested until Kevin got to the next day and explained that he had given a presentation on seed breeding in Changchun. They asked to see it.

Kevin retrieved his laptop and set it up on the table. The outline alone took up three slides. In China, his inborn thoroughness was amplified by the need to translate everything into Mandarin. Presenting the file had taken him three and a half hours.

The presentation was highly technical, and the agents soon looked lost. Kevin was used to seeing people's eyes glaze over when he talked about plant science. But, he thought, if they were investigating anything connected to corn breeding, the men were remarkably uninformed. Among the terms he had to explain was "inbred seed."

He recounted the rest of his schedule in Changchun, detailing discussions about weed control he had with other breeders, the trip he took with his hosts to a hot springs resort, and the boozy dinner that followed. Kevin treated conversations about details like an endurance sport. For an FBI agent looking for a friendly source with the patience to explain scientific concepts, he was ideal. For an agent hoping for a slip or an omission, he was a nightmare.

After an hour or two, the agents took off their jackets, but still they would not accept anything to drink. As he knocked back two more glasses of lemonade, Kevin could see that they were fading. Finally he got to the end of his China trip, to his visit to Beijing to see DBN's headquarters. When he talked about arriving at the airport and meeting Mao Li, DBN's assistant, the agents perked up.

"Tell us about Mao Li and the company she works for," said the lead agent.

Kevin had not told the agents that Mao Li worked for a company, or that she was a woman.

Now the lead agent asked for a host of minor details. How much did the hotel cost? Who paid for the room? As he took notes, the other agent watched Kevin intently, searching, the agronomist later reflected, for a shift in facial expression or body language. It was only when Kevin said the name Robert Mo that the agents leaned in and began scribbling intensely.

"Did Mr. Mo ever give you any seed?" the lead agent asked.

"No."

"Did you ever give Mr. Mo any seed?"

"No." Kevin explained that the hybrids he sourced for DBN had all been planted at the Monee farm.

"Were you ever asked to obtain or acquire seed or technology which you were not authorized to have on Mr. Mo's behalf?"

A wave of nausea swept over Kevin as he realized that the FBI was investigating his primary contact at DBN. He managed not to vomit, but only because he had not consumed anything except lemonade since breakfast.

The questioning lasted for more than five hours. After a while, the lead agent's questions lost their edge, and Kevin intuited that the men actually believed that he had no knowledge of illegal activity. But Robert, it seemed, was in deep trouble. It was only toward the end of the interview that Kevin got a hint of what Robert had done.

"Mr. Mo," the agent who talked said, "has an unhealthy interest in Pioneer seeds and technology."

Then he made a pitch. He asked Kevin to keep working for DBN—but to report back to the FBI with details. "We're not asking you to spy," the agent told him. "Just go about your business."

It was precisely the sort of appeal that is made when one is, in fact, asking someone to spy.

EIGHTEEN

SUMMER 2012

Ye Jian gazed out the window of the Chevy Tahoe. It was just before Labor Day in 2012, and the fields were mature and just a few weeks away from harvest. The air that reached his flared nostrils smelled faintly of manure.

The view had been like this for miles, with only the texture of the road, the occasional switch from asphalt to gravel or back to asphalt, to break the punishing monotony. To go this long without seeing other people in China, you had to venture far from the congested cities of the east, to Inner Mongolia or the Himalayas. And yet here were he and Lin Yong, his DBN colleague, just a few hours from Chicago. Finally a group of cyclists sped into view. "Oh, my," Ye Jian said in Mandarin. "These people are keen on sports. Look at their cool bikes."

Lin Yong seemed grateful for the small talk. "The bikes even have flashing lights at the tail," he mused. His buzzed hair came to a peak in the center of his forehead, just above his teardrop-shaped birthmark.

"Those are required," Ye Jian said, with unjustified authority. "First, you have to wear a helmet. Second, your bike has to have such a taillight." Ye Jian was the bigger presence, with a chubby build and an outsized personality. Although he was younger than Lin Yong, most of the time—and the men did not lack for time—he played teacher to his colleague's willing student.

In Chicago they had done some sightseeing, but in rural Illinois the diversions that existed were reminders of unfinished business. Hoopeston, home of a sixteen-foot-tall corn stalk sculpture, was giving away fifty tons of corn in its annual town festival that very weekend. Dr. Li wanted only the cutting-edge varieties found in research fields, though, so slowly, driving at the bare minimum speed, Ye Jian and Lin Yong traced a squiggly path across Illinois, making a dozen or so pit stops to collect ears of corn outside obscure towns: Arrowsmith, Foosland, Rantoul.

Along the way, their banter spanned a wide range of topics. They gossiped about their co-workers, talked about corruption in the Chinese government, and established what to do if stopped by police while in a field (claim that they were students working on surveys). Eventually, they plunged into that conversational hole that anyone who has ever been on a road trip has experienced. They talked to fill the silence. They quoted liberally from Jackie Chan movies, discussed why Walmart opens when it does, and speculated about why Americans drive such large vehicles. "Americans buy big cars because they often need to carry stuff," Lin Yong ventured, momentarily forgetting that he and Ye Jian were carrying a load of corn in the trunk.

A FEW DAYS LATER, Ye Jian and Lin Yong pulled up alongside a field in Earlville, a town of 1,600 people in north central Illinois. The sky was overcast, with intermittent rain. Meticulously they collected whole ears of corn, tagging them so that they wouldn't get mixed up with the other samples sitting in the back of the Tahoe.

They had managed to get to the male inbreds at a key moment, just after machines mowed down the rows, leaving a sprinkling of escapes on the ground. Nearly a year had passed since Robert Mo, Dr. Li, and Wang Lei were stopped by a sheriff's deputy outside Bondurant under similar conditions. Here, at least, the forlorn location provided some cover. Earlville consisted of a run-down gas station, an ancient grain silo, and a few blocks of houses with chipped siding.

Nonetheless, Lin Yong was nervous. Several months earlier, he and Ye Jian had been pulled over and asked to provide ID while driving through Chicago with Robert. After they finished tagging the ears, they climbed back in the car. As the sun arced toward the horizon, Lin Yong worried that all of his labor that year was for nothing. The collection effort was moving faster now that Robert refused to join them—his colleagues agreed that he tended to slow things down—but still Lin Yong guessed that half of the male samples they had collected this season were duplicates, varieties that had been swiped on earlier trips. He worried that they would need to return to the Midwest again next year and repeat their corn tour. The whole operation was turning into a lengthy and pointlessly risky endeavor.

Ye Jian wasn't helping his mood. "You can forget about ever coming to the U.S. again, assuming things go wrong," he said.

"If it's just not being able to come to the U.S. again—" Lin Yong started.

"That's no biggie."

"That's no biggie? I don't think it's that simple. I actually—the law in the U.S.—I studied law! These are actually very serious offenses," he said.

Ye Jian agreed that what they were doing was a serious crime. "They could treat us as spies," he said.

"That is what we've been doing!" Lin Yong exclaimed. He listed the potential charges. "Trespassing on other people's private property—that's one. Second, theft or larceny, and third, violation of IP law. All criminal offenses. Not just blocking us from visiting. Dr. Li, he—"

"Hasn't he considered this?" Ye Jian asked.

"He knows," Lin Yong said.

Chinese leaders, Lin Yong knew, had little patience for the way Western diplomats crowed about intellectual property rights. Officials in Beijing liked to point out how far China had come in protecting intellectual property by pointing to a few highly publicized arrests. At other moments leaders would bring up the history of technological theft. Had China charged the West for borrowing gunpowder and the printing press? The shift in the U.S. stance over time, from enthusiasm for stealing technology to ambivalence toward spying on others to moral outrage, met with cynicism in Beijing. Leaders alleged that the United States was simply trying to prevent China from emerging as a world power.

But like Dr. Li, Lin Yong also knew that in the eyes of U.S. law enforcement, none of that mattered. Tensions were running high. Earlier that year, the cover of *Bloomberg Businessweek* had read HEY CHINA! STOP STEALING OUR STUFF. Industrial espionage was now among the most critical issues in the U.S.-China technology relationship. A month before Lin Yong and Ye Jian started their tour of the Midwest, National Security Agency director Keith Alexander had called intellectual property theft "the greatest transfer of wealth in history."

Lin Yong soon grew distraught. "My family just has no clue what I am doing here," he lamented. "My old man asked me, 'What are you guys doing staying in the U.S. for so long?' What can I say? Can't say anything."

"Can't say anything that will make your family worry about you," Ye Jian agreed.

"Right! He also said, 'When you are in the U.S., you can't even communicate well for such a long time. What are you going to do?'"

Ye Jian laughed.

"Yeah," Lin Yong continued. "When I think about it, what he said makes sense." He went on for a while before concluding: "Nowadays, the U.S. is very hostile to China on this matter. If this time they opt to—"

Ye Jian sighed audibly.

"If they max the punishment," Lin Yong continued, "then we are done. I can't think of this. Whenever I think of this, I just can't do anything."

Half an hour later, though, Lin Yong was still thinking about it. "Going into others' fields. IP theft. Any one term is very severe."

Ye Jian laughed again. "Others think we are spies sent from China."

"We are surely considered as such," Lin Yong said. He did not laugh.

NINETEEN

SUMMER 2012

The agents who showed up on Kevin's doorstep on that blazing July day made one follow-up visit. When Kevin met with the FBI a third time, the two were replaced by a supervisory agent from Chicago. The new agent was a woman. She told Kevin that they had profiled him ahead of the first encounter and guessed that he would respond better to a man, but that the bureau now felt that maybe that assumption was wrong. Kevin could guess how he looked on paper: Midwestern male from downstate Illinois, raised on a farm. He would respond well to someone who knew something about seed breeding, male or female, he thought. Fortunately, the new agent did.

Now that he no longer had to explain the most basic details about corn breeding, his relationship with the FBI brought a degree of much-needed certainty to his life. For months, he had wondered what his status was at DBN, and whether the company valued his knowledge. The FBI, by contrast, was fairly clear with him, at least when it came to laying out his role as an informant.

He was not asked to wear a wire, but he was expected to notify the new agent in Chicago every time he communicated with anyone at DBN. Should he forget to tip her off, he figured, the FBI was monitoring all of his communications anyway.

Even without a wire, maintaining an air of nonchalance was difficult for Kevin. In more normal times it was his brutal honesty that got him in trouble. Now it seemed that a related trait—his poor command of deception—might do him in. He didn't fear repercussions from DBN if he was found out; Robert wasn't a thug. But he knew that a slip-up could botch the FBI's investigation.

Kevin tried to follow the FBI agent's advice and pursue business as usual. While checking on his hybrids at the Monee farm, he noticed that his breeding project had been overshadowed by a remodeling job that was going on at the farmhouse. Kevin watched in amazement as a crew gutted the interior, tore out the fixtures, and built a new two-car garage alongside the house. Robert informed Kevin that he had plans to add an office, a conference room, and a bedroom.

His test fields, meanwhile, had been invaded by pigweed and velvetleaf, which in some places had grown as tall as the corn. Robert had hired someone to spray the field for weeds, but the man didn't show, so one day Kevin drove out to the farm with a hoe and a gas-powered weed whacker to take care of it himself. When he arrived, it struck him that something was off. Vandals had taken note of the remodeling effort and broken into the house. They had swiped copper fixtures and all other parts of value. Swaths of drywall were now punctuated by abrupt holes. Lightbulbs dangled from thin electrical wiring. Kevin wasn't entirely shocked—the house had sat conspicuously vacant for weeks—but he was struck by the totality of the destruction. It was hard to tell where the remodeling ended and the vandalism began.

He emailed Robert offering advice on how to ward off vandals. Mow the lawn, he suggested. Park a vehicle on the property. Make it look like someone lives there, even if no one does. In his response, Robert let on that the timing of the break-in was inopportune. He was preparing to host visitors from China. Kevin passed on the news to his contact at the FBI.

DESPITE EVERYTHING, Kevin still held out hope that some of the hybrids planted in the Monee plot would be exported to South America and from there sent on to China. All he knew was that DBN was being investigated and that Robert, as the FBI agent had put it, had an unhealthy interest in Pioneer seeds. His handler didn't share with him the details of the FBI's investigation, or the extent of the activity that had interested agents in Robert. Because Kevin had set up the seed licensing arrangement surrounding the Monee hybrids, he knew that it was legitimate. DBN was a large company, and it was possible that the FBI investigation was limited to one aspect of its work. Plus the Chinese company was still paying him.

Kevin wrote to a winter nursery in Chile to arrange for shipment of the hybrids, then pestered Robert about which ones he should send on. The nursery required contact information for someone in China so that it could obtain an export permit. Whom should he list as a contact? Kevin asked. When Robert didn't respond to his emails, Kevin called him and asked him for an address over the phone. A long and awkward pause ensued.

"So when can you send the seed?" Robert asked finally.

"When you give me an address," Kevin said.

Robert hung up.

A few weeks later, Robert did something that truly annoyed Kevin. He mentioned that he had hired another breeder to go through the plot that Kevin had tended all summer to select hybrids to send on to Chile.

Nearly forgetting he had become an FBI informant, Kevin dashed off an indignant email. "I would like to know how and when the independent testing/observation was conducted and just as important, why was I not involved?" The memory of Robert's telling him that he wasn't his first choice for the job still stung. He continued: "Are you dissatisfied with my performance or involvement in this project? Has my role changed?" He never got a reply.

The conversation turned Kevin against Robert once and for all. Trade secrets theft was one thing. Insulting his scientific ability was another.

TWENTY

SUMMER 2012

D r. Li and Ye Jian holed up in their storage unit and reluctantly got to work. On the asphalt outside, boats and RVs sat parked in wait of outings. The lot stretched the length of a soccer field, ending abruptly at a chain-link fence. In the distance, beyond the fence, was a row of rural businesses that was as close as New Lenox, Illinois, got to a downtown. Temporary storage outfits see all sorts of people: a drug cartel looking for a place to stash heroin; thieves attracted to a trove of unwatched loot. And yet in some ways food is a more pernicious storage threat, as it could attract rodents that might burrow into other units. When the manager of the Infinite Self-Storage learned that the men were storing whole ears of corn in their shed, he told them he wanted the crop out. He gave them forty-eight hours.

They had rented the shed only a few weeks before, and already it held hundreds of ears. When Ye Jian and Dr. Li finished boxing it up, they loaded the containers into the back of a rented silver Dodge

Journey and drove nine miles along unswerving roads to the farm in Monee.

Robert arrived at O'Hare on a flight from Florida soon after and checked into a hotel near the airport. He spent the evening exercising in the gym and lounging by the pool, trying to postpone his trip to the farm as long as possible. When Ye Jian and Lin Yong had toured cornfields several weeks earlier, he had happily stayed in Florida. *Ninety-five percent chance that the FBI is watching us*, he had told Dr. Li. But now the seeds were almost out of the country. Lin Yong had already returned to China, and Dr. Li and Ye Jian were preparing to fly to Beijing as well. And the next day was Mid-Autumn Festival, an important holiday in China that is usually celebrated with a nice meal. Robert felt obligated to at least show his face.

In the morning, Robert set out for the farm bearing mooncakes, the sweet and savory pastries that are eaten to celebrate the holiday. Dr. Li and Ye Jian were already there. They were joined by Michael Yao, the balding real-estate agent, along with a man named Wang Hongwei, who lived in Quebec and had flown in for the weekend. The house was a mess from the vandalism and the renovation, so the men stayed outside in the gravel clearing, gathering around the newly built garage. It was there that they divided the seeds.

They worked steadily. Some seeds they slipped into small manila envelopes, of the sort hardware stores use for copied keys. Others they wrapped in plastic bags or rolled up in napkins they had swiped from Subway. One by one, they coded these packets so that breeders in Beijing would be able to distinguish the seed lines: 2155, 2403, F1, F2. Then they hid the envelopes in boxes of Pop Weaver and Orville Redenbacher microwave popcorn, taking care to lay bags of popcorn on top and re-glue the boxes shut so that they appeared factory-sealed—a corn swap that rivaled the FBI's FedEx switch in its ingenuity.

In the afternoon they broke for a meal at Monee's lone Chinese restaurant, where the chef cooked them a feast for the holiday. When night fell, Ye Jian returned the Dodge Journey to an Enterprise rental outfit. The men checked into a nearby hotel and rested for their flights.

It had been an eventful month. Ye Jian and Lin Yong in particular had tested fate with their conversation as they toured corn country. *Theft or larceny*, Lin Yong had said. *Violation of IP law. All criminal offenses.* Dr. Li, they had agreed, understood all of this deeply. *He knows.* And even if the two low-level employees had been the ones to take corn from the fields, it had all been Dr. Li's idea. He had been in the getaway car at the very beginning, when Robert was stopped by the sheriff's deputy in the Monsanto field outside Bondurant, Iowa. Now Lin Yong was back in China, and Dr. Li and Ye Jian were preparing to take stolen corn out of the country. It would be difficult for either man to claim complete ignorance. But they were just hours away from a flight to Beijing, where U.S. law enforcement couldn't reach them. Only Robert would remain on American soil.

BEFORE LEAVING FOR THE AIRPORT the next day, the men stood around Robert's rental car discussing how to divide up the seed. They decided to send a set of seeds with each group of travelers. That way, if one didn't make it for some reason, they'd still have the other sets.

When they had distributed the contraband, Dr. Li got in Wang Hongwei's car, and Ye Jian climbed in next to Robert.

"Your Z-1 F-1 is a set?" Robert asked the younger man.

"Yeah."

"Z-2 F-2 is the second set," Robert asserted, as much for himself as for Ye Jian. "The key is to ensure safety. They were also divided into three batches last year. Three batches and all arrived safely."

Safety was critical. As the U.S. crackdown on industrial espionage intensified, there were more and more cases involving Chinese defendants. A few days earlier, a federal jury in Newark, New Jersey, had convicted a Chinese national who formerly worked for a U.S. defense contractor of nine felony counts, for trying to take information about the design of missile guidance systems and other unmanned aerial vehicles back to China. In Detroit, meanwhile, a husband and wife accused of stealing hybrid car secrets from General Motors were about to go on trial. They faced the prospect of decades in prison.

As the two men neared O'Hare, Robert nervously instructed Ye Jian on the importance of cleaning the rental cars. *Remove any traceable marks or clues. Wash the car yourself, and then wash it again. Vacuum it twice. Clean it inside and out.*

"The car has been washed many times," Ye Jian assured him.

Robert persisted. "Last time, when we returned the car, you guys finished and left, and I went back and vacuumed it one more time. Because I—well, I am very attentive to details."

"Right. Not a single kernel of corn was left behind."

AT O'HARE, THE MEN PARTED WAYS. Robert Mo boarded a plane to Fort Lauderdale, and Wang Hongwei got on a flight to Burlington, Vermont. Ye Jian and Dr. Li headed for the international terminal.

As the two men checked their bags and walked to the gate, they could have been any other boss and employee duo heading out of the country. They passed people running to catch flights and others killing time in duty-free shops. Here, finally, they were among other foreigners. No more sideways glances, no more arming themselves with a story at every turn. They could blend in. Perhaps they thought ahead fourteen hours to their arrival in Beijing—a city where men like them could sail through life with VIP club memberships and hired help, where their nationality would be an asset rather than a hindrance. Even as they were transporting contraband through the airport, there was reassurance in knowing that they were almost home.

In the rear passenger door of the rental car, though, were a number of items that Ye Jian had overlooked. These included a plastic bag filled with rubber bands, a roll of cellophane tape, and a napkin inscribed with numbers close to the day's date: 9-5–9-13, 9-19–9-22.

Ye Jian had also neglected to vacuum the trunk. Scattered throughout were loose kernels of corn.

TWENTY-ONE

FALL 2012

f Ye Jian and Dr. Li felt at home in the airport, the FBI agents on their trail felt even more comfortable. United States law allows searches and seizures at international borders without a warrant. Customs and Border Protection (CBP) officers are permitted to search any traveler at random. They can riffle through luggage, log in to phones and laptops, and scroll through photos on digital cameras. The U.S. Supreme Court has ruled that the Fourth Amendment, which protects citizens from unreasonable search and seizure, doesn't apply in such cases. This is called the border search exception, and it has been liberally used since September 11, 2001. The CBP is often merely the outward-facing authority in a border search. Behind the scenes on this particular day was the FBI.

When Ye Jian and Dr. Li arrived at their gate, CBP officers watched as they separated, taking seats in different sections. Elsewhere in the airport, other agents offloaded the men's checked bags and examined the contents. Amid their clothes and toiletries, the agents found the Pop Weaver and Orville Redenbacher boxes containing hundreds of small envelopes of seed, each neatly labeled in code.

Shortly before boarding started, an airline worker paged the two men. Separately, in their distinct seating areas, Ye Jian and Dr. Li ignored the announcement. A few minutes later their names crackled over the loudspeaker a second time. When the men still did nothing, CBP agents approached the men to question them about the seed in their luggage, using the guise of U.S. agriculture regulations, which prohibit passengers from taking seeds and plants out of the United States without a permit.

Stopping suspects under the premise of a routine border search was a common strategy in trade secrets theft cases. On another day at O'Hare five years earlier, former Motorola engineer Hanjuan Jin had attempted to fly back to China with storage devices containing more than a thousand company documents. In her case, the airport search was swiftly followed by arrest—and, after a trial, four years in federal prison.

But the corn case presented an added wrinkle: Agents couldn't arrest the men on the spot. The bureau had bugged the rental car that Ye Jian and Lin Yong drove around the Midwest, capturing their conversation about what laws they were breaking. Agents had also recorded audio of Robert and the other men talking about how to divide up the seeds. But Mark Betten's team hadn't yet analyzed the audio; they didn't know what they had. The FBI had opted for more conventional bugs because live wires that could be monitored in real time required either the constant presence of a nearby surveillance team equipped with radio transmitters or consistent cell phone signals, and in the rural Midwest both were difficult to arrange. At the time of the airport encounter, the audio hadn't yet been translated into English. Then, too, a case built entirely on potentially incriminating statements might leave a defense lawyer with plenty of opportunities to poke holes. To leave an airtight case for prosecutors, investigators needed to test the seed. Because that could not be done immediately, agents would have to let the men fly back to China. And if they were too obvious about either the search or their questioning, the men might never return.

Mark knew the risk the FBI ran by seizing seed and questioning the DBN employees without arresting them. But it was clear that the men were carrying more than microwave popcorn, and that their stash likely included Pioneer and Monsanto products. Letting the men leave the country with stolen intellectual property would defeat a two-year investigation on which the bureau had blown untold funds.

When the CBP agents confronted Ye Jian, he lied and said he was traveling alone. Dr. Li lied as well, but with certain details he was more forthcoming. He bought his stash of seed, he told the agents, from a man named Mo Hailong.

IN ANOTHER TERMINAL AT O'HARE, Wang Hongwei, the Canadian man who had helped package seed at the Monee farm, boarded a United flight to Burlington, Vermont. When he arrived, he retrieved his car from an airport parking lot and headed north for the U.S.-Canada border. CBP agents have no authority to search passengers on domestic flights, but at the border they would have free rein—provided they caught him before he crossed.

The drive from Burlington to the southern edge of Canada normally takes less than an hour. The FBI was on Wang's trail from the time he set off. But as dusk fell, the agents lost sight of him when he turned without signaling into a mall parking lot. Agents alerted the border patrol at two nearby crossings, providing Wang's license plate number. Soon after, he reached Highgate Springs Port of Entry, at the northwestern tip of Vermont.

As the terminus of Interstate 89, Highgate Springs is one of the largest border crossings between the United States and Canada. The crossing sees heavy traffic, which makes it a good choice for a man hoping to be waved through speedily. But this is not what happened to Wang. Instead he was flagged for a search.

In his car, agents found a notebook filled with what appeared to be latitude and longitude coordinates, a digital camera storing hundreds of pictures of cornfields, and, stashed underneath a seat, forty-four small brown bags containing manila envelopes filled with seed. CBP officers copied the photos of cornfields to an external drive and seized the envelopes of seed. Then they let Wang cross.

TWENTY-TWO

FALL 2012

As Wang Hongwei drove north through Quebec, crossing the Pike River, Dr. Li and Ye Jian soared over the Arctic Ocean on their way to Beijing. Their moods had dimmed. They, too, had been allowed to leave the United States. But like Wang they, too, had been forced to forfeit their seed.

Robert, meanwhile, landed in Florida. He retrieved his car and drove home to his Boca Raton cul-de-sac, cruising past gardens lined with palm trees, unaware that everything about the operation was now in danger.

SOON AFTER ROBERT ARRIVED, Ye Jian called him and frantically explained that he and Dr. Li had been stopped by agents and their luggage thoroughly searched. Robert tried to reassure him. *It's normal for them to check*, he said, as if he himself had not been a bundle of nerves for the preceding months. But Robert's attitude changed when he found out that Dr. Li had given his name to the authorities.

He had never much liked Dr. Li, but now his boss had really gone too far. Robert was the one who had made a life in the United States—the one with fully American children, the savings in U.S. dollars, a mortgage to pay off. And now his colleagues at DBN were safely back in China, leaving him uniquely vulnerable. He opened a document on his computer and drafted an indignant note to his brother-in-law. Shao Genhuo needed to know what Dr. Li had done.

In the letter, Robert lamented the loss of the seized seeds. He explained the danger that the FBI or some other authority might compare the seeds seized from Dr. Li and Ye Jian at the Chicago airport with those seized from Wang's car at the Vermont-Canada border and discover that the codes matched up. "The team led by Dr. Li worked very hard in the U.S. this time and received sizeable results," he wrote, starting on a positive note. He added that the seeds "unfortunately were seized by U.S. customs, and the resources were confiscated."

He continued:

> Because each set of the resource had one to two thousand small bags with clear sequential marks, if Li's and Wang's resources were combined, it would be very easy to determine they were two sets of the same things. That would make the matter very severe. The accumulated work done in North America could be completely destroyed by Dr. Li's aggressive decisions.

At the first sign of trouble, Dr. Li had needlessly sacrificed him. Robert felt that his brother-in-law had tolerated Dr. Li's antics for too long. It was time for him to get tough.

Robert had not bargained for all of this stress. On top of the close call with the U.S. authorities, his health was suffering. A groin injury he had suffered years ago in a basketball game was bothering him. When he felt around just above his left thigh, there was a small lump. He made a mental note to get it checked.

TWENTY-THREE

2015-2016

I had set out to report on one very specific story—that of the man found in a field where he didn't belong. But it quickly became clear that Robert's case was wrapped up with those of other defendants like him. In just my first year back in the United States, the U.S. government brought industrial-espionage-related charges against thirteen people. All of them were ethnic Chinese.

Some of these cases involved technologies of clear national security importance and were accompanied by extensive court documents detailing serious crimes. But in other cases, charges were announced with breathless press releases and heated rhetoric and then a few months later were dropped entirely. In the federal court system, the conviction rate is 93 percent, and U.S. attorneys typically don't waste resources on cases with thin evidence. By the time defendants are charged, prosecutors are usually confident that they can win a conviction. But these cases were different. One minute the accused were enemies of the state, and the next minute it was as if nothing had happened.

I started to wonder whether in these botched cases there might be echoes of the Wen Ho Lee investigation. In time I realized that I wasn't the only one who felt that way. A whole community of activists had sprung up around the issue.

Among them was Haipei Shue, president of United Chinese Americans, a D.C.-based federation of community groups around the country. One morning in May 2015, Shue was reading the news in his office in Washington when he came across a *New York Times* article about a woman named Sherry Chen, a National Weather Service employee who had been accused of passing information about the U.S. dam network to a Chinese official. The previous October, the FBI had arrested Chen at her office, charging her with four felonies. She faced twenty-five years in prison and $1 million in fines. Now, Shue read that prosecutors had dropped all charges.

"It was shocking to me that the government would throw this much power and resources and intensity behind a case, when it's fundamentally something that she did not do," he told me. "I thought, Wow, could there be more like this?" He recalled what had happened to Wen Ho Lee in 1999. Shue had been working in D.C. on trade issues when the case unfolded. He scrambled into action.

Within days, Asian-American community organizations came together to demand answers on the Sherry Chen case. Specifically, they wanted to know whether what happened to Chen was part of a pattern of racial profiling.

On May 21, 2015, twenty-two members of Congress signed a letter to Attorney General Loretta Lynch requesting an investigation into whether federal employees were being racially targeted. Representative Ted Lieu of California, one of the letter's signatories, bemoaned the targeting of innocent scientists as "a constitutional and civil rights problem." In July 2015, the group received a reply from the Justice Department denying the existence of racial profiling. But then news broke of additional botched investigations involving ethnic Chinese scientists.

That is how I found myself at a café in Minneapolis, sitting across from Joyce Xi, as she recounted how everything imploded for her family.

IN MAY 2015, Joyce was a senior at Yale majoring in chemistry. She had just finished her spring classes and was home in Penn Valley, Pennsylvania, looking forward to the summer. She had one semester left of college, and she was trying to figure out what to do after graduation. Then one morning the FBI showed up at her family's house with a battering ram, guns drawn, and hauled her father off in handcuffs.

Xiaoxing Xi was the interim chair of the physics department at Temple University in Philadelphia. He had emigrated from China in 1989 and was a naturalized U.S. citizen. Unlike Robert Mo, Xi was not some middling researcher in desperate need of money. A world-renowned expert on superconducting thin films, he oversaw a team of fifteen people and received more than $1 million a year in U.S. government research funding. His team had just obtained breakthrough results on two separate topics, which he was preparing to submit to *Science* and *Nature*. On the way home from her father's bail hearing later that day, Joyce read a copy of the indictment that had been brought against him. He was charged with trying to transfer to China designs for a device called the pocket heater, which makes thin films of the superconductor magnesium diboride. He faced eighty years in prison and $1 million in fines.

The family arrived back home to find FBI agents milling around outside, waiting to execute a search warrant. The agents soon fanned out through the house, collecting the family's possessions: documents, cameras, laptops. As they worked, television news crews filmed segments from the front yard. A well-meaning agent taped a bedsheet to the front window so that the crews couldn't film the family inside, but later that night, when the FBI finally left, reporters rang the doorbell.

It eventually became clear that prosecutors had proceeded without checking the science behind their charges. Xi was charged with wire fraud, which one prosecutor described to me as a backstop charge that is used when economic espionage is difficult to prove. The purported evidence against him consisted of four emails he had sent to labs in China in which he had discussed legitimate collaboration efforts with scientists there. One project involved a thin film deposition device, but it was not the pocket heater. Experts submitted strongly worded affidavits in his defense. One of them, Paul Chu of the University of Houston in Texas, told me Xi's offer to collaborate with Chinese colleagues on basic research was perfectly normal in the field of superconductivity. Another, physicist David Larbalestier at Florida State University in Tallahassee, called the entire case "just completely misconceived." About the type of thin films at issue in the case, he said: "The whole idea that there are huge pots of money that anybody is making out of magnesium diboride is just wrong. I am mystified as to why the case was brought."

Four months later, the U.S. attorney's office in Philadelphia abruptly dropped all charges against Xi, noting only that "additional information came to the attention of the government." Commentators were quick to fill in the gaps. Xi's crime, according to one legal blog, was "emailing while Chinese-American."

Four months is long enough for lives to be sent into a tailspin. Xi was released after putting up his family's home as collateral for bail, and throughout the summer, he and his family stayed inside, limiting contact with friends and neighbors out of fear that someone could turn against them. They worried that people might want to physically harm them. They didn't know whom to trust, Joyce told me, her voice quavering.

The ordeal marked her political awakening. "This is not the America I thought I knew," she wrote in an op-ed article for *USA Today*, seven days after the charges against her father were dropped. "As our country faces increased anxiety over China, the government is targeting innocent Chinese Americans."

In addition to Xi and Chen, it turned out that three other ethnically Chinese defendants had seen charges dropped in trade secrets theft–related cases since 2013. In one of these cases, prosecutors accused Guoqing Cao, a Chinese-born U.S. citizen formerly employed by Eli Lilly, of being a traitor. One of the trade secrets Cao was accused of sharing turned out to be a broad description of his job responsibilities on his résumé, which he sent to a Chinese company when applying for a job. Other alleged trade secrets were findings that had appeared in published papers years earlier. The man's crime, it seemed, was that he had run afoul of a former employer by taking a job with a competitor. "The word is not treason," the attorney for his co-defendant told reporters. "The word is overreach."

The urgency surrounding economic espionage was so great that charges were being brought without much vetting, advocates alleged.

"The U.S. government put two and two together and came up with five," said D.C.-based intellectual property lawyer Peter Toren, a former prosecutor with the Justice Department's Computer Crime and Intellectual Property Section who helped draft parts of the Economic Espionage Act, of the Xi case. "And I think that's very troublesome." Peter Zeidenberg, an attorney with the law firm Arent Fox who represented both Xi and Chen, told me, "As a former prosecutor, I can tell you that if you're looking for a crime and that's what's rewarded, you're going to find it. There is an overreaction to a legitimate concern, which is leading to people being victimized." Technology theft cases involved what one attorney described as a trifecta of challenging topics: China, complicated technologies, and intellectual property law. Given the FBI's institutional history of racial profiling, cases like Xi's suggested a real problem: Faced with a complex investigation, an agent might be subconsciously swayed by a suspect's ethnicity.

The campaign led by Asian-American community organizations now shifted into high gear. Congressional leaders redoubled their entreaties to Attorney General Lynch on the issue of racial profiling. Activists who had worked on the Wen Ho Lee case took leading roles. In the early 2000s, Jeremy Wu had handled complaints about racial profiling as Department of Energy ombudsman. Now he started a legal defense fund for Chen. Civil rights lawyer Aryani Ong had raised concerns about the Lee case with high-level government officials. Now she helped organize regular conference calls for groups to share information and ideas. "Fifteen years had passed since Wen Ho Lee," Ong told me. "How did we get here again?"

Organizations staged "know your rights" seminars for scientists across the country. In these sessions, attorneys outlined the laws governing trade secrets theft and economic espionage. Assume that all communications with researchers in China are being monitored, they said. Assume that your devices will be searched at the border. Assume that anything that can be misinterpreted will be. They emphasized that even having a trade secret in your memory can be a crime.

Many participants walked out more worried than reassured. "The indictments have instilled a great deal of uncertainty and anxiety in our community," Albert Chang, a physicist at Duke University in Durham, North Carolina, told me. "People are wondering, 'Is this going to happen to me?'"

Their worries were understandable. Andrew Chongseh Kim, a visiting scholar at South Texas College of Law, analyzed 136 cases brought under the Economic Espionage Act between 1996 and 2015. He found that 21 percent of defendants with Chinese names were never proved guilty of spying or other serious crimes, about twice the rate of defendants from other ethnic groups. While other factors might account for charges being dropped or downgraded, Kim wrote, "These findings raise the possibility that as many as one in five accused Asian 'spies' might actually be innocent." Harvard law professor Noah Feldman compared the rash of economic espionage cases to anti-Communist cases in the McCarthy era, noting that both had "an ethnic cast." In the McCarthy era, he noted, many secret U.S. Communists were Jewish. But that fact did not justify profiling people, because the vast majority of Jewish people were not Communists. The same went for Chinese-American scientists today, he added.

Activists pointed out that bungled prosecutions could backfire, creating a hostile environment and propelling talented scientists back to China out of necessity or fear. According to the National Science Foundation, students from China account for 10 percent of all science and engineering PhDs earned at U.S. universities—more than any other nationality. As the Chinese Communist Party tries hard to recruit talented overseas Chinese scientists, sloppy charges make it easier for them to decide to leave. In the years following the Wen Ho Lee debacle, so many disillusioned Chinese-born weapons scientists returned to China that they became known as the Los Alamos club. Critics worried that in the name of protecting innovation, the U.S. government was singling out for scrutiny the very people who powered America's labs.

The media picked up on the story. *60 Minutes* aired a segment on the botched cases, and *The New York Times* published an editorial calling for Chen and Xi to receive a formal apology, alleging that FBI agents and federal prosecutors "acted with reckless haste." In March 2016, the Department of Justice instituted a rule change stipulating that all cases involving national security issues, including ones involving tangential charges like wire fraud, be overseen by the National Security Division. But an apology never came.

Chen, meanwhile, petitioned the U.S. Commerce Department, which oversees the National Weather Service, to get her job back. In April 2018, a judge with the U.S. Merit Systems Protection Board ruled in her favor. She then sued the federal government. "An unsubstantiated and patently racist accusation set into motion a modern-day witch hunt where hundreds of thousands of our tax dollars were spent to try to prove a 'Chinese national' a spy," her attorney, Michele Young, told news outlets. Xi took his case to a law firm in Philadelphia, which brought a suit against the FBI agent who oversaw his investigation. (The American Civil Liberties Union later joined the suit.) In late 2019, both cases were in litigation, and

Xi's family was still paying off legal fees connected to the erroneous pocket heater charges.

For Joyce, the experience prompted a realization that the U.S. justice system often failed people. "We had to deal with a lot of lingering issues, all for nothing," Joyce said. "And all because of some incompetence that was not our fault." After graduation, she ended up going into racial justice work.

The damage from these cases extended beyond the lives of people like Joyce Xi, to the larger community of foreign-born scholars who contributed to the project of American innovation. Prominent researchers told me of aspiring PhD students from China who worried about the wisdom of studying in the United States. Canada and Europe offered attractive alternatives—as did China, where botched cases became powerful ammunition for the state propaganda machine. In the wake of Sherry Chen's arrest, the Chinese state-run English newspaper *Global Times* ran a strident editorial headlined WASHINGTON'S SPY CHARGES PARANOID. "The U.S. has a history of indulging in persecution of certain groups of immigrants," it read. "We hope Chinese-Americans won't suffer from this because of China's rise." Return to China, the article implied to scholars, and your work will be celebrated rather than vilified.

Unlike Xiaoxing Xi and Sherry Chen, Robert Mo was not the sort of defendant who inspired people to call their congressperson. Even so, his situation underscored that in economic espionage cases, investigators and prosecutors were willing to go to extremes.

TWENTY-FOUR

FALL 2012-SUMMER 2013

In the weeks following the airport bust, Mark's team obtained a warrant to test the haul of corn seized by the CBP. Investigators now had in their possession twenty-five thousand seeds. But they now had to confirm that the seized seeds were in fact trade secrets. That was a gargantuan task.

In trying to crack the code used on the envelopes, FBI analysts first tried the obvious, comparing the labels—2155, 2403, F1—against product numbers used by Pioneer and Monsanto. When they didn't find a connection, they looked at GPS coordinates. The tracking device attached to the Tahoe had logged the coordinates of the fields where Lin Yong and Ye Jian had stopped, and there were more coordinates in the notebook border agents had taken from Wang Hongwei's car. But the numbers on the envelopes still didn't match up.

For Mark, the FBI's inability to break the code was frustrating because it meant that the seeds, assuming they were stolen, could belong either to Monsanto or to Pioneer—or even, perhaps, to a third company. GPS tracking information from the rental cars the men had driven wasn't much help. In some areas where the men stopped, there were inbred fields belonging to different companies on both sides of the road. Because the cars typically remained parked on the asphalt, it was impossible to know without other evidence what side of the road they had targeted. In order to test the unidentified seed, prosecutors would have to get Monsanto and Pioneer to agree on a protocol. And the two companies agreed on almost nothing. The process of brokering a consensus would make trailing suspects over dusty farm roads look simple. It didn't help that at the time the seed was seized, the Justice Department's Antitrust Division had an active investigation into Monsanto's business practices.

THE WORKSHOP CONVENED by the Justice Department and the USDA in 2010 in Ankeny, Iowa, had proved that there was significant public support for breaking up big agriculture. The action appeared to have legal grounding as well. Antitrust enforcers have historically been harsher on companies like Monsanto, which expand through acquisitions, than on those that grow more naturally. But after the workshops, the Justice Department released very little information about its investigation. In November 2012, the department quietly dropped the inquiry. The news came as only a short note on Monsanto's website. The investigations initiated by state attorneys general fizzled as well.

The Justice Department dropped investigations of other agriculture companies around the same time. Still, it was noteworthy, at least, that the department abandoned its effort to break up Monsanto's monopoly precisely as it was developing a major economic espionage case on behalf of the company. It may have helped that

Monsanto spent more than $6 million a year on lobbying, more than any other agribusiness company, and that it employed a number of former U.S. government officials.

But while the conclusion of the antitrust inquiry removed one barrier to Monsanto's cooperation, the company's lawyers had other reasons to worry about allowing the seized seeds to be tested. With regulators retreating, the agricultural giants had resumed their acquisition spree, and Monsanto and Pioneer were locked in a battle for market share. Their main foes were now each other.

One battlefront in this war centered on a trade secrets spat far removed from China, involving Pioneer's use of Monsanto's Roundup Ready trait in its genetically modified crops. The company accused Pioneer of "stacking" additional traits onto the gene, a tweak the company claimed was not allowed by the licensing agreement. In August 2012, shortly before the airport bust, a jury in Monsanto's hometown of St. Louis agreed, awarding Monsanto $1 billion in damages. Lawyers for Pioneer vowed to appeal.

Now the twenty-five thousand seized seeds became a new source of anxiety. Monsanto's counsel feared that if the seeds were sent out for testing in one batch, Pioneer would learn which seed lines the company had in development. Pioneer's lawyers had the same concern about Monsanto. As they gobbled up smaller entities in a battle for market share, the agrochemical giants were existential threats to each other in a way that DBN was to neither.

The other issue was that in any court proceedings, the defense would be entitled to see some version of the results. Neither company wanted to expose sensitive intellectual property to the very people accused of trying to steal it. A number of questions were under debate. Did the federal government have to test *all* of the seized seeds? What kinds of tests should be done, and what lab should perform them?

To hash out a solution, Mark worked closely with Jason Griess, an assistant U.S. attorney in Iowa's southern district. In his time as a federal prosecutor, Griess had worked on international drug trafficking cases and biological weapons threats, but he still didn't quite look the part. A fellow Nebraska native, he was thickly built and bearlike, with a shaved head. He had followed the FBI's investigation since the beginning, and he had invested enough time in the case that he didn't want it in jeopardy because of a dispute between the victim companies.

For a while, the battle over how to test the seeds subsumed the actual trade secrets theft investigation. Then, in April 2013, Monsanto and DuPont ironed out their differences in the stacking suit. In exchange for Pioneer paying licensing fees, Monsanto agreed to throw out the $1 billion jury verdict and give its competitor access to coveted research. Antitrust advocates read the agreement as an ominous sign. In a market with many players, licensing arrangements can raise the overall quality of research and boost competition. In a market dominated by a few giants, they tend to be anticompetitive.

In the end, Monsanto and Pioneer agreed to go forward with testing in the Robert Mo case if each seed line was assigned a generic code and the seeds were then sent to an independent lab, to limit the chance that either company could glean information about the competition's products. With the process finally worked out, Mark and Griess sent out 652 seed samples to a Wisconsin laboratory called BioDiagnostics. Then Mark noted the dates of seed conferences, spring planting, harvest time—any events that might draw Dr. Li and his team back to the United States.

· · ·

BACK IN CHINA, meanwhile, talk of assimilating foreign technologies continued unabated. In September 2013, Xi Jinping led the
twenty-five-person Politburo on an excursion. Wearing navy blue
windbreakers, navy blue trousers, and sensible leather shoes, the officials filed onto a bus with tinted windows and rode to a white-tiled
building in Zhongguancun, the city's tech quarter. It was the eve of
National Day, a holiday that commemorated the 1949 founding of
the People's Republic, and the visit to the National Indigenous Innovation Demonstration Zone Exhibition Center was part of a na-
tionalistic media blitz.

The Politburo holds monthly study sessions for committee members and other government officials on an array of topics. Typically
these are led by professors and researchers at the party's complex
in central Beijing. The Zhongguancun visit was the first ever held
off-site.

Inside the center, Xi took the podium. Faced with an international audience in Des Moines the year before, he had talked of international cooperation. Now, as China's most powerful leader, he
stood before a very different crowd. He spoke of technological ascendance and of using science to strengthen China. In the audience
sat dozens of men and two women, taking notes. Among them was
Shao Genhuo, the farmer's-son-turned-CEO of DBN.

Xi urged the audience members to master "core technologies,"
a category that encompassed everything from semiconductors to
seeds. "We must seize the opportunities presented by this new
phase of technological revolution and industrial change," Xi avowed.
"We cannot wait, we cannot watch from the sidelines, we cannot
slack off."

Afterward, Xi toured the exhibition center. When he came to DBN's exhibit, he stood next to Shao, watching as a DBN employee in a white lab coat tinkered with a microscope. The state press snapped photos.

Despite the note of urgency that Xi struck in his speech, DBN's employees held off on U.S. trips. Months rolled by, and the dates on Mark's calendar passed uneventfully.

Ye Jian briefly returned to the United States, but the FBI passed up the opportunity to arrest him, reasoning that a bust would squander any chance of snagging others. Robert traveled to Iowa to attend the World Pork Expo, the Super Bowl for the swine industry, but he stayed away from cornfields. Dr. Li didn't show.

The FBI's investigation of seed company insiders continued. Mark and Griess believed that it was possible that DBN planned to use information gleaned from the seed theft to improve its negotiating position in legal licensing agreements with companies like Stine. But that wasn't enough to land people like Lily Cheng in jail.

Mark and Griess considered the visits to test fields growing inbred corn, the UPS packages labeled CORN SAMPLES, and the farms that DBN owned in Redfield, Iowa, and Monee, Illinois. They pondered the bags of commercial seed that Robert Mo had purchased from dealers across the Midwest—including the six bags he bought from Joel Thomas at Crossroads Ag. They analyzed the FBI's interviews with Kevin Montgomery and other sources across the Midwest, along with the transcripts of Robert's intercepted phone calls.

Just a few months earlier, the FBI believed that DBN planned to chase the self on the company's U.S. farms, by planting bags of seed, letting it grow, and then identifying by height the critical 1 percent that was rogue female inbreds. But as Mark amassed more evidence, he and Griess began to doubt that earlier conclusion.

Neither farm appeared to be critical to the reverse engineering effort. The corn Robert Mo had hired a contract farmer to plant at the Redfield farm was all harvested and sold at the end of the season to a local granary. Robert was barely involved in the process, and the granary records checked out. Not much happened with the seed that Kevin planted in Monee, either. Chasing the self would have required several researchers with PhDs in agronomy, and DBN had not apparently sent anyone over for that purpose. Robert had not even tried to co-opt Kevin—and now Kevin was working for the FBI.

Over time, Mark and Griess pieced together a new operating theory. DBN's plan had changed somewhere along the way, they concluded. Ye Jian and Lin Yong had collected male inbreds from production fields across the Midwest. But to derive the female inbreds, the men had apparently decided to ship large amounts of seed to China and chase the self there. The company might have hung on to the farms to use them as cover when buying seed, or in the case of the Monee farm to house DBN employees visiting from Beijing.

As the months ticked by, Mark worried that DBN might have enough information to start reverse engineering. Griess shared his concern. Dr. Li or no Dr. Li, they could wait no longer.

TWENTY-FIVE

FALL 2012-SUMMER 2013

Even as Kevin's contacts at the FBI told him little about their investigation, he was independently coming to his own conclusions about DBN's scheme. By noting what his handler at the bureau asked and didn't ask, he picked up small bits of information. Her questions triggered memories of incidents that hadn't seemed remarkable at the time. Now they suddenly seemed portentous.

He deduced that Robert and others at DBN were planning to plant out the hybrids to chase the self and derive the female inbred parent. As he pieced together the details of this reverse-engineering operation, his feelings of betrayal and anger gave way to astonishment at the sheer stupidity of the plan. It wasn't just the brashness of messing with companies like Monsanto and DuPont. It was the fact that if DBN wanted to steal seed, the approach its executives had chosen was the least efficient one he could imagine. And the notion that U.S. investigators ever thought Kevin was involved with the scheme offended his ego. The plan was apparently not devised by a plant scientist. There was, he knew, a more straightforward way to reverse engineer inbred seed.

Using this method, Dr. Li and others could have avoided sneaking through fields. All they needed was a single bag of seed for each hybrid they wanted to reverse engineer—or, if they wanted to challenge themselves, a single seed from within that bag. There was a way to determine both the male and the female inbreds through that one seed.* That method would have required a lot of work, but it would also have avoided a lot of risk-taking.

The lies and obfuscations, the encounters with deputies and other authorities, the speeding off through the ditch: All of that could have been avoided if DBN's researchers had the necessary breeding knowledge. The thought that they didn't reinforced a fear he had about the state of modern corn breeding. Because the money was in genetic modification, young breeders were taught the ins and outs of GM traits—even in China, where GM corn couldn't yet be legally sold. They could expound on molecular biology while standing on their heads. But the youngsters lacked a command of the basics of corn breeding.

To Kevin, who remembered when reverse engineering was common practice at seed companies, the faster approach was obvious. Stealing ears off the ground, in particular, struck him as silly. He even briefly wondered: Could DBN's cornfield antics be a cover for some deeper, more sophisticated operation? But most of the time he just thought the plan was foolish.

The absurdity of DBN's plan stuck in Kevin's mind in Decem-

---

*Kevin wavered on whether to explain the process to me. He worried that a dishonest seed company executive could read the explanation and see in it a blueprint for trade secrets theft. Then when he finally did explain the process, it nearly put me to sleep.

ber 2012 as he met with Robert on the sidelines of the American Seed Trade Association Seed Expo in Chicago. Held in a seventy-thousand-square-foot exhibit hall at the Hyatt Regency overlooking the Chicago River, the meeting was usually an important networking opportunity for Kevin. The few small seed companies that remained afloat exhibited their work, as did farm machinery outfits and magazines like *Seed Today* and *Seed World*. But this year he was distracted by his dealings with DBN.

He and Robert retreated into one of the less trafficked ballrooms. A few dozen people milled about, chatting by the coffee table or browsing the posters tacked to the wall at one end of the room, which covered such scintillating topics as "Nutrient Accumulation Patterns in Soybean Cultivars Released over 90 Years." The two men took a seat at an empty table, outside earshot of the other conference-goers.

At the previous year's Seed Expo, Robert had formally offered Kevin the consulting job. So much had changed since then. Now Kevin was an FBI informant, Robert was suspicious of everyone, and an unspoken tension lay between them.

Kevin was sick of being strung along as the foreign face in an illegal operation. DBN had thrust into jeopardy his relationships with contacts in the seed industry. He'd had to inform the people who provided seed for the Monee plot that all of their efforts to provide hybrids had come to nothing. "My contact is the CEO's brother-in-law," he said, by way of explanation. "He doesn't have a background in agriculture." Most people were understanding. Everyone knew of poorly managed seed companies. Nonetheless, it was Kevin's reputation that was on the line. He couldn't explain that the man who hired him was under investigation by the FBI.

Robert started their meeting by telling Kevin that he was disappointed that the agronomist hadn't managed to send any hybrids to South America. Kevin countered that despite asking on multiple occasions, he hadn't been given a contact in China, a budget, or a timeline. And why was another breeder brought in without his knowledge?

Robert shrugged off Kevin's questions, for once passing up the opportunity to talk. He seemed to be avoiding eye contact. If he wanted Kevin to continue working for DBN, Kevin thought, he wasn't trying very hard. He didn't know that Robert had his own grievances—that he, too, wanted to distance himself from the more questionable aspects of DBN's work.

Despite his frustration, Kevin could see reasons not to quit. His handler wanted him to keep feeding the FBI information. And the investigation hadn't stopped him from hoping that the work he was doing for DBN might translate into projects for other Chinese seed companies. He had begun supplementing his studies of fortune cookie phrases with a Mandarin-language guide he found at a discount bookstore. After everything, he still dreamed of one day retracing his father's footsteps in Shanghai.

AFTER MEETING ROBERT at the Seed Expo, Kevin decided to stay on at DBN, but under one unspoken condition: He would make the relationship work for him. When spring arrived in Illinois, he planted his hybrids in the small plot in Monee, which by then looked entirely abandoned. Robert had stopped replying to his emails, but Kevin decided that he might as well use the land. If he continued to cultivate the hybrids, he figured, he might be able to provide them to other clients.

DBN's ambitious renovation plans for the farm appeared to have been scrapped. Not long after he finished planting, drought hit the area, sucking the water out of the soil and turning it to dust. Fissures spliced through the earth, mirroring the cracks in the farmhouse from the break-in the summer before. As the growing season wore on, Kevin saw no hint of visitors. Even vandals left the place alone.

The FBI believed that if DBN managed to obtain both Monsanto and Pioneer seed, its scientists wouldn't need to stop at simply re-creating existing American products. They could combine the best inbreds in the world to create new super seeds—products that were better than the sum of their parts. But Kevin knew that more established U.S. companies had legally swapped inbreds with that aim and had failed to produce interesting new hybrids. Typically, it took years of experimentation to arrive at the best pair of parent seeds. The FBI's fear assumed a level of sophistication that, in Kevin's view, DBN's scientists lacked.

At times his mind went to the Keystone Kops, the group of incompetent policemen made famous by early silent films. Where the FBI saw an elaborate effort to steal intellectual property and threaten national security, Kevin saw a collection of inept criminals bumbling around cornfields. He wanted to rant about it to someone who understood, like another breeder. But he still couldn't say anything about the investigation.

It wasn't just that there was a much better way to reverse engineer corn. It was the fact that Robert and his colleagues had spent untold amounts of money trying to obtain a few top-notch seeds. Dr. Li had aimed for one hundred varieties of corn, but in reality DBN probably got far fewer than that. Corn breeding was an industry in which companies were expected to constantly improve on their varieties. If DBN's executives had instead directed all that effort into improving their breeding program, Kevin believed, the company might actually thrive long term, perhaps even to the point where it ended up on the other side of the trade secrets battle-ground: with intellectual property of its own to protect.

Kevin's concerns raised an important issue: Even if a company manages to steal a technology, a few years later the technology is obsolete. To keep up, it either has to learn from the theft or steal again.

He approached the question as a scientist primarily interested in research outcomes, though. There were other factors that mattered. While intellectual property theft was not a viable long-term strat-egy, when combined with central government policies that gave do-mestic companies an edge in the Chinese market, it could boost sales long enough for a company to gain a significant foothold in the market. Obtaining a handful of superior inbreds might give DBN a short-term advantage and perhaps a few years of healthy profits. And if those few years coincided with a concerted Chinese govern-ment effort to support domestic agricultural technology, DBN might edge out Monsanto and Pioneer, at least in China. From there the company could move on to other markets where farmers were eager for lower-priced alternatives to Western seeds, like develop-ing countries in Africa and other parts of Asia.

The plan that to Kevin seemed so foolish could actually work, at least in the short run. But with many of the stolen seeds already overseas, it wasn't at all clear that a few FBI arrests could stop the operation—let alone solve the larger problem of intellectual prop-erty theft.

TWENTY-SIX

WINTER 2013-2014

At 6:00 A.M. on December 11, a squad of agents in bulletproof vests encircled Robert Mo's house in Boca Raton, their boots cutting into the vibrant lawn. As neighbors in the cul-de-sac rose to make coffee and let the dogs out, they cracked open curtains and rolled up blinds, puzzling over the commotion at the Chinese scientist's home.

Mark Betten was elsewhere that day, but he'd helped arrange the arrest date with the FBI's Miami field office. The bureau was preparing to apprehend another Chinese national in an unrelated agricultural espionage case in Kansas, and bureau leaders had decided to coordinate the arrests for the same day so that neither suspect would spook and flee. Mark might have wanted to arrest six men on an airtight indictment, with the identities of the seized seeds clear and a direct link to Beijing established. But he had to make do with apprehending one—the man who had sparked the whole investigation when he showed up near a field where he didn't belong.

"FBI!" the agents shouted, banging on the front door. Robert's wife, Carolyn, got there first; he was close behind her, half clothed. A stream of agents rushed inside, past a Christmas tree decorated in anticipation of the upcoming holiday. They placed Robert under arrest, handcuffed him, and marched him outside to a government vehicle.

Back in the house, the FBI was just getting started. Investigators ransacked the place, collecting anything that might be evidence— laptops, flash drives, external hard drives, a portable GPS navigator. More than twenty devices in total. They seized tax records and other financial documents, and a collection of assorted scientific papers, including a folder that contained inexplicable clippings about Sasquatch sightings. The ruckus roused Robert and Carolyn's two children, who watched with their mother, confused, as a sketch artist pulled out a pad and drew the layout of the house.

The arrest set off a flurry of activity across the country. Agents from the FBI's Miami field office searched DBN's office in Boca Raton, seizing the sign-in log, property tax receipts, and several computers and hard drives. Across the Midwest, the FBI descended on people with any connection to the case. In Johnston, Iowa, agents dropped in at the homes of ethnic Chinese breeders working for Pioneer who were suspected of being insiders. To the southwest in Adel, they rolled open the door on DBN's storage locker, cataloging the bags of seed and stray corncobs that the men had left behind.

Outside Chicago, agents pulled in next to a vasectomy clinic and searched the mortgage brokerage headed by Michael Yao, seizing eleven hard drives.

Back in Florida, Robert rode north in the government car. At Gun Club Road, the car turned right, onto a small lane. On the other side of a barbed-wire fence was the gaudy Trump International Golf Club, which carried a $250,000 initiation fee. The club had just taken on a new importance with the news that Donald Trump was toying with a run for president. But Robert would not be golfing. The car came to a stop at the Palm Beach County Main Detention Center. After years of work by dozens of agents in five states building a case against him, Robert Mo was in U.S. government custody.

TWENTY-SEVEN

WINTER 2013-2014

Robert looked up at the jail, a nine-story monstrosity with tiny slits for windows. More than fifteen hundred inmates were housed inside. He was only twenty minutes from his house, but he felt light-years away.

It was 4:30 P.M. on the day of his arrest. In his account, he hadn't eaten anything since dinner the night before. When he awakened that morning to loud knocks, he briefly wondered if he was dreaming. Then, after the shock of the arrest, there was the wrangling over inane details with agents while sitting in the government car. No, he couldn't put on proper clothes; a T-shirt, boxer shorts, and slippers were sufficient for where he was headed. No, the agents couldn't explain the charges against him. Yes, he could be escorted back into his house to get his hypertension pills.

The scene he would never forget came when he returned to the house for his medication: his son and daughter, sitting mutely on the sofa in their pajamas, a blanket over their laps. The sight of

Robert in handcuffs prompted his son to throw the blanket over his head. His daughter just stared at him in disbelief.

He fetched his meds in shame, then turned to his children. "Don't be scared!" Robert entreated as the agents yanked him out of the house. "Always trust your dad, as I always trust you."

In jail, the memory haunted him. His stomach churned. Finally, someone brought him a meager sandwich—a single slice each of meat and cheese between thin slices of bread. Processing took hours. At around 11:00 P.M., the lawyer Carolyn had called showed up. Valentin Rodriguez looked like he hawked used cars rather than defended accused criminals. His website, www.defenderforme.com, featured a gigantic image of his face photoshopped in front of a courthouse. But they needed to act fast, and Rodriguez happened to be available when Carolyn called.

A few months earlier, when Robert saw the photos of Shao Genhuo meeting with Xi Jinping at the Zhongguancun innovation center, he had grown nervous. *The more famous you are, the more trouble it brings*, he warned Dr. Li. Now his fears were borne out. DBN's fame had brought trouble—for Robert, at least.

Just before midnight Robert was given his prison uniform—a thin scrubslike pants and shirt. As he slipped the clothes on, the fabric brushed past the lump in his groin. A doctor he had seen on a recent stint in Beijing had recommended removing it, but another medical professional thought the lump was merely a hernia. He had intended to consult a third expert on his planned trip to China. That medical visit, like all of his other plans, had been foiled.

Many of the other men in the jail had committed drug offenses. A few men were in for murder. The conditions in which inmates were held varied wildly. A few years earlier, millionaire sex offender

Jeffrey Epstein had been given a private wing of the jail after striking a deal with the U.S. attorney's office. In Robert's account, he was shoved into a cell that housed around twenty inmates. That night, he shifted about, shivering, as the air-conditioning blasted through a vent. He tried to sleep, but the image of his son hiding under the blanket looped on repeat in his head.

Four days later, Robert was charged with conspiracy to steal trade secrets under the Economic Espionage Act. A complaint filed by Mark Betten laid bare the FBI's extensive bugging and GPS tracking of rental cars used by DBN employees as they drove around the Midwest. Mark listed the fields that Lin Yong and Ye Jian had visited on their trips through corn country, quoting liberally from their conversation about how they were engaged in a criminal offense. The complaint also covered Robert's early run-in with Polk County sheriff's deputies in Bondurant, Iowa; his visits to FedEx facilities in Illinois and Iowa; and the storage spaces that the men had used to stow corn. Even his appearance at a World Food Prize event, wearing another man's name tag, was mentioned.

Robert faced a maximum sentence of ten years in prison and a $250,000 fine. For the U.S. government, this was not the preferred offense. Jason Griess had been hoping to show that Robert had acted at the behest of the Chinese government—a charge that would have meant a maximum of fifteen years in prison and a $500,000 fine. But for Robert it was unthinkable. Ten years meant missing his daughter's high school and college educations, his son's adolescence. Because he was not a U.S. citizen, a felony conviction would also mean the end of his life in America. Upon serving out a prison term, he would be deported, sent back to China in disgrace. The indictment also charged other DBN employees, including Ye Jian, Lin Yong, and Dr. Li. But all of them were in China, which had no extradition treaty with the United States. They were unlikely to ever spend time behind bars. Only Robert faced any real prospect of time in federal prison.

A judge deemed Robert a flight risk, denying his request to be released on bail. A few weeks after his arrest, guards shackled his hands and feet, chained him to another inmate, and shuttled him aboard a plane to Atlanta operated by "Con Air"—the nickname for the fleet of rickety jets operated by the Justice Prisoner and Alien Transportation System. From Atlanta he took a second plane to Oklahoma City, where he stayed for three days in a county jail. He continued by bus to a private jail in Kansas City, Missouri, spending a week there before finally moving on by van to Des Moines, where he would face trial. When transporting inmates in federal custody, he learned, speed is not a priority.

Other prisoners informed him that the grueling cross-country trips were called the diesel treatment. Chained to another inmate, hot and hungry and needing to pee, Robert thought back to the time he had spent sourcing animal feed for DBN, before all the drama started. A pig transportation expert had told him that it was good practice to keep crated pigs in lower temperatures. They were less likely to get sick and die that way. Now he understood firsthand what the expert had meant.

TWENTY-EIGHT

WINTER 2013-2014

The day after Robert Mo's arrest, *The Des Moines Register* and *USA Today* carried the news. From there it hit *The Wall Street Journal* and the Chinese press. Most of the American coverage centered on one image: a man in a suit in a cornfield with fully grown corn. In Iowa, meanwhile, commentators had a more immediate concern: that the arrest of Robert Mo could jeopardize the state's lucrative relationship with China.

Xi Jinping's visit to the World Food Prize Hall the year before had cemented Iowa's dependence on Chinese agricultural imports. In the wake of Xi's sojourn, officials in Hebei province had announced plans to construct what they called the China-U.S. Friendship Farm—a full replica of the farm that the Chinese leader had visited in Maxwell, Iowa. At a ceremony held just two months before Robert's arrest, Iowa companies signed twenty cooperative trade agreements with Chinese counterparts, covering some $1 billion worth of goods.

Now Governor Terry Branstad was confronted by the fact that

as he shook hands with Chinese dignitaries the year before, an accused criminal had watched from the audience. In his weekly news conference, journalists questioned Branstad about Robert's arrest. "I believe it may present some additional challenges in terms of our relationship, but this is a particular incident," he said. "I don't think this should prevent us from continuing to work together."

In fact, the same day that Robert was arrested, the FBI apprehended a second Chinese agricultural researcher in an unconnected case in Kansas. Weiqiang Zhang was a rice breeder with the biopharmaceutical company Ventria Bioscience, which uses rice seeds to develop specialized medicines. Zhang was accused of filching hundreds of these souped-up seeds from his employer, stashing them in his freezer and his bedroom closet, and passing them off to a delegation of visiting Chinese crop scientists. His case bore enough similarities to Robert's—the visiting agricultural delegation, the seeds stashed in luggage—for the FBI to suggest that agricultural espionage was, to use the bureau's phrasing, a growing threat.

Kevin was at the America Seed Trade Association's annual meeting in Chicago when his FBI handler called him to inform him that Robert was in custody. Two years earlier, Robert had formally hired him at the conference. The year before, he had met Robert there for a tense discussion about DBN's seed-breeding plans. This year, he learned that his strange stint as an FBI informant was over. He was happy to no longer be carrying secrets, whether for DBN or the FBI.

After he arrived home, Kevin opened Facebook to unburden himself. "This may be the strangest post you will ever see on my wall," he began. Linking to an article on Robert's arrest, he went on to detail the events of the previous two years:

> I was interviewed by the FBI on 5 occasions. The fact that you are reading this now means that I had NOTHING to do with this. My suspicions started prior to my 1st of 5 interviews with the FBI; the kinds of questions Robert Mo asked were indicative of how little he understood and every request from me for agronomic information was ignored. Robert seemed to have no grasp of the experimental requirements, equipment needed and time to conduct legitimate plant breeding research.

His tone was almost gleeful. In truth, he was satisfied that Robert had been arrested, but disappointed that after such a lengthy investigation no one else had. Much of his relief was due to the fact that after seventeen months as an FBI informant, he would no longer have to be so careful about what he said. "I am glad that they did not try to involve me in this industrial espionage and (allegedly) theft activity," he concluded. He published the post.

The responses were quick. "Wow. . . . I now know a celebrity!!!" a friend wrote. "Thanks for not giving away our stuff to China!!!"

Kevin replied: "Not a celebrity; just a farm boy trying to help others grow more food for themselves." Then he added, "Legally."

TWENTY-NINE

2016

At times it seemed to me that Mark Betten, Robert Mo, and Kevin Montgomery were merely actors in a play directed by someone else. As the special agent overseeing the investigation, Mark had control over what leads he pursued, but the bureau's larger priorities were beyond his control. Robert had enlisted for a very different sort of work, and he went along with DBN's plan only reluctantly. And Kevin had never signed up to be either a stooge or an informant. In order to truly understand the case, I realized, I needed to get a sense for high-level discussions surrounding industrial espionage and China. One July, I traveled to a breathtaking resort in Aspen, Colorado, to attend the Aspen Security Forum, a conference frequented by U.S. intelligence and defense officials.

The list of speakers the year I attended included the secretary of the Department of Homeland Security, the CIA director, the U.S. central commander, several cabinet undersecretaries, and a smattering of foreign ambassadors to the United States—so many big names that I wondered whether for a few days of the year Aspen had to implement heightened security measures. The audience was filled out by CEOs, journalists, and spooks.

After years of attending Chinese science conferences, where lukewarm buffet food and lukewarm conversation were the norm, I found the atmosphere fascinating. There was an espresso bar, an afternoon chocolate service, and a caterer who elevated ancient grains to fine cuisine. Between events, participants traded war stories over superfood balls and lemon-raspberry water, or went for hikes in the surrounding mountains.

Despite the relaxing setting, a nervous energy pulsed through the gathering. At the Republican National Convention the week before, delegates had selected Donald Trump as the party's nominee for the presidential election in November. At rallies, Trump frequently called out China, sometimes for vaguely delineated offenses and at other times for trade or intellectual property abuses. "We can't continue to allow China to rape our country," he said in Fort Wayne, Indiana, in May 2016. Then, channeling General Keith Alexander and sidestepping colonialism, he added, "It's the greatest theft in the history of the world." No one I talked to at the forum admitted to favoring Trump, though one man did tell me that if the celebrity candidate won he'd be the first to line up for a job. "He doesn't have anyone to fill positions," the man said jovially. I wandered off and I never learned whether he succeeded in getting a job in the White House. I ended up chatting with a goateed British man who said he had been a spy for Scotland Yard. The conversation turned to cybersecurity, and to illustrate a point he took out his phone and started scrolling through a list of all the devices that participants had connected to the resort's unprotected Wi-Fi, as if toying with the idea of snooping on them.

Many participants had thoughts on the U.S.-China technology

relationship. But none wielded as much influence over economic espionage prosecutions as John Carlin, who was then assistant attorney general in charge of the Justice Department's National Security Division. He oversaw work on industrial espionage cases—including the case brought against Robert Mo.

The National Security Division was created in 2006 to prevent some of the mistakes that led to the September 11 attacks. The idea was that by combining the counterterrorism and counterintelligence units, the Justice Department could guard against future intelligence failures. From the start, this was controversial. The first head of the division took office amid protests against warrantless wiretapping and U.S. prisoner detention practices. As the years passed, though, the controversy died down. By the time the division's mandate broadened to include acts that did not physically endanger Americans, such as the theft of corn, the critics had mostly retreated.

I sat down with Carlin one afternoon on a balcony overlooking a lush mountain landscape. He was clean-cut and boyish, and he smiled as he talked. The handler he brought along did not. As a Justice Department rookie in the 1990s, Carlin was assigned cybercrime cases because, as he told it, he could use email and operate the printer. Later he became chief of staff for FBI director Robert Mueller. Then he returned to the Justice Department, filling several roles within the NSD before being confirmed as assistant attorney general in 2014. To his young daughter, he explained that his new job meant fighting the wolf in "Three Little Pigs."

Soon after he took office, he announced the indictment of the members of Unit 61398, a Chinese People's Liberation Army hacking outfit that was accused of penetrating giants like Alcoa, U.S. Steel, and Westinghouse Electric. At the press conference where Carlin and other officials unveiled charges, the hackers' faces were

splashed across FBI WANTED posters. Justice Department attorneys
under Carlin's direction had spent two years building the case
against the men, who went by colorful monikers like KandyGoo
and UglyGorilla, but since they were in China, there was little hope
that they would ever be apprehended. National security experts
were quick to question the utility of the indictment. At an event at
the Brookings Institution in Washington, D.C., senior fellow Benjamin Wittes asked Carlin whether it was "a very sophisticated form
of legal PR." Others speculated that the bold move was an effort by
the NSD to carve out a new mission as terrorism cases declined.

"There was immense skepticism in certain quarters after we
brought the case," Carlin told me on the balcony. "Time has shown
that it made a difference." He argued that the indictment sent a
message through "naming and shaming" the perpetrators. "The
approach is a giant 'no trespass' sign," he had explained on stage in
Aspen. "It's, 'Get off our lawn.'"

Carlin became the public face of the Justice Department's economic espionage effort. He spearheaded a reorganization of the department that increased resources for technology theft cases, and
he traveled the United States trying to persuade CEOs to cooperate
with federal prosecutors and with the FBI. "Right now, companies
that have been breached can be reluctant to come forward because
they're afraid they're going to suffer civil or regulatory consequences," he told me. "The big concern that I don't think has been
fully addressed is, 'If I come forward to the FBI, is that going to get
fed somehow to a regulator and used against me?'"

I knew that there was truth to what Carlin said. Regulators were
one threat. Executives also worried that if they pressed charges
in industrial espionage cases, their company's stock price would

plunge, or they would lose market access in China. As the head of China operations for a Fortune 500 firm put it to me, "In China you can face significant retaliation. The fact that your second latest technology is stolen is no longer as important as the fact that you are generating $5 billion in revenue and $1 billion in earnings. Very few CEOs will seize the problem and say, 'Enough is enough. Fix it.'"

But over time, some in the U.S. business community in China had grown dissatisfied with the limits on their market access. As upstart Chinese competitors began challenging U.S. companies in other markets, American CEOs calculated that assisting with trade secrets actions might be worth their time. Corporations with little China business had even less to lose.

In fact, some critics feel the problem is not too little cooperation between the Justice Department and the private sector but too much. In seminars, printed material, and even dramatic films, the FBI's Strategic Partnership Program emphasizes its close relationship with business. Around the time of Robert's arrest, the office published a brochure on agricultural espionage. The cover featured a tiny seedling, glowing against a black backdrop. "You and the FBI: Sowing the seeds of cooperation to defeat the IP threat," it read. At moments, the FBI has gone so far as to stage international sting operations to defend U.S. companies' technology. In one of these stings, an informant lured to the United States two Chinese entrepreneurs who had targeted trade secrets connected to the Missouri-based company Pittsburgh Corning's glass block insulation. In a film that the FBI produced about the sting, a gong sounds as the villains enter the scene. Later, the hero's wife intones, "Just say no to the Chinese!"

In arguing to executives that they should cooperate on technology theft investigations, Carlin sometimes pointed to the case of Robert Mo. "Hailong and his co-conspirators brazenly stole inbred corn seeds from production fields," he said at a roundtable discussion on intellectual property at Iowa State, referring to Robert by his given name rather than his surname. "Our entire nation, including Iowa, is under constant attack from foreign adversaries and competitors who try to steal trade secrets and other intellectual property—at the expense of our economy and national security."

Close cooperation between government and business meant that companies' claims about their technologies might be accepted uncritically—and that prosecutors could become front men for companies interested in suppressing competition. "What the government should do when it gets one of these cases is not take the word of the obviously interested company that this is proprietary or trade secret information," said John Cline, a defense attorney in San Francisco who represented Wen Ho Lee and who briefly worked on Robert's case. "The government ought to get an independent expert to carefully examine the technology at issue. But it rarely seems to do that." A failure to seek out independent experts could lead to errors like the one committed in Xiaoxing Xi's case, in which innocuous exchanges are read as nefarious because of a misreading of the science behind them.

Like other U.S. national security officials, Carlin sometimes talked about industrial espionage in moralistic terms. "We didn't help Boeing get a leg up by learning what Chinese aviation firms were doing or help Monsanto learn about Chinese agricultural systems," he wrote in his book, *Dawn of the Code War*. China, he added, "uses the power and assets of the government to create an unfair playing field for businesses." He told Lesley Stahl of *60 Minutes*:

"They're targeting our private companies. And it's not a fair fight. A private company can't compete against the resources of the second largest economy in the world." But I wondered, wasn't bringing cases on behalf of large corporations its own type of assistance?

OUTSIDE THE REALM of Chinese intellectual property theft, there are plenty of examples of trade secrets cases that have played out in civil court as battles between two giants, or sometimes as brutal whompings, with Goliath going after David. Starwood sued Hilton over luxury boutique hotels. Google Waymo sued Uber over self-driving cars. Kraft sued Schwan over self-rising pizza dough. When I spoke with attorneys in the field, they pointed out that intellectual property law is often wielded to the advantage of the powerful, and more protections are not necessarily good for innovation. Restrictions can prevent something called knowledge spillover, which is critical to the dissemination of new ideas. One of the reasons often cited for Silicon Valley's success is California's ban on noncompete agreements, which has allowed talented employees to break off and start their own firms.

In civil suits, legal costs are borne by the companies that bring them. In federal cases involving economic espionage–related charges, though, corporations often figure behind the scenes. One area in which companies wield significant influence is in the question of value, or how much a stolen technology is worth—a number that affects how much a perpetrator has to pay in restitution.

One oft-cited statistic, for example, holds that the intellectual property stolen by China every year is worth more than $300 billion. Some estimates go as high as $600 billion. I set out to find a reliable source for this figure. The exercise became a lesson in statistical manipulation. The number $300 billion first showed up in a 1997 survey of private companies conducted by the American Society for Industrial Security, an industry association for corporate security officers. The society asked members how much they had lost to both domestic and foreign spies. Reports sourced from ASIS information suggest that members reported domestic theft as the bigger threat. Beyond that, ASIS gave little insight into how the number was calculated, claiming, with no hint of irony, that the methodology was considered proprietary information. A group of analysts who later analyzed the survey concluded that the results were likely "laden with company bias."

In 2002, the number $300 billion appeared in the Office of the National Counterintelligence Executive's Annual Report to Congress on Foreign Economic Collection and Industrial Espionage. In 2010, General Alexander began using it in speeches. In 2013, the figure cropped up in a report from the IP Commission, an independent body headed by former ambassador to China Jon Huntsman, Jr. Somewhere along the way, it morphed from an estimate of all intellectual property losses suffered by U.S. companies to an estimate of the damage inflicted by China alone. One scholar bemoaned efforts to calculate total losses as "based on anecdotes, extrapolation, and bad math."

Nor were estimates of losses in cyberspace any better. In 2011, a report from the cybersecurity firm Symantec put the cost of intellectual property theft from cyberattacks at $250 billion. Its competitor McAfee claimed that cybercrime cost the global economy $1 trillion a year. One expert who conducted research for McAfee described the rigor of the $1 trillion estimate as "below abysmal." Others in the field wrote that surveys on cybercrime losses "are so compromised and biased that no faith whatever can be placed in their findings." Much as ASIS is in the business of promoting corporate security, Symantec and McAfee are in the business of selling cybersecurity products. None of these organizations are impartial observers.

In federal economic espionage cases, estimates of the value of a stolen technology often come from the company whose technology has been targeted. Companies frequently argue that value is whatever they spend on research. But the market isn't guided by that logic. If a company spends $50 million researching a product, and a competitor with a legitimate research program gets the same product to market first, the investment is lost. The real value of a technology is in the profit it generates, and when a trade secret is stolen, profit becomes a matter of speculation. More to the point, the company that produces the technology has a stake in estimating high.

As I lunched with CEOs and intelligence officials in Aspen, allegations of close cooperation struck me as apt. Anti-Monsanto activists often focused on the millions the company spent on lobbying and its adept use of the Washington revolving door. The opaque conclusion of the Justice Department's antitrust investigation hadn't helped this impression. Now, the U.S. government's work to protect the company's trade secrets stirred up other charges of machination. For activists who loathed the very name Monsanto, the corn seed case became further proof that the company was in bed with the federal government. Anti-GMO sites trawling for conspiracy were quick to pick up on Robert's indictment. A headline on one of these sites read: THE FBI IS NOW WORKING FOR MONSANTO.

THIRTY

SPRING 2014

Robert ran in circles around the moldy Des Moines basement, a pair of location-tracking bracelets on his ankles. Spring had arrived, and he longed to breathe fresh air. Instead, he was stuck with this improvised routine in the only room in the house large enough for any sort of real exercise. Jog a few paces, turn. Jog a few paces, turn.

House arrest was supposed to be an improvement on the Polk County Jail, where Robert spent the first few months after his transfer to Iowa. His lawyers had worked hard to get him this deal. His family in China had sent over $50,000 for bail, and now they were helping pay the rent and the exorbitant costs of the full-time security detail that was a condition of his release. Every day that he was here, he racked up $1,000 in charges from a private security company.

During the day the guards mostly sat around watching movies. As Robert lay in bed at night, they shone flashlights onto his face, to check whether he had somehow managed to wriggle free of the tracking bracelets and circumvent the sensors that surrounded the house. *I was asleep until you came in with the light*, he wanted to say. When he did manage to sleep, he dreamed of death.

In Robert's account of his house arrest, the guards didn't even allow him to speak Chinese on the phone. What was he going to do, he thought, summon People's Liberation Army commandos from the sky? It was a funny thought, him trying to signal for help from Iowa, smack in the middle of America, but he wasn't in the mood for humor now. House arrest was spiritual torture, and all on his own dime (or his family's, at least). He was allowed to call Carolyn and his kids and talk to them in English—which was his kids' primary language anyway—but he felt distant.

The visits with his lawyers and doctors were his only contact with the outside world. He had a conflicted relationship with both categories of professional, and not just because the security company slapped on an additional $500 for transportation each time he left the house. While in the county jail, he had noticed that the rubbery lump in his groin had grown. The jail clinician did an ultrasound and assured him that the lump was a benign growth called a lipoma. He handed Robert a two-page pamphlet and told him there was no need to do anything. But every time he examined it the lump seemed to be larger. Benign or not, it looked as if an alien had laid eggs under his skin. Now that he was out of jail, he booked appointments with specialists in an effort to figure out what was wrong, but he mistrusted their advice.

Then there were his lawyers. He knew he didn't stand a chance at trial with a public defender, so colleagues at DBN helped direct him to Mark Beck, a former federal prosecutor in Los Angeles whose firm had done some work for the company. Beck brought a second Mark onto the team: Mark Weinhardt, a Des Moines attorney who wore bow ties and shirts monogrammed with his initials, MEW, and who worked out of an office decorated with cover images from 1950s dime-store thrillers.

The defense had the right to review all of the evidence the federal government had collected against Robert, and Beck and Weinhardt soon amassed thousands of pages of documents, including intercepted emails, transcripts of bugged conversations, and legal briefs. They brought on attorneys in Beijing to help.

The fees for all of this cost Robert—or rather his family—a small fortune. He had gotten involved with DBN in the first place because of his financial troubles. The job had brought him a few years of reprieve after he'd failed to secure a steady academic job, but now he was more beholden to his rich family members than ever. Jason Griess and other prosecutors working the case looked at his high-powered legal team and saw seemingly unlimited reserves of wealth, but Robert remained painfully aware of the debt he was accumulating. The way the Chinese favor wheel worked, he might not have to pay it all back, but he would carry around the emotional burden of owing his relatives for years. And if his family ever cut him off and he fell behind on the bills for his house arrest, he knew, he'd be thrown back in jail. Robert's inborn flair for drama became more pronounced. He started telling people that the doctors and lawyers were vampires perched on his shoulders.

As a condition of his release, Robert was permitted to resume his work for DBN, provided he stuck to tasks that everyone agreed were legal. And although it had been his job that got him into this mess, he needed the money. Going online in his private prison, he sourced ingredients for animal feed and brokered purchasing contracts. The guards mainly left him alone while he worked, though he figured his internet connection was monitored. There was a saying in China: *Use a long line to catch a big fish.* Now that he had a modicum of freedom, he suspected that it would be used against him.

While online, he frequently drifted to news articles on his case. In many articles, as in the court system itself, the order of his name was reversed. First name Mo, last name Hailong. It would be an easy task to establish the surname in his case—Chinese surnames are almost always one syllable—but no one seemed to care enough to do so. When Carolyn testified at his bail hearing, her Chinese name was misspelled in the court record as well.

Then there was the notion that Wang Lei had been found in the Monsanto field outside Bondurant wearing a suit, the corn towering high above his head, when in fact he had worn more casual garb, and the field had been mostly cleared. An error in a police log had metastasized and been enshrined as truth. Other press coverage explained, pulling the detail directly from the indictment, that Robert had been found on his hands and knees digging in the Tama County field. Robert maintained that he was in the car at the time, and that Wang Lei was the one doing the digging.

It was unlikely, of course, that jurors would care whether Robert should be addressed as Mr. Hailong or Mr. Mo, or whether Wang Lei had been wearing a polo shirt and trousers or a suit when he sneaked onto a Monsanto field, or whether Robert dug for corn or merely drove the getaway vehicle. But to Robert, who had a taste for conspiracy, the inconsistencies were threads in a grand tapestry of deception. He had been duplicitous in his work for DBN, but now he was outraged at what he saw as the U.S. government's duplicity in its treatment of him.

Back in China, Robert's parents were ill. His father had throat cancer, and his mother suffered from high blood pressure. They lived in Beijing with his sister Mo Yun, who had more time to devote to family now that she no longer worked for DBN. But she had two school-age children, and even with hired domestic help it was a lot for her to handle. Most nights Shao Genhuo didn't return home until eight, and he often worked weekends. And here was Robert, under house arrest in America, in a situation that would make any parent's blood pressure soar.

When Mo Yun told Robert that she was planning a trip to California, he tried to warn her. Mo Yun was normally sympathetic to his requests, and she had stood by him after his arrest. But this time she didn't listen. She had promised the kids she would take them to Disneyland. She wasn't going to let her brother's arrest stand in the way of their vacation.

THIRTY-ONE

SUMMER 2014

I n the basement of Los Angeles International Airport's Terminal 2, Mark Betten gathered law enforcement officers to explain the arrest they were about to carry out. Mark and his team had a dilemma: They had to figure out what to do with the kids.

The week before, Mo Yun had arrived in Los Angeles with her two children. Because she had overseen a division at DBN and was married to the company's CEO, Mark had designated her as a person of interest in the case. When she passed through customs on her way into the country, her name triggered an alert. CBP officers notified Mark of Mo Yun's arrival, and he had digital forensics specialists search images of Robert's devices for evidence that might implicate her. On a hard drive seized from DBN's Boca Raton office, the FBI found copies of MSN chat conversations between Robert and DBN staff in Beijing extending all the way back to 2007, to the inception of the seed operation. Someone—presumably Robert—had cut and pasted the conversations into Word and text documents. Several of the chats were with Mo Yun.

In one chat, Robert and Mo Yun discussed the purchase of farm-land in the Midwest. In another, Mo Yun asked if Robert had managed to get any corn yet. In a third, Dr. Li told Robert that Mo Yun "is in charge of the specifics from the home country side" and that he would speak with her about getting additional people to help Robert with seed collection.

That might be enough on which to hang an indictment, Mark believed. He hightailed it to Los Angeles, arriving in time for Mo Yun's return flight to Beijing.

Mark had a warrant for Mo Yun's arrest, but he wanted to first see if she might offer some useful or incriminating information in a casual encounter. FBI agents could freely question people as long as the people agreed. If suspects declined or seemed unwilling to talk, agents were required to read them their Miranda rights. Reciting those rights tended to make people close off. *You have the right to remain silent.* And often, they would. So Mark again planned to work through the CBP. Border patrol agents not only had significant leeway with searches; they could also question foreign nationals at will.

Around noon, Mo Yun and her kids arrived at the airport, checked their three suitcases, and cleared security. They walked to the gate area, bags of souvenirs dangling from their arms. When they arrived, almost every chair was occupied. People lounged on the floor with their phones plugged into outlets, charging them before the long haul. The terminal was under renovation, and its cheap carpeting and low ceilings gave it the feel of a developing-world airport, plopped into America's second-largest city. Mo Yun stopped at a bland Hudson News to buy snacks, and the line snaked around the register. Agents watched as she paid and returned to the gate with her kids. Then, as she moved toward a pair of open seats, CBP agent Gerome Esguerra approached her.

"We need to ask you some questions about your visa application," he said. He was in full uniform. His colleague Edward Becerril stood next to him, in plainclothes chinos and a button-down shirt, untucked to conceal the gun in his waistband. Mark watched discreetly from a short distance away, wearing a suit. If not for his military haircut, he could have been any other American businessman on his way to Beijing.

At forty, Mo Yun was slim, with long side-parted hair framing a narrow face. When she reached the seats, she plopped down her bags and retrieved her passport, handing it to the agents. She sat down, and her daughter, who was five, crawled onto her lap. Her twelve-year-old son took the seat next to them and started playing video games.

"We just have some questions we need to ask you, OK?"

"OK."

"For your visa. When you applied for your visa." This wasn't such a farfetched premise for an encounter. At airports along the U.S.-Mexico border, agents often pick out people for questioning as they wait for their flights.

"Oh, my visa," Mo Yun said.

"Yes, remember?"

"You speak English—a little bit?" Becerril interjected. He and the other agents knew from her entry interview, and from the transcripts of her online chats with Robert, that her English was passable, but they had an interpreter on hand in case she feigned incomprehension.

"Uh-huh." She nodded.

"Do you still work for DBN?" Esguerra asked. And with that, he signaled that the agents were interested not just in her visa, but in her brother—and her husband.

IN THE INTERVIEW THAT FOLLOWED, the border patrol agents played nice. Esguerra asked Mo Yun about her PhD, joking, "I should call you Dr. Mo." Softening to the comment, Mo Yun laughed and thanked him. Then she stood up. Before she could move away, Mark joined the group and told her that he was working on her brother's case. He did not mention that he was with the FBI.

"While you were here during this visit, did you meet with your brother at all?" he asked, as a discreetly placed audio recorder picked up the conversation.

"No, no, no, no. Just for vacation."

"Disneyland? How was it, by the way? Did the kids like it?"

"It was good, yeah."

"First time there?"

"Uh, we are the first time."

They talked about Universal Studios, and the challenges of navigating around Los Angeles, and then Mark cut off the small talk. He knew other passengers could hear what he was saying, and even after nearly eighteen years in the FBI, he still felt awkward questioning someone in public. But finally he got it out. As part of his work on her brother's case, he told Mo Yun, "If there's any kind of information or evidence that is helpful to him, we have an obligation to determine that and tell him about it and give it to his defense lawyers. So one of the things I wanted to talk with you about is some information that could potentially be helpful to him."

It was technically true that the FBI was legally obligated to turn over evidence or testimony that might help an individual under investigation. But investigators hardly went out of their way to do so. Instead, he was trying to get a statement from Mo Yun before officially putting her under arrest. Suggesting that he was on her brother's side might make her let down her guard.

He started by asking about Dr. Li. "One of the things that we've discovered looking at your brother's case is that it looks like he was put under some pressure by Dr. Li to go out and—"

"I don't know," Mo Yun said quickly. "I'm very surprised for this."

Mark brought up the chat logs that had been found pasted into Word documents on Robert's computer. He produced an excerpt from a 2007 conversation and pointed to the characters for her name, 莫云.

"Do you remember writing these chats with your brother, and having these conversations?" Mark asked.

In the chat, Robert had told Mo Yun about his marital problems, and about how he was struggling to make ends meet financially. Mo Yun encouraged him to support his family no matter what. Mark had chosen the conversation carefully. There was no suggestion of illegal behavior here, just sisterly concern for Robert's troubles. Admitting her involvement would not seem, on its face, to imply any guilt. But if Mo Yun confirmed here, outside an official interrogation, that she recognized the conversation, it would be hard for a lawyer to later claim in court that the Word documents containing other chats had been manufactured.

"Maybe," Mo Yun said.

"It looked like it was probably Yahoo chat that you were using for these chat sessions," Mark offered.

"Maybe, maybe."

"Did you usually write in English, too?" he pressed.

"Um, yeah. Maybe." Mo Yun said as her daughter squeezed her mother's nostrils.

Mark moved on to other topics, trying to get on tape as much detail as possible while the element of surprise was still fresh. He started to bring up another chat in which Mo Yun appeared to discuss with her brother a plan for chasing the self of a seed line but was interrupted by a flight attendant announcing over the loudspeaker that the plane to Beijing was about to board.

"Can we talk to you away from your kids, just real briefly?" Mark asked. "You'll be right here. She'll be able to see you," he added, indicating her daughter.

"She always want to sleep. Sorry. My brother has a lawyer. Maybe we—you—can talk with them."

Mark lowered his voice. By now the other passengers had grown curious about the commotion. "What we want to tell you, though, is we do have a warrant for your arrest." He explained that she would have to be separated from her kids. "I can assure you we're going to take good care of your two children."

"No. No. No."

Agent Becerril piped up to reiterate what Mark had just told her. "There's no choice," he said, and then, when Mo Yun shook her head, "Yes."

"No."

"Yes."

"*No!*"

The agents explained that she had two options: Put her children on a plane back to China alone to be met by a friend or relative, or keep them in Los Angeles, where they would be given to child protective services.

Mo Yun burst out crying. "No," she said. "Such a fun vacation! A holiday vacation. No!"

"You're going to need to make a decision, OK?" Becerril said. "Or we can make the decision. It's up to you."

"We would rather not put you in handcuffs in front of your kids," Esguerra said. "If you could just walk with us, no handcuffs. But if we have to, we will put you in handcuffs." The girl started to cry.

Finally, Mo Yun chose to put her children on the flight to Beijing, alone. An FBI agent who had been standing back from the operation surfaced to help her fill out the necessary forms. Her daughter screamed.

Eventually Mo Yun said a tearful good-bye to her kids, and airplane personnel pulled the girl from her and escorted both children onto the plane. The CBP agents led her to a processing facility in the basement of the airport, Mark following close behind. Only then did he hand Mo Yun a document laying out her Miranda rights in Chinese. *You have the right to remain silent. Anything you say can and will be used against you in a court of law. You have the right to an attorney.*

The FBI finally had someone close to DBN's leadership in custody. Mark's plan had worked. Or so it seemed at the time.

THIRTY-TWO

FALL 2014

For a few months following her arrest, Mo Yun lived with Robert in the secured house in Des Moines, but she chafed under the restrictions imposed on her, and her lawyers managed to get her let out in Iowa on supervised release. Before long Robert was alone with his problems.

A few months after his sister's arrest, as his guards waited outside a hospital operating room in Des Moines, Robert lay on a table, slipping out of consciousness. After he went under, the surgeon took a scalpel and made an incision straight down his inner thigh. He disconnected the lump from the blood vessel it was attached to and removed it. With that, the tumor that Robert had been told was a benign lipoma was gone. Except that in the process of removing it, the doctor started to suspect that maybe it wasn't what he had thought. Lipoma is yellow and slimy, like chicken fat. Robert's growth was a mess of dark blood clots.

The biopsy results came back three weeks later. The tumor

turned out to be an aggressive cancer called synovial sarcoma. An oncologist explained that the disease was far along, and that the procedure had made the cancer worse. When the surgeon cut it open, some of the tumor had escaped and lingered in his body. Robert needed to start chemotherapy immediately. Even then, the chance of recurrence was high.

In most cases, cancer means carcinoma. The most common cancers—those of the lung, breast, and colon—are almost always carcinomas. Every year more than a million such cases are diagnosed in the United States. But there is also a second, much rarer category of cancer called sarcoma. While carcinomas form in the skin or tissue cells that line our organs, sarcomas thrive in connective tissue cells, like muscles, bones, and nerves. Often they do not respond to chemotherapy. Synovial sarcoma, Robert's specific kind, can be lethal, but many patients, curiously, experience little pain. The number of cases diagnosed annually in the United States is fewer than one thousand.

The ignorance of Robert's doctor was not particularly unusual; most oncologists have never encountered the condition. But that didn't make the news any easier to handle. Robert's lawyers persuaded a judge to let him move from Des Moines to Houston to receive treatment at MD Anderson Cancer Center, which has the top sarcoma experts in the world. He found a new place to rent and a new security team and soon settled in to the extent that he could. With the restrictions governing his house arrest, it mattered little whether he was in Iowa or Texas. Either way, he was far from Carolyn and the kids.

The sarcoma center at MD Anderson exuded a soft, gentle vibe, like the headquarters for a gardening club. The walls were lavender, and the halls that held patient rooms were distinguished by flower names: Freesia and Hibiscus and Jasmine. In a waiting area lined with plush chairs, magazines were arranged just so. But design could not cancel the fact that everywhere people were battling death. Patients roamed the halls wearing face masks, their hair lost to chemo. Toddlers trudged the grounds with oxygen tubes clipped to their shirts. In this bastion of grief, Robert was finally surrounded by people who could match his mood.

Many of them were Chinese. As people in China ate more like Americans, with diets heavy in corn-fed meat, rates of cancer had skyrocketed. MD Anderson had become the preferred destination for care—so much so that agencies had cropped up to offer all-inclusive packages that comprised airfare, hotel, interpreters, and even personal shoppers while in Houston. Just next to 1 Mid Campus, MD Anderson's corporate headquarters, a Chinese developer was at work on a $94.7 million hotel, with sixteen stories of rooms aimed at mainland patients. MD Anderson also brokered research and clinical care partnerships with Chinese universities and hospitals, some of them led by the many Chinese-born researchers on staff. The institution was emblematic of just how deeply the United States and China were entangled in both commerce and science.

Robert became a patient of Dejka Araujo, the only doctor in the country who specializes in synovial sarcoma. On Christmas Day, he started treatment: six cycles of chemo, followed by five weeks of daily doses of radiation, with only Sundays off. Dr. Araujo explained that even if his cancer was to go into remission, he would face significant risk of it recurring within two years. As with his legal case, the prognosis seemed dim.

THIRTY-THREE

2017

From outside the U.S. Courthouse Annex, I could see a bridge leading across the river to the heart of downtown Des Moines, where men and women clad in business casual bought their morning coffee and hustled into office towers. Where I stood, police cars outnumbered people. The windows of the building before me were tinted green, obscuring the view of what was inside.

I walked through the door and passed through a metal detector, taking the elevator up three floors to the U.S. attorney's office for the Southern District of Iowa. The ceilings in the space were low, and the walls were decorated with airbrushed paintings of bland nature vistas. In the one that hung in the conference room where I met Jason Griess, a seagull swooped into a puff of turquoise sea foam.

Next to Mark Betten, Griess was the man who knew the most about the corn theft investigation. It was his first economic espionage case, and it had dominated his life for two and a half years. "These are just tremendously valuable secrets, and it's a national security issue that we not allow those to leak out," he told me.

He explained to me the process of poring over reams of documents. As Robert's case moved toward trial, the sheer resources expended in the investigation had become clear. Over the course of two years, dozens of agents had worked on catching him. Griess's team had at their disposal seventeen thousand intercepted emails, detailed GPS logs, boxes of documents taken from Robert's home, hundreds of hours of audio recordings and intercepted telephone calls, and numerous FBI 302s—the bureau's official accounts of interviews with sources. When the results from BioDiagnostics came back, a portion of the samples appeared to match Pioneer and Monsanto seeds that the companies considered trade secrets, so that evidence, too, had to be carefully considered. Early on, an attorney was sent from the Justice Department's National Security Division to help. Even so, combing through all this entailed an immense amount of work, and the case came to consume his life.

Griess was amiable and open. He spoke freely until, in a followup call, I asked him about the Foreign Intelligence Surveillance Act warrant—the secret, expansive permit that was used to collect some of the evidence in Robert Mo's case. "I don't want to get into the whole FISA thing," he said.

FISA WARRANTS ARE the product of a 1978 law enacted in the wake of Watergate and other intelligence scandals. The law was among a suite of reforms intended to prevent such abuses from happening again. The idea was that a secret body—the Foreign Intelligence Surveillance Court—would be put in charge of issuing the warrants needed to combat the most extreme national security threats, allowing intelligence officials to obtain permission quickly and discreetly while also reining in spurious surveillance. FISA was never meant to be used solely to monitor domestic communications.

Over time, though, the court fell prey to a powerful case of mission creep. As international calls became cheaper and people began sending dozens of emails a day, the volume of data available exploded. In their investigations of people overseas, intelligence agencies ended up intercepting increasing amounts of information on Americans. FISA court judges operate in secret, with only the numbers of warrants applied for and approved made public, and the judges sign off on the vast majority of requests. Between 1979 and 2013, the year Robert was arrested, the FISA court granted 35,434 warrants and rejected only 12 requests. The law might have been designed to target international terrorists, but in practice the warrants were also used to spy on Americans who had any communication, however slight, with people deemed suspicious. By the 2000s, the court had become a rubber-stamp body, used to justify the very same sort of surveillance that it was designed to prevent.

Shortly before Robert's arrest, a document leaked to the press by Edward Snowden showed that the NSA had used FISA to collect bulk data on many Americans' phone calls and emails. That leak revealed a disturbingly wide range of surveillance activity. But even by those standards, it was unusual for FISA to be used in an economic espionage case like Robert's where no weapons secrets were at stake. As far as Robert's lawyers could tell, his case marked the first time in U.S. history where such warrants had been used to investigate a trade dispute between privately owned companies.

Typically, the warrants and evidence from an investigation are made available to a defendant when a case goes to court, but the very issuance of a FISA warrant is classified. In Robert's case, the government was required to tell his lawyers only that the collected evidence would be used, not to specify what that evidence was. Robert's lawyers guessed that the warrant was used to eavesdrop on his cell phone calls with Lily Cheng and others, perhaps with assistance from the NSA. But there was no way to know for sure.

FISA was by then so expansive that it's possible that Robert's name did not appear on any FISA warrant applications, and that he was simply collateral in an investigation of some other target. Another agency might have looked into someone he had contacted once, and after he came under investigation, the mere fact of that contact would have allowed the FBI to go digging.

"We don't know what we're fighting about," Robert's attorney Mark Weinhardt complained in a pretrial hearing. "Imagine a garden-variety drug case in which the prosecutor tells the defense, 'I have a glassine packet, a plastic bag containing crack cocaine, and your client's thumbprint is unmistakably on that bag.' And the government says, 'I'm not going to tell you where I got it, but it's really, really good evidence. Can't tell you where I got it. National security. You just can't know.'" That was the situation they were in with FISA, he said.

Robert's lawyers tried to push for more information, but the matter was settled with an affidavit from U.S. Attorney General Lynch asserting that it would harm U.S. national security interests to hold a hearing on the matter.

In the months leading up to Robert's arrest, the FISA court had quietly issued a series of rulings that vastly expanded the definition of foreign intelligence, making targets on U.S. soil fair game. Nonetheless, civil rights activists and legal scholars were appalled by the use of FISA in a trade secrets theft case. An attack on corn was not an attack on the nation, they felt. As Weinhardt put it in a filing, quoting from one of the statutes governing FISA, "The government has no 'significant need' for information about the alleged theft of corn germplasm to protect the United States against 'clandestine intelligence activities' by 'an agent of a foreign power.'"

If Robert's case became precedent, it would mean that the government could use FISA warrants to bring charges against people who were involved in purely commercial activities. "If this becomes an accepted practice, the implications for civil liberties are huge," Kening Li, an intellectual property attorney with the law firm Duane Morris who submitted an affidavit in Robert Mo's case, told me. "If you are on the wrong side, you're screwed." For some people I interviewed, FISA was the defining issue in the case. But the details surrounding its use were, like the seeds at the heart of the court proceedings, a secret.

AS THE CASE MOVED TOWARD TRIAL, the U.S. government proposed calling as witnesses experts on corn seed, including one professor from Iowa State who held the title of Pioneer Chair in Agribusiness. Robert's attorneys, meanwhile, subpoenaed Pioneer and Monsanto, demanding that the companies provide evidence that the seed lines he and his colleagues had targeted were actually trade secrets. They sought documents connected to every field that the men were alleged to have visited, including the plot in Bondurant where Robert, Wang Lei, and Dr. Li were stopped by a sheriff's deputy and the fields that Ye Jian and Lin Yong visited on their road trip through Iowa and Illinois. They asked for copies of the contracts that the companies brokered with the farmers who planted the fields and details on the results of lab testing, including which seed lines had matched products that the companies claimed as trade secrets. The hope was to prove that the targeted corn was patented. If described in detail in a public filing, it could not be a trade secret.

But Pioneer and Monsanto had no intention of sending any more information about their seeds to Robert's defense team, let alone to each other. The companies fought back in filings filled with bold italics: *"confidential and sensitive information . . . irrelevant to the charges . . . not subject to disclosure."* The government did not actually need to prove that the corn varieties in the targeted fields were trade secrets, a lawyer for Monsanto argued—only that Robert thought they were.

"Since this is a conspiracy to steal trade secrets case, it may not matter at all whether it was a regular cornfield," an attorney who represented Monsanto told a magistrate judge. "The fact that the defendant was illegally in that field and stealing seed is evidence of intent."

This statement struck me as surreal. It was technically true that the U.S. government needed only to prove that Robert Mo intended to steal trade secrets, and not that he actually did. But if the Economic Espionage Act existed to protect innovation, and there was no need to prove that the technology under assault actually was highly coveted intellectual property, it raised questions about the law's utility. Robert called it a case of "the emperor's new clothes"—everyone was pretending to see a trade secret that was not there—and for once one of his overwrought metaphors seemed apt.

"Monsanto is a victim in this proceeding," a lawyer for Monsanto said one day in court.

"Let me be straight," a lawyer for Pioneer added. "We're a victim."

THIRTY-FOUR

SPRING 2015

All rise," said the clerk. Feet shuffled and papers rustled as everyone stood up, and then a hush fell over the small courtroom. In walked a woman of medium height and build, with prominent cheekbones and long brown hair.

"Good morning," said U.S. District Court Judge Stephanie Rose. "You can be seated. We are here today in the matter of *United States v. Mo Hailong and Mo Yun*."

Judge Rose's career had been marked by both spectacular rise and persistent controversy. In 2008, as a young U.S. assistant attorney in the Northern District of Iowa, she was criticized for her role in charging hundreds of undocumented immigrants following a raid at a kosher meatpacking plant. Rose prosecuted the workers in fast-track hearings held on a cattle fairground. Despite the opposition of immigration lawyers around the country, the next year she was confirmed as U.S. attorney for the district. She went on to charge the slaughterhouse manager with bank fraud, asking the

judge for a life sentence. That extreme request invited a public rebuke from six former U.S. attorneys general and more than a dozen
former U.S. attorneys.

In 2012, when she was appointed to the federal bench by President Obama, Judge Rose became the youngest federal judge in the
country and the first woman to serve in Iowa's southern district.
Then, just nine months into the job, she handed down a sentence in
a drug case that was a full two years longer than what the plea
agreement called for and sent an email to a prosecutor comparing
herself with the Hulk. "You know how Bruce Banner says, 'You
won't like me when I'm angry'? There's a lesson in there for all attorneys." The lesson for all judges came when the U.S. attorney's
office made the exchange part of the public record, and Rose's email
was splashed across the pages of *The Des Moines Register*.

As she presided over the courtroom, calling the pretrial hearing
to order, Judge Rose looked decidedly un-Hulk-like. The interior of
the courtroom was windowless and filled with dark tones: mahogany wood, gray suits, the long black robe hanging stiffly off Judge
Rose's shoulders. Mo Yun sat to the judge's right, wearing a white
blouse and black trousers. Since the hearing mainly concerned her,
Robert called in from Houston instead of traveling to Des Moines
for the occasion.

Mo Yun had hired a high-powered legal team from Los Angeles,
independent of Robert's, a move that was fairly common in cases
involving multiple defendants. Her lawyers had flown in to argue
that Mark Betten's airport questioning of her was illegal, because
it happened before the agent had read her Miranda rights. Officers are allowed to be duplicitous—they can gather information
undercover—but they can't threaten a person, or back her into a

corner, in order to get answers. Her lawyers aimed to prove that her airport encounter with Mark was effectively coerced. In the exchange, Mo Yun had conceded that she *might* recognize her MSN chats with Robert and that she and her brother *might* have chatted in English. Those weren't grave admissions, but getting them thrown out would nonetheless severely weaken the case against her.

Jason Griess was off preparing for another hearing, so prosecutor Marc Krickbaum called a series of witnesses to the stand in an effort to prove that Mo Yun freely consented to questioning. When Mark took the stand, he explained that the gate area was crowded and that he had worried about others overhearing the conversation, so he stood closer to Mo Yun than he might have otherwise. At no point leading up to the arrest did he take her phone, or handcuff her, or direct her to do anything, he said. Then Krickbaum sat down and Mo Yun's attorney Gary Lincenberg rose for cross-examination. He asked Mark to draw a diagram of the gate area, marking out the locations of the window and the boarding gate, along with where he and Mo Yun had stood.

"Now, Agent Betten," the defense attorney probed, "during the interrogation Ms. Mo also had a five-year-old daughter for large parts of it hanging on her, correct?"

"I would say probably the entire part of it."

"And it's still your testimony that you believe that there was a risk that she could leave that area and run away from the questioning; is that your testimony?" Lincenberg asked.

"No, that's not my testimony," Mark said. "I'd consider it highly unlikely that she would try to run away, so because of that we didn't position ourselves in any strategic location to try to prevent that.

We positioned ourselves in a manner that was conducive to conducting a consensual interview."

In his closing statement, Lincenberg alluded to the diagram that Mark had drawn. He argued that Mo Yun was backed against a window in a crowded boarding area and questioned in a foreign language while her children watched: "Three much larger male agents in deep voices with a gun showing and the baton showing then stood in front of her," he said with a flourish. "She was physically constrained. And Agent Betten even testified that they were probably even closer in Ms. Mo's face than they would have ordinarily been because of the background noise. She, faced with walls in front of her, posts to the left, agents in front of her, a daughter hanging around her neck and seats behind her, had no place to go."

Judge Rose agreed. Few of the travelers picked out by CBP agents for questioning have the impression that they can just walk away, she noted. "We've got at least four officers with this one woman—one of whom is in uniform wearing a gun and baton—approaching this woman, who is a citizen not of any country but of China, that has some of the worst human rights violations out there, and in which you, as a citizen, do not challenge the government," the judge said. "If the government says to you, 'You'll answer our questions,' you'll answer their questions." Mo Yun, she ruled, was entitled to have her Miranda rights read.

It was a remarkable development, and not only because Judge Rose, whose involvement in the slaughterhouse raids had earned her the eternal wrath of immigrant advocates, had ruled in favor of a noncitizen. The decision meant that all of Mo Yun's statements in the airport were inadmissible as evidence. Two months later, the judge threw out the MSN chats as well.

On July 28, 2015, the U.S. attorney's office dropped charges against Mo Yun and removed her name from the indictment. Investigators didn't have much else on her, and Griess and colleagues no doubt knew that in the absence of highly incriminating evidence, a jury was not likely to look kindly on the government's forcibly separating a mother from her children. Almost as quickly as the case against Mo Yun was built, it was dismantled. After a four-year investigation involving offices around the country, the government was back to one defendant: Robert.

THIRTY-FIVE

WINTER 2015-2016

Kevin expected that when Robert's case finally went to trial, he would be called as a witness. As the trial date neared and he learned more about the investigation of DBN, he reflected on some of the oddities in his relationship with the company. He thought back on the deflections, the unanswered emails, the feeling that he was swept aside whenever he tried to make serious progress on his assigned tasks. He recalled the attempts during his Beijing lab visit to prevent him from asking certain questions. He thought about Robert's lack of interest in the experimental hybrids growing on the Monee farm. Finally, it dawned on him that the Monee hybrids were a ruse. His participation had helped DBN maintain a front of legitimacy. He was a useful stooge.

He felt betrayed. All of the time he had spent mining his contacts and poring over fortune cookie messages was for nothing. He realized that his disposition as a scientist, always interested in finding an empirical solution, had led him to overlook warning signs, leaving him prone to manipulation. His ego hadn't helped. He had been seduced into thinking that a major Chinese agricultural company might actually be interested in the seeds he had developed in his backyard. He was so focused on the prospect of commercializing some of his seed lines that he ignored the signs that he was being played.

He tried to focus on breeding again, turning his attention to his backyard research plot. He worked on an ambitious project to breed corn that could tolerate cold weather during germination. A friend in Texas refrigerated seeds in thirty-eight-degree water, let them soak for three weeks, and shipped the seedlings that survived to Kevin, who transplanted them into his plot and monitored their growth. Kevin later "selfed" the best plants, or turned them into inbreds, with the goal of crossing pairs of inbred parents to make hybrids. He did this all without chemicals. To discourage ground squirrels from digging up seedlings, Kevin scattered mothballs around the plot. They dotted the soil like marshmallows on a chocolate cookie.

Kevin's efforts ran in opposition to the general trend in agriculture. As agribusiness companies grew larger and more industrial, the variety of seeds available to farmers had decreased. They had to make do with planting the same seed whether they were in Illinois or Nebraska. And here Kevin was developing seeds for specific weather conditions, and then in some cases hand-planting them.

By then the number of global seed companies was dwindling from six to four. DuPont had announced that it was merging with the chemical company Dow. Monsanto executives were contemplating a similar deal with the German conglomerate Bayer. Some of Kevin's neighbors prided themselves on buying American seed.

Now, as American companies joined with others beyond their borders, it wasn't even clear what that meant. Multinationals' ultimate allegiance was to their shareholders, not to Washington.

One of Kevin's old classmates was caught up in this shift. At the inception of the corn theft investigation, William Niebur had overseen DuPont Pioneer's Asia operations. He told an agricultural reporter that China was "unlike any other environment in the world when it comes to intellectual property." Then, in February 2016, he confused industry observers by becoming CEO of the Chinese seed company Origin Agritech. The company brokered a licensing deal with Pioneer and prepared to open its first branch outside China, in Des Moines. Chinese companies, too, were becoming global in ways that tested traditional alliances.

One trend was universal: As the companies grew, they became even more litigious. Kevin's 1980s brushes with flashlight breeding had made him wary of messing with other companies' intellectual property, and he felt certain that he would have walked away the minute it became clear that DBN was trying to reverse engineer seeds. Kevin figured that Robert had not trusted him from the start, that his DBN contact had intuited his blunt honesty and lack of talent for spy craft and decided not to make him part of the scheme. But there were some breeding efforts that fell into a legal gray area. Kevin knew that the FBI, like the multinational seed companies, was generally not interested in nuance. He felt lucky that his work had stayed squarely on the margins of the operation.

THIRTY-SIX

WINTER 2015-2016

R obert looked on, resigned, as Dr. Robert Leonard took the stand. On one side of the courtroom was an empty jury box, which would soon be filled with the Iowan office clerks and teachers and salesmen tasked with deciding his fate. His trial date was a month away. Following his treatment at MD Anderson, his sarcoma had gone into remission. There was a risk that it could come back in his groin or could spread to his lungs, but for the moment the cancer was the least of his worries.

As the trial approached, his lawyers left no argument unexplored. After charges were dropped in Mo Yun's case, they had tried to squeeze every last piece of evidence out of the U.S. attorney's office—including the Orville Redenbacher boxes that had been seized by CBP. They also launched a valiant effort to get evidence excluded in the case. In one filing, they pointed to the twenty-two congresspeople's inquiry in the wake of the Sherry Chen case about whether federal investigators and prosecutors singled out Asian Americans. They quoted from the *Newsweek* article by Jeff Stein calling Robert one of the "locusts in a swarm," and referenced the warrant application in which Mark Betten had suggested that Robert and Lily Cheng's conversing in Mandarin was suspicious. And they mentioned an offhand comment from Joel Thomas, the owner of Crossroads Ag, that Robert had seemed suspicious because of his ethnicity and because he spoke accented English.

So explosive was the atmosphere surrounding economic espionage investigations, Robert's lawyers argued, that his case was at risk of being marred by racism and xenophobia. The argument convinced Judge Rose, who forbade unnecessary mention of Robert's ethnicity and nationality at trial. Mere mention was too loaded, because that ethnicity was Chinese.

But the other motions brought by the defense failed. And Judge Rose's checkered record with immigrants, combined with her propensity to hand out long sentences, did not bode well for Robert.

Robert's lead attorney, Mark Weinhardt, knew that the prosecution had witnesses—sheriff's deputy Cass Bollman, Crossroads Ag owner Joel Thomas, Kevin—who could place Robert in cornfields and seed stores. He knew that Jason Griess and the other prosecutors would give the jury transcripts of the incriminating conversations captured as Ye Jian and Lin Yong drove across the Midwest in the rented Tahoe, seeking out cornfields. *Going into others' fields. IP theft. Any one term is very severe. . . . Others think we are spies sent from China. . . . We are surely considered as such.* If Ye Jian and Lin Yong knew they were committing a crime, it seemed likely that Robert did, too. But Robert's lawyers sensed an opening. Perhaps they could discredit the Tahoe conversation with help from a colorful expert witness. They were in court today so that Judge Rose could determine whether he would be allowed to testify.

Robert Leonard had once been the lead singer in the greaser revival band Sha Na Na. At Woodstock in 1969, he belted out a cover of "Teen Angel," wearing a gold suit open over a bare chest. Sha Na Na opened for Jimi Hendrix, the Kinks, the Grateful Dead, and Bruce Springsteen, and performed with John Lennon at Madison Square Garden. By the time the group appeared in the movie *Grease*, Leonard had left to pursue an academic career. He eventually became a professor at Hofstra University in Hempstead, New York, where he specialized in the field of forensic linguistics, an area of language analysis used in solving crimes.

Now a bespectacled man in his sixties, Leonard explained on the stand that he helped juries make sense of language, much as a radiologist might help them understand an X-ray. He might, for example, match a ransom note against the writings of an accused murderer by observing that the suspect frequently left out apostrophes in contractions like *cant* and *dont*, and that so, too, did the killer. Leonard was esteemed within his field and was frequently called as a witness in federal cases, though the expert testimony he gave in some cases seemed tenuous. He had once been hired by the defense in a federal case against a man accused of having sexually explicit conversations with an undercover agent posing as a fourteen-year-old girl. Leonard testified in a pretrial hearing that because the undercover agent did not properly mimic the language of a teenage girl, the man may have believed he was chatting with an adult woman. The judge threw out that testimony, on the grounds that Leonard was not an expert on fantasy role-play. But for Robert's lawyers, he was worth a try. The charges against Robert also came down to language—in the form of hours and hours of intercepted audio. His lawyers hoped that some of this dialogue might be dismantled using forensic linguistics.

In an earlier hearing, Judge Rose had acknowledged that there was "some weirdness" to the Tahoe conversation. What criminal, worried about being caught, meticulously lists the crimes he is committing? And when Ye Jian returned to the United States several months after the airport bust, why did the FBI not arrest him? Why, if he was a target in the investigation, was he allowed to return to China?

The answer, the defense planned to suggest at trial, was that Ye Jian and Lin Yong were agents of the U.S. government, co-opted in service of the investigation. Either that or they were trying to get recruited as U.S. government agents. To succeed with this line of argument, the defense didn't need to prove that the men were in fact working for the FBI. They merely needed to poke enough holes in the government's argument to instill doubt in the minds of the jurors.

If admitted as an expert witness, Leonard would take this smidgen of doubt and give it academic backing. Because he didn't speak Mandarin, he had hired a former U.S. Census Bureau linguist named Yuling Pan to help him analyze audio from the case. Robert watched as Leonard explained on the stand that Chinese is diglossic, meaning that distinct variants are used for formal situations and casual conversations. Together he and Pan determined that the Tahoe conversation was an odd mixture of "high" Mandarin, used in formal or literary settings, and "low" Mandarin, used in casual conversation. When a bird dive-bombed the SUV, Leonard said, Lin Yong and Ye Jian had been speaking in high, stilted Mandarin—suggesting a rehearsed conversation. The surprise of seeing gray excrement splatter across the windshield jolted them into a more normal dialogue. "They snap into L, spontaneous conversation," the linguist explained, "and they talk about the bird and they make jokes about it and the dive-bombing, and then they go right back into H again." Expert witnesses are not allowed to give opinions, but the implication of Leonard's testimony was clear: The incriminating portion of the conversation was staged.

Robert watched in silence. Every time he shifted his position or crossed his legs, his pant legs slid up, revealing the clunky ankle bracelets that tracked his every move. He listened as Leonard and a prosecutor had a nonsensical exchange about the Mandarin word *yinwei*, which means "since" or "because." The prosecutor tried to make analogies to English. Leonard resisted; Chinese was different, he maintained, but he couldn't offer details on precisely how. Robert thought that the argument that Lin Yong and Ye Jian were government agents was dubious. He actually rather liked Lin Yong. And here in the courtroom were two men tussling over a language neither one spoke. It was a surreal twist in a case that Robert felt had been characterized by misunderstandings throughout—starting with the image of the man in a field, wearing a suit.

Judge Rose ultimately sided with the prosecution, ruling that Leonard could not testify. Putting him on the stand at trial, she noted, would bring a risk of "confusion and waste of time." And with that, the most imaginative defense Robert's legal team had left vanished.

NOT LONG AFTERWARD, the U.S. attorney's office offered Robert a plea deal. Conspiracy to steal trade secrets carries a maximum sentence of ten years in prison and a $250,000 fine, but in exchange for a guilty plea, prosecutors would keep it to five years in prison, with no fine.

Robert considered the offer. He had closely watched another

case involving DuPont, in which two men were accused of stealing
the company's process for producing titanium dioxide, a whitener
found in everything from house paint to Oreo cookies. A jury in
California had convicted both men. The lead perpetrator, a Malay-
sian national of Chinese descent, was sentenced to fifteen years in
prison—the same sentence handed down to Boeing engineer Greg
Chung for stealing rocketry secrets. And that had happened in San
Francisco, a progressive place with a large Chinese-American population, where people were presumably less prone to leap to assumptions because of a person's ethnicity. His lawyers had explained
to him the risks of facing a jury in Iowa. In addition to racism, he
would be up against a seed company that some farmers still considered local, despite it being owned by DuPont.

Because Robert had decided that the American justice system
was rigged, he believed that a trial would merely delay his inevitable
conviction. Years earlier he had transformed himself from a scientist into a businessman. What was a plea arrangement but another
business transaction? He decided to take the deal.

The agreement did not cover restitution, and Robert learned
that following his sentencing he might be required to pay Pioneer
and Monsanto large sums of money. And because the federal government alleged that they were purchased as part of the conspiracy,
DBN's farms in Illinois and Iowa would be forfeited—notices of
possession attached to their front doors, the weeds left to grow even
longer, vandals all but invited back in. But Robert would, at least, be
guaranteed a shorter prison sentence.

On January 27, 2016, the two sides gathered in court again. Four
and a half years after Robert was first found in a field, and two years
after his arrest, Judge Rose laid out his rights one last time. If he
went to trial, she noted, he would have the right to review all the

evidence that the U.S. government had against him. He could choose not to say anything or he could present his own defense.

"If you plead guilty here today, you give up all of those trial rights," she concluded. "There will never be a trial on this matter. Do you understand that?"

"Yes, Your Honor."

Then she asked, "Formally and for the record, how do you plead to Count 1 of the fourth superseding indictment, guilty or not guilty?"

"Guilty."

THIRTY-SEVEN

FALL 2016

At 9:00 A.M. on the day of Robert's sentencing, the stiff wooden benches in the courtroom gallery were full. With the exception of a retiree who showed up in jeans and sneakers, clutching a book, most of the onlookers had a close connection to the case. They kept to their respective sides in the gallery, like guests at a wedding—friends of the prosecution to the right, friends of the defense to the left.

On the prosecution side, Mark Betten chatted with other law enforcement officers about where they'd gone for drinks the night before. He was jovial, as if settling in to watch a film. For Mark, Robert's sentencing marked the culmination of years of hard work. His gaze eventually fell on Jason Griess, who sat at a heavy oak table, shuffling papers and talking in a low tone with the other prosecutors. He had grown a thick beard in the preceding months. "Like Grizzly Adams," Mark whispered to the guy next to him, chuckling.

At the table across from Griess was Mark Weinhardt, with his bow tie and monogrammed attire. The two attorneys looked like actors who had been cast in the wrong roles: Weinhardt resembled a straitlaced prosecutor, while Griess looked like a fiery defense attorney.

Robert sat next to Weinhardt, wearing a gray suit and a red tie. Because he no longer needed frequent treatments at MD Anderson, Judge Rose had allowed him to move back in with his family in Florida on supervised release. He had returned to Boca Raton to find his backyard garden neglected, his fruit trees dying. The damage to his children was even more profound. His teenage daughter had suffered emotionally with all the upheaval brought on by his case. Now, at this crucial moment, he and Carolyn had decided to keep the kids away from the drama. They were awaiting the decision back in Florida, far from the courtroom. He would have to face his sentence alone.

Judge Rose took her seat and called the courtroom to order. She reviewed the evidence before the court, looking down at her notes as she spoke. Robert's guilty plea hadn't stopped the deluge of filings, and the exhibits the attorneys had sent her ahead of sentencing ran to more than twenty-five hundred pages. Prosecutors tried to back up their claim that Pioneer and Monsanto had suffered steep losses because of the stolen seeds. The defense, meanwhile, submitted letters of support from Robert's friends, family, and even the security guards who had watched him during his house arrest, who apparently never suspected the dark thoughts he harbored about vampires sucking the life out of him. ("In my forty-three years in public and private law enforcement security work, I have never dealt with a more respectful or compliant individual," one read.) If Judge

Rose had ever relished inserting herself into lawyers' work, as her
Hulk email exchange suggested, she had lost some of that energy
over the duration of this case. She sounded weary.

Griess listened carefully as she spoke. In securing a plea, the U.S.
attorney's office had stopped the drain of resources and obtained a
conviction. He and other prosecutors had pushed the defense to the
limit, to the point where the lawyers had called a former rock star
to the stand to pursue a line of reasoning that Griess found highly
specious. And yet, on a personal level, Griess was bothered by the
abrupt conclusion of the case after investing years of his life in it.
He funneled all the energy he had left into drafting a two-hundred-
page memo, arguing for giving Robert the maximum sentence al-
lowable under the plea deal: five years in prison.

By contrast, Weinhardt asked that Robert be put on probation
and given "draconian community service obligations." A sentence
restricted to community service would allow him to stay with his
family and get sufficient medical care. It was an unusual request,
Weinhardt noted, "but this is in so many ways an unusual case and
in so many ways an unusual individual." Another factor made the
request particularly urgent: Because Robert was not a U.S. citizen,
a term of more than one year would trigger his deportation upon
release.

THE SENTENCING HEARING lasted for three days. On the third day,
Judge Rose gave each side a final chance to make its case. Griess
shifted the focus back to the crime, arguing that the impact of the
seed theft would not end with Robert Mo's sentencing. Pioneer and
Monsanto might suffer losses for years to come, he speculated. Sales

of their products in China could decline. Americans might lose their jobs. "This is market share that Pioneer and Monsanto have earned through years of research and development, innovation, trial, and hard work," he said. "And unlike other types of theft, once those trade secrets are out, there's no getting them back." Then he zoomed out, moving from a cornfield in Iowa to the world beyond. With her decision today, Judge Rose had the power to deter future economic spies, he said. "We need to impose a sentence, or the court does, which doesn't lead other would-be thieves, whether they're foreign or domestic, to conclude that stealing a competitor's trade secrets is worth the risk," he said.

Some people felt that as a solution to industrial espionage, sending individual perpetrators to prison for years had about as much effect as locking up drug runners in the fight against drug trafficking. It was a game of whack-a-mole: One person went to prison, and another took his place. Arrests of individuals also got mired in questions of discrimination and selective prosecution. In the long run, there were more productive ways to safeguard innovation: Improve education, subsidize health care, boost interest in science and engineering fields, liberalize green card requirements so that the United States had an adequate supply of talented workers. But these were systemic changes that didn't have the sexiness of an urgent foreign threat. They were far beyond the purview of Griess as he stood in court, making the case for the man in the field to get as much prison time as possible.

When Griess finished, Weinhardt rose to argue that Robert was a family man: active in his church, devoted to his wife and kids, giving of his time to others in need. In his job at DBN, he performed a number of entirely legal functions. His involvement in the corn theft scheme, Weinhardt explained somewhat improbably, was due to his overtrusting nature. The defense lawyer quoted a letter from a friend: "'Although Robert is extremely smart and intellectually curious, he sometimes seemed child-like, naive, and gullible.' And I'm sorry, Robert"—Weinhardt glanced at his client, pausing for effect—"but all of us on the defense team have had the same reaction, that we struggle to find a combination of someone of such immense intelligence and academic achievement on the one hand and naïveté and lack of street sense on the other."

After Weinhardt finished, Robert got up to speak. It was the first time that he had said more than a few words in court.

"Dear Honorable Judge Rose," he began, reading from a paper he clutched in his hands. "I'm writing to you, to Your Honor, for the only purpose of admitting my mistakes and in taking full responsibilities without any complaints or excuses." He talked of once being taken with the American dream, of moving with Carolyn to the United States to build a future for his children. "Now I have destroyed everything that I wanted: my reputation, job security, and my family's respect." He started to sob.

"Mr. Mo, you can take some time if you need it," Judge Rose said. "Just continue whenever you're ready, OK?"

"Yes," he said slowly. "I'm ready." He resumed reading. "In my mind, the cancer that developed in Des Moines was a punishment for my crime." He talked about how his family had suffered in his absence. "My heart is broken because I know that I am to blame." And then he slipped into the comfort of metaphor, explaining how when he returned from house arrest he took his sickly garden as an omen. He threw his energy into reviving it. Finally, the rosebush flowered a deep crimson, and the mango and avocado trees yielded fruit. He relished the sight of his children eating this bounty. "It reminds me how precious it is to stay at home," he said. Poetry and music held new meaning, as did life itself. He was, he suggested, already a changed man. "I have learned a lesson and will never put myself in a situation like this again."

As she prepared to announce her decision, Judge Rose was solemn. The case, she said, "was one that started with a man in a field and grew into something that internationally is an enormous case for both China and the United States." It was, she added, "undeniably part of a larger trend that is being seen across the United States. I do think we have to send a message to China that this kind of criminal behavior is not going to be tolerated."

And then, midspeech, the judge suddenly began addressing Robert directly. "I have debated more hours than I could count what to do in this case," she said. Faced with a single perpetrator, her certainty about sending a message slipped away. "And less than many other cases, I am not sure that I'm going to get it entirely right. I'm not sure there is a good or right answer." It was a remarkable admission for a judge who had once compared herself with a superhero.

"Ultimately, I think the appropriate sentence in your case is thirty-six months' imprisonment," she said, "and that is what I'm going to impose." If Robert Mo had been entirely healthy, she added, she would have imposed the full five years.

And then, as if to soften the blow, she gave Robert a pep talk. "I know you've said that you destroyed everything in your life. I don't think you have. You certainly hit a bump in the road, but you are still a young man and you still have an incredible brain and you still have a good family. You can put this back together." He looked at her, and for a moment the mood in the courtroom turned hopeful. The judge added: "You just learned a really harsh lesson."

. . .

KEVIN'S IMPORTANCE TO THE CASE had diminished when it ended in
a plea deal, so he learned about Robert's sentence only after a friend
sent him an article from *The Des Moines Register.* The news inspired
mixed feelings. He recalled all of the intellectual property issues
he'd heard about in his days as a seed breeder: the flashlight breeding of years past, the case of Holden and the stolen Pioneer inbreds.
He could not recall anyone ever spending a day in jail. In that sense
Robert's sentence was an improvement over previous cases.

But on another level the disconnect between Robert's sentence
and the punishments in those previous seed theft cases also bothered him. He wondered if the reason for the discrepancy was Robert's ethnicity.

THIRTY-EIGHT

2017-2019

Mounted next to a door at FBI headquarters in Washington, D.C., is a light-up ON AIR sign left over from an era when radio was king. On the day I visited, the light was off. On the other side of the door, a floor-to-ceiling blue velvet curtain hung as the backdrop to two flags: one American and one featuring the intricate emblem of the FBI. The space felt like the set for a community theater production. It was here, in the J. Edgar Hoover Building's midcentury media room, that I interviewed Mark Betten.

That FBI headquarters is still named after the director who was responsible for some of the bureau's worst abuses is a matter of significant controversy. A number of civil society groups and some former FBI agents have pushed for a change. But wrapped up in that conflict is the strange endurance of the building itself, a concrete behemoth that routinely tops lists of the world's ugliest buildings. The FBI plans to eventually build a new headquarters. In the meantime, the tight corridors and fortresslike floor plan of the current building make it hard to forget the bureau's history.

Arranging a meeting with Mark had taken months of correspondence with the FBI's media relations department. Donald Trump had been sworn in as president earlier in the year. Shortly afterward, he fired FBI director James Comey. Now that we were finally here, Mark had brought along his supervisor, acting Economic Espionage Unit head John Hartnett. On top of overseeing hundreds of other cases, Hartnett helped manage the investigation of Robert Mo and DBN.

We sat at a small wooden table in the center of the room, Mark and Hartnett on one side and me on the other. His face expressionless, Hartnett talked about the corn theft investigation in broad strokes. "From the unit's perspective, it ended up being a very important case," he began.

I asked him how it connected to theories about Chinese industrial espionage. China, he said, had challenged the nature of the Western research system by embracing a nontraditional collector model, which he explained meant focusing on "the individuals who have access to the information—typically engineers, scientists, researchers, and so forth." He continued: "Other countries typically use their intelligence officers to recruit sources that have access to information. That's a spotting and assessing cycle, which is a traditional counterintelligence approach. The Chinese approach is a little bit different. They utilize people of Asian or Chinese backgrounds that have come to the U.S. or to Western countries."

This sounded a lot like the thousand grains of sand theory, so I mentioned the case of Xiaoxing Xi, the Temple University physicist who had been arrested at gunpoint before being cleared of all charges. "Is there a concern with these cases that you might ensnare people who are innocent?" I asked.

"Certainly it's a concern," Hartnett said. Then he backpedaled.

"There can be certain portrayals of the FBI that may not put us in a favorable light, so it's certainly a concern."

I brought up allegations of racial profiling from community organizers.

"If there's a larger percentage of one group that appears to be investigated or charged, it doesn't mean they're being targeted," Hartnett told me. "The investigations are properly predicated. The FBI is just following the evidence."

In the case of Robert Mo, the evidence had led the FBI to spend two years bugging rental cars, intercepting phone calls, and flying surveillance planes overhead. The case that started with a man in a field had swollen into something much larger. There was the FISA warrant, the border searches, the arrest of Mo Yun while her children were escorted onto an international flight without her.

Despite the vast resources expended in the case, in the end only one of the seven people charged was sent to prison. The company at the center of the scheme, DBN, had not suffered any serious consequences. Lily Cheng and other suspected insiders had not been charged. Dr. Li, Lin Yong, Ye Jian, Wang Lei, and Wang Hongwei remained on the FBI's Most Wanted list, where together they accounted for nearly a third of all counterintelligence suspects at large.

I turned to Mark and asked about the investigation's limitations. Whether Robert was a tentacle of a foreign government or a cog in middle management who had been caught up in a harebrained plan, it seemed to me that there was no denying that the outcome of the case did not match the FBI's ambition.

"Do you feel frustration at all that you have these suspects in China who won't be extradited in the case?" I asked him.

"I think any agent is frustrated when you're unable to get in custody the person charged," Mark told me frankly. "But there are lots of member countries in Interpol. I haven't ruled out the possibility that we could still get one of these individuals."

In the meantime, some of those individuals—Dr. Li, Ye Jian, and Lin Yong—were safe in Beijing, where the Chinese government had gone on the counteroffensive by hyping its own foreign espionage threat. In 2016, April 15 became National Security Education Day in China. Posters appeared around Beijing featuring a comic strip titled "Dangerous Love." The story line starred a delicate young woman named Xiao Li, who had the misfortune to meet a dodgy-looking white man named David. Claiming to be a scholar, David persuaded her to hand over confidential documents—and then, as soon as she delivered them, he promptly disappeared. The encounter landed Xiao Li in trouble with the Ministry of State Security.

The Beijing state security bureau unveiled a hotline and offered awards for tips on foreign spies. The bureau's website explained that espionage had increased as China opened to the outside world. It was as if the Ministry of State Security's publicity managers had closely studied the tropes of the FBI's Strategic Partnership Program. Had the two agencies been corporations, one might have sued.

Shortly after this campaign, I flew to Beijing to see what I could dredge up on DBN. One day I hired a taxi driver to take me to the village of Shenjiaying, fifty-five miles outside the capital. As we left the city on the expressway, the smog thinned and the terrain grew hilly. I glimpsed a stretch of the Great Wall crisscrossing the green slopes, fog hanging over the wall's stone towers. Eventually we arrived in the village, where I knew there was a large farm that grew DBN seeds.

It was harvest time, and there was dried corn everywhere. In

Iowa, grain is typically transported to a silo or granary after being harvested by machine. In Shenjiaying, ears of dried corn were heaped in haphazard piles or spread clear across the road. Most of the village's residents lived in bland cinder-block housing lining the fields. The only building of any size was an outlandish castlelike structure that looked like it had been transported from a second-rate Disneyland. A villager informed me it was the local elementary school.

I located the farm I'd found online and walked toward a large house with whitewashed walls and a neat tile roof. There was no one in sight. As I watched a cat climb a sapling in the yard and contemplated what to do, a man with a weathered face and sandpaper hands appeared from an adjacent field. He introduced himself as Mr. Liu and confirmed that he planted DBN seed. "They work with the Chinese Academy of Agricultural Sciences," he said proudly.

He emphasized that the seed he grew was not genetically modified, adding that he believed GM seed was bad for people's health, and from this I deduced that the seed lines he planted were not the ones that so interested the FBI. But Mr. Liu's allegiance to DBN echoed what I had found elsewhere: that the company was doing just fine, despite several of its employees being charged with felonies in the United States. When news of Robert's 2013 arrest first broke, the company's share prices on the Shenzhen Stock Exchange had taken a hit. But they recovered within a few months, after it became clear that the case would have little impact on DBN's day-to-day operations. Government planning documents continued to emphasize the importance of China's agriculture and biotechnology sectors, and in 2014 DBN was selected by China's Ministry of Agriculture as one of twenty companies to receive funding for "innovation demonstration" labs—signaling that the central government, like the company's shareholders, didn't care about the criminal case winding its way through America's court system. By mid-2015, DBN's shares had more than doubled in value compared with 2013.

In February 2016, the state-owned petrochemical company ChemChina announced a $43 billion bid for Syngenta, a Swiss agricultural company. The largest ever Chinese takeover of a foreign company, the acquisition was a natural outcome in an industry in which Western multinationals held little real allegiance to the nations that had spawned them. (A few years earlier, the Chinese meat producer Shuanghui International had purchased the American meat-processing outfit Smithfield Foods.) For Chinese leaders, ChemChina's acquisition of Syngenta was momentous. It meant that ChemChina would acquire Syngenta's impressive portfolio of genetically modified seeds, and leaders would finally achieve their goal of having a seed company that could compete with DuPont and Monsanto. Industry consultants took it as a sign that a change in Chinese government policy was imminent, and that genetically modified corn would soon be commercialized.

There was a certain irony to the fact that ChemChina had managed to do legally what DBN had spent several years trying to accomplish through theft. But if government policy changed, Shao Genhuo's company stood to gain as well. DBN could soon begin selling genetically modified seeds in China—no matter their source.

A few months after the Syngenta deal was announced, and several weeks before Robert's sentencing, Kings Nower staged a flashy fifteen-year anniversary bash. Six hundred employees, contract farmers, and other friends of DBN gathered in a large event hall in Beijing. Crimson banners hung from the ceiling declaring KINGS NOWER, RED UNDER HEAVEN.

DBN CEO Shao Genhuo watched approvingly from the audience as Dr. Li took the stage, smiling his taut grin. His speech took the theme of "dreams, journeys, and futures." The seed industry, he proclaimed, was "a major battleground for defending the country and a strategic sector for realizing the great rejuvenation of the Chinese nation." Shao had once told Chinese journalists that by 2023 DBN would become a world-class firm and by 2033 it would be the top agribusiness company in the world. Robert's conviction apparently had little effect on this ambition. As far as I could tell from coverage of the event, no one mentioned him.

IN 2018, FBI DIRECTOR CHRISTOPHER WRAY revealed that the bureau had active economic espionage investigations in all fifty states. "The volume of it, the pervasiveness of it, the significance of it is something this country cannot underestimate," he said at the Aspen Security Forum that year. In a briefing before the Senate Intelligence Committee, Wray said that Chinese students and scientists were "exploiting the very open research and development environment that we have." The FBI viewed China, he added, as "a whole-of-society threat."

Some counterintelligence analysts argued that Wray's remarks were a reference to a speech Xi Jinping had made at China's 2017 Party Congress calling for "a whole-of-society" effort to secure China's rise. That same year, China enacted a national intelligence law that obliged citizens, businesses, and other organizations to assist with a broad variety of intelligence work. But Wray had singled out ethnic Chinese scientists and students in the United States, and U.S. community organizers interpreted the phrase to mean that they were part of the problem—and that ethnic Chinese scholars were guilty until proven innocent. Several Asian-American organizations coauthored a letter to Wray's office, expressing concern. They never got a reply. Instead, Wray doubled down on his remarks in a later appearance.

At the field office level, the FBI was more receptive to dialogue, and individual offices started responding to requests to meet with Chinese-American community groups. In November 2018, I attended an FBI event on economic espionage in St. Paul, Minnesota, hosted by the local chapter of the Chinese American Alliance. A few dozen people sat on folding chairs in a gymnasium hung with giant red lanterns. Many kept their jackets on to insulate them from the Minnesota cold. Jeffrey Van Nest, chief division counsel for the FBI's Minneapolis office, stood before the group, giving a lighthearted tour of FBI lore that glossed over the abuses of the Hoover years. Then he warned the audience members that they might be approached by people seeking industrial secrets for China. He went over what they should do: Tell their employers first, then go to the FBI. "We simply can't do our job without your help," Van Nest entreated.

His presentation was measured and respectful. He was careful not to suggest that audience members were in any way involved with technology theft. Instead, he stressed that they might find themselves approached by people with bad intentions.

But the FBI had not altered its messaging at the highest levels, and when Van Nest broke for questions, a man in the audience asked whether the bureau had played a role in rounding up Japanese Americans during World War II. More than 120,000 people had been interned in camps, the majority of them U.S. citizens. Van Nest claimed that the FBI had not been involved, eliding the bureau's role in arresting nearly 1,300 Japanese Americans in the days after the Pearl Harbor bombing. But I was more struck by the man's question, and the fact that he had asked it at this event. He seemed to be suggesting that internment could happen again, this time with Chinese Americans. As tensions between China and the United States escalated, I came to understand his apprehension.

By then the FBI crackdown had spread to universities and research institutions, as the bureau worked with the U.S. National Institutes of Health to address fears that China was taking advantage of federally funded research. For years, the Chinese government had tried to recruit ethnic Chinese scientists by offering lucrative grants and incentives for those who returned. The most well known of these programs was called Thousand Talents. Scientists often accepted the money and took short trips to China to visit friends and relatives while keeping their jobs at U.S. institutions. Some reported the Chinese grants. Others did not—a clear violation of NIH policy. In a handful of cases, grant recipients took technologies back to China, prompting the NIH and FBI to view the talent programs not as double-dipping vacation plans but as a path for U.S.-based scientists to set up "shadow labs" overseas. After working closely with the FBI to identify perpetrators, the NIH sent out letters to more than sixty institutions, asking them to investigate researchers who were suspected of violating agency policy. One of these institutions was MD Anderson, where Robert had received cancer treatment.

In November 2017, the center's administrators gave the FBI access to the network accounts of twenty-three employees. A week later, two senior researchers were marched out of their offices and put on administrative leave. They lost access to their research teams, email accounts, and labs. More scientists were put on leave soon after.

Months of confusion ensued. The FBI installed a video camera near the office of one Chinese-born researcher. After investigators examined copies of his devices and found images they claimed were suspicious, he was charged in state court with possession of child pornography. But then, ten months later, the charges were dropped after his lawyer proved that the images in question did not in fact depict minors.

In the end, MD Anderson invoked termination proceedings with three researchers, two of whom resigned before they could be fired. Other scientists left under a cloud of suspicion or simply because the atmosphere had grown too toxic.

When I flew to Houston in the wake of the investigations, I found a campus roiled by fear. The lavender-hued halls labeled with flower names that Robert had encountered during his treatment did little to soothe researchers' worries.

I placed public information requests seeking documents from MD Anderson connected to the FBI investigation. Weeks of wrangling ensued. In one surreal response, an MD Anderson lawyer asked me to define the word "between." Instead of releasing the requested documents, administrators gave a handful of redacted investigative files to another reporter, Todd Ackerman of the *Houston Chronicle*.

Ackerman and I decided to team up. The files he had received suggested that several of the researchers had violated NIH policy, for example by sharing papers under review with people not authorized to see them. But they also showed that in carrying out the inquiries, MD Anderson administrators had wide discretion and seemed determined to find nefarious intent where there was none. In one case, a Chinese-born researcher kept up a flirtatious correspondence with a former postdoctoral fellow of his who had moved back to China. As a favor to her, he filled out a Thousand Talents application to work in Beijing. But he never completed the application process, nor did he receive any payment from the Chinese host institution. (Researchers at MD Anderson were allowed to participate in foreign research programs as long as they reported the income and affiliation.) The center's ethics and compliance officer concluded that because the scientist had offered his services, it was "immaterial" whether he was actually paid.

After Ackerman and I published our stories, MD Anderson administrators called a town hall meeting for faculty. Someone later passed me an audio recording of the event. One researcher asked administrators whether "an increasingly xenophobic and isolationist" federal government was prompting MD Anderson to act rashly. "How can you—and I plead, please—reassure all of our employees that we as an institution and academia are not being manipulated as part of a centralized policy to practice and to act in ways that are diametrically opposite to our core values?" he asked.

"Really excellent point," an administrator responded. "We follow due process."

Ethnic Chinese researchers at other institutions soon lost their jobs as well. Some were deported. Scholars warned of a coming nationwide purge. Soon it emerged that the FBI was urging U.S. universities to monitor students from select Chinese research institutions, and even interviewing Americans on study-abroad programs in China.

The researchers who departed MD Anderson in the wake of the crackdown included tenured professors who made sizable salaries, along with the institution's vice president for research. Several took jobs at elite universities in China. A number of affected scientists had technically violated NIH policy, but their punishments seemed

out of sync with their offenses. The crackdown was also highly
counterproductive. "These are the top talents that foreign countries have been trying to recruit unsuccessfully," said Steven Pei, an
engineering professor at another institution in Houston. "MD Anderson is helping foreign countries to accomplish what they could
not do by themselves."

In an effort to bolster its Chinese patient population, in fact, MD
Anderson's administration had spent years cultivating ties to the
Chinese government. In 2015, China's State Council gave the institution an International Science and Technology Cooperation Award,
in a ceremony attended by Xi Jinping. In 2017, an MD Anderson
vice president flew to Beijing to meet with the director of the State
Administration of Foreign Expert Affairs, the very agency that ad-
ministers the Thousand Talents program. But when the crackdown
came, administrators purged ethnic Chinese scientists while offering little explanation to the broader academic community—a move
that, in the global battle for talent, played neatly into the Chinese
government's hands.

INVESTIGATIONS OFTEN HAVE unintended consequences. The stress
of seeing a son arrested for drug possession might propel a father
to start drinking. In seeking justice in court, a victim of a violent
attack might have to relive a horrifying episode. But the investigation of Robert Mo had a particularly ironic footnote. Brought in the
name of protecting agricultural innovation, it ended up hurting an
American farmer.

After selling Robert six bags of seed, Iowa seed dealer Joel Thomas
cooperated with the FBI, spending hours answering questions about
the transaction at Crossroads Ag. Prosecutors prepped him to be a

witness if the case went to trial. But then Pioneer management learned that Thomas had sold seed without a tech agreement on file. The company revoked his dealer permit. Without a license, he managed to remain in business only by cutting in a middleman, which meant giving another dealer a slice of his revenue.

"It's a corporate deal," he told me. We were in the warehouse behind Crossroads Ag. Thomas wore a Carhartt work shirt and jeans, and as he spoke he leaned on the bed of his pickup truck, a Big Gulp soda at his side. Once it came out that Robert had managed to buy Pioneer seed to send back to China, he said, the company needed someone to blame. "Everything goes downhill, and I'm at the bottom. They have to have somebody to throw under the bus."

Thomas said that when Robert was arrested, an FBI agent called him to say that in the long run the investigation would prove its worth, by deterring trade secrets theft. Thomas didn't buy it. He was a Trump supporter, and he wasn't particularly attuned to arguments about racial bias. His comments were among the factors that prompted Judge Rose to ban unnecessary mention of Robert's ethnicity and nationality at trial. But he was skeptical that the investigation would ultimately prevent the leakage of secrets. "The FBI thought they won," he said. "I don't think so." He had heard that in China counterfeit Pioneer seed was still everywhere.

He added: "I'd hate to guess how much taxpayer money they spent on this."

THIRTY-NINE

SPRING 2018

Plastic coyotes stalked the lawn at Butner Low Federal Correctional Institution, scaring away any geese that might contemplate making the prison their home. Two-dimensional and tinged a brownish orange, the decoys were frozen into position—backs arched, yellow eyes wide, mouths open in a menacing grin. To give some semblance of movement, they pivoted on stakes protruding from their bellies, swiveling frantically with every gust of wind. Before he ordered the fake predators from Amazon, the warden fought a constant battle against goose droppings in his quest to keep the lawn clean for visitors. Now the birds stayed on the other side of the towering barbed-wire fence, where stark institutional design gave way to the forested hills of North Carolina.

"Best forty dollars I ever spent," the warden told me.

The warden walked on, and a correctional officer led me deeper into the prison. A heavy glass door thudded behind us, then another. I entered a large room filled with overturned chairs. To one

THE SCIENTIST AND THE SPY   247

side were vending machines stocked with overpriced soda and snacks. In the center of the room, a thick glass door opened onto a patio that held a cluster of picnic tables. In the distance, I glimpsed coils of razor wire.

A guard sat on a platform high above the space, inspecting her nails. I started to wonder about this uniformed woman in a prison full of men, but my thoughts were interrupted when a correctional officer escorted in Robert Mo.

He smiled weakly. The officer led us into a small room that held two tables and two plastic chairs. On one of the tables was an un- plugged monitor, the screen turned to face the wall. The carpet was strewn with litter. A window in the door enabled guards to look in.

"Should I leave it open?" the officer asked. The subtext was *Are you comfortable being alone with him, with this man who has stolen corn?*

I said that he could close it.

We sat down. I had first made eye contact with Robert at his sentencing as he walked into court. He didn't know me then, and yet he flashed me a smile. I remembered reflecting on how confi- dent he appeared, given that he was about to receive a prison sen- tence. For months afterward we corresponded on CorrLinks, the federal prison email system. Now that I finally faced him, I could see that he was a slight man, with teeth stained a yellowish brown.

He wore khaki prison garb emblazoned with 04617–104. He had answered to several names over the course of his life. First the man born Mo Tian had become Hailong, then Robert. Now he was re- duced to eight digits.

When Robert began serving his sentence in January 2017, he told me, he vowed to make the best of a difficult situation. The trial was finally behind him. So was the stress of working for Dr. Li. Prison entailed a lot of waiting—waiting in line for lunch, waiting in line for medication, waiting for the guards to complete the hourly inmate check. But the rest of the time he was unencumbered. Gone were the worries about ballooning medical and legal bills. Gone were the pressures that came with his job: sourcing swine feed at competitive rates, brokering international acquisitions and licensing agreements, breaking the law.

Butner Low is part of the Butner Federal Medical Center complex, and its inmates have either serious health conditions or lawyers powerful enough to argue persuasively that they are ill. Some call it Club Fed. The hedge fund manager Bernie Madoff was incarcerated at another prison in the complex, and for a while Matthew Kluger, a charismatic corporate lawyer convicted of insider trading, also served time at Butner Low. Robert won assignment to the institution because of his cancer. For his checkups he had access to oncologists from Wake Forest and Duke universities. As far as prisons went, it could be much worse.

Every morning he went for a jog around the yard. He played chess and ping-pong with other inmates, and he wrote poems about his incarceration in the Tang dynasty style. One poem, "Exile March of the Penal Battalion," began: "Look back upon three years of wind and rain—dense and deep."

At Butner Low there were two other Chinese inmates of around Robert's age, both of them scientists who had also once led middle-class American existences. One was Greg Chung, the Boeing researcher convicted of stealing secrets connected to the Delta IV rocket. Chung was perhaps the most famous economic espionage perpetrator in recent history, and he and Robert had become fast friends. They talked about Chinese history and poetry, leaving the stories of their cases undiscussed. As Robert saw it, they were two men of culture, brought together far from their birthplace by the Economic Espionage Act.

THERE IS A FAMOUS SCENE in Alfred Hitchcock's *North by Northwest* in which Cary Grant's character ends up in a Midwestern field, ducking between stalks of corn as a crop duster dive-bombs him from above. *North by Northwest* is about mistaken identity; the man in the field is either a government spook or a man for whom things have gone terribly wrong. As I wrapped up my research, I realized that Robert's case embodied a similar ambiguity. It was a Rorschach test for views on the Chinese technology threat. In the inkblot of the corn seed case, one person might see an imminent national security threat. Another might see an instance of corporate influence gone awry. As tensions escalated, though, it became harder for some in the U.S. government to come away with anything except the most heinous interpretation.

In December 2016, shortly after he was elected as president, Donald Trump appointed Terry Branstad as ambassador to China. The appointment smacked of political favor trading. As the governor of Iowa, a crucial primary state, Branstad had stood behind Trump throughout his presidential campaign. Still, people in both parties saw Branstad's appointment as a wise move. His decades-long friendship with Xi Jinping, they hoped, would help him advance American interests in China. A Chinese foreign ministry spokesman hailed the governor as "an old friend of the Chinese people," and at his confirmation hearing Branstad vowed to work hard to open up Chinese markets to more U.S. agricultural goods. But it wasn't long before U.S.-China policy was pulled in multiple directions.

Soon after Branstad's appointment, Trump appointed as trade adviser Peter Navarro, an economist who had authored books titled *Death by China* and *The Coming China Wars*. In March 2018, White House aide Stephen Miller pushed internally for a ban on all students from China, citing concerns about spying. According to the *Financial Times*, the plan was dropped only after Branstad faced off with Miller in the Oval Office, arguing that a ban would hurt states like Iowa, where universities needed large numbers of Chinese students paying full tuition in order to stay afloat. Trump nonetheless seemed to have internalized the message. Over dinner at his private golf club in Bedminster, New Jersey, he told a group of CEOs, in a thinly veiled reference to China, that "almost every student that comes over to this country is a spy."

Meanwhile, the White House announced plans for tariffs on $60 billion worth of Chinese goods. "When a country (USA) is losing many billions of dollars on trade with virtually every country it does business with, trade wars are good, and easy to win," Trump tweeted in March 2018. "Example, when we are down $100 billion with a certain country and they get cute, don't trade anymore—we win big. It's easy!"

Beijing fought back with its own tariffs. A headline on Xinhua's website read CHINA IS NOT AFRAID. Among the retaliatory tariffs levied by China was a 25 percent tax on soybeans and corn imported from the United States. When the measures finally took hold, it was clear that farmers in Iowa—the same people who helped to elect Trump—would be hard hit. According to a study from Iowa State University, Iowa's corn and soy industries stood to lose hundreds of millions in revenue a year. On trips home to Iowa, Ambassador Branstad tried to quell anxiety, urging farmers to take the

long view of the situation. But it was hard to stay calm when *Corn &
Soybean Digest* warned that grain prices would continue to slide as
China looked elsewhere for cheaper crops.

As the trade war halted the shipment of hundreds of millions of
bushels, grain elevators across the Midwest overflowed with corn
and soy. Elevator managers held on to the crop until the spring,
hoping that it would stay fresh long enough to be sold then. In the
meantime, lower spending from farmers rippled across the economy, leading to an estimated $1 billion to $2 billion decline in
Iowa's $190 billion gross domestic product. That meant less money
for schools, parks, and infrastructure. Even before the tariffs, farmers in the Midwest had struggled to stay afloat. The Trump administration unveiled bailout packages totaling $30 billion in aid, but
when the bailout checks were issued, some corn growers got less
than $5. Much of the money went to large agricultural companies.

Soon Branstad waded in again, this time to turn attention back
to the crime of Robert Mo. "Many Iowans remember the case in
which a Chinese agent attempted to literally steal the seed corn
from our fields," he wrote in an op-ed in *The Des Moines Register*.
It was true that industrial espionage was among the justifications
Trump gave for placing tariffs on Chinese goods, and that the tariffs had spawned the retaliatory trade actions that led to Iowans'
suffering. Ultimately, though, the trade war affected farmers much
more acutely than did the theft of a few Pioneer seed lines. Some
began to worry that as Trump obsessed over winning the trade war,
he had lost sight of the concerns that prompted the tariffs in the
first place.

There was talk of protracted conflict. As the Trump administration took on the Chinese telecommunications firm Huawei,

pressuring U.S. allies not to partner with the company on construction of 5G infrastructure, some corporate executives spotted an opportunity to use the conflict to their advantage. On Capitol Hill, tech company representatives cited Chinese controls on information to argue against regulating them. If we don't allow our tech companies to remain large and unregulated, this argument went, China will win the tech cold war. It was a race to the bottom.

No one now talked of breaking up big agriculture. Dow and DuPont had clinched their merger in 2017, becoming DowDuPont. Soon afterward, Trump picked a former Dow executive to lead research at the USDA. In June 2018, meanwhile, Bayer closed a $66 billion deal to buy Monsanto. As part of the acquisition, executives decided that the Monsanto name would finally be ditched. That was an unusual move in the acquisition of an established firm, but for all the money Monsanto had spent on lobbying, it had long ago lost the battle for the public's support. An already abysmal reputation had become worse in 2015, when the International Agency for Research on Cancer, a cancer agency affiliated with the World Health Organization, determined that Roundup was a probable carcinogen. The company was being hit with lawsuits by farmers and gardeners who alleged that exposure to the herbicide had given them cancer. A new name was probably an asset.

More significant for the war on industrial espionage, the deal also meant that the company the Justice Department had worked so hard to protect was no longer even American. "Monsanto appreciated all of the efforts that were taken by the U.S. Government to protect intellectual property," a spokeswoman for Bayer wrote me after the merger. "Innovations in the agriculture sector help provide abundant, affordable, and safe food for our growing world."

. . .

IN PRISON, ROBERT READ *Dream of the Red Chamber*, a Chinese classic. The winding twenty-eight-hundred-page epic details the Jia clan's descent from wealth. Rife with power struggles, love affairs, and infighting among servants, it is like a Chinese *Downton Abbey*. Robert told me that he loved the vividness of its images, the playful double meanings.

But one of the book's themes is loss. A song that is central to the plot contains the lines:

> Like a great building's tottering crash,
> Like flickering lampwick burned to ash,
> Your scene of happiness concludes in grief:
> For worldly bliss is always insecure and brief.

If his case was a tragedy, Robert saw himself as the hero. He spoke of the irony in industrial agriculture: Soybeans originally came from China, but then due to accidents of history and trade, the major seed companies gained control of the crop and made money selling the seeds back to China. What was the soybean but another of the Middle Kingdom's inventions for which it never collected royalties? Wasn't corn, on the other hand, a public good? He talked of the imperial envoy Zhang Qian, who in the second century B.C.E. brought corn seeds back to China from overseas. In China he was celebrated. Perhaps in the United States he would have been vilified.

I had heard from others that Robert had a flair for hyperbole, and in person he did not disappoint. The story surrounding his case was the work of an "evil mastermind," he told me. Although he had never been one to decry racism in American culture, he now saw it everywhere. "No consequence for law enforcement personnel to lie, especially for serving the purpose of evilizing Chinese," he said.

The Trump administration helped reinforce this worldview. Months after we met, State Department director of policy planning Kiron Skinner warned that China was a special foe. "This is the first time that we will have a great power competitor that is not Caucasian," she said. The Justice Department announced a project called the China Initiative, promising even more emphasis on economic espionage prosecutions. Meanwhile, a cast of right-wing Trump administration characters, including former adviser Steve Bannon, revived the Cold War group Committee on the Present Danger. In the 1970s and 1980s, committee members had railed against the Soviet Union. Now the enemy was China, and the group's approach involved mingling national security concerns with xenophobia. The committee's website warned of the Chinese Communist Party's "control, domination and exploitation of Chinese diaspora communities," a message with echoes of earlier national security alarmism. A vice chair of the committee, Frank Gaffney, had founded a think tank that argued that American Muslims are part of a "stealth jihad."

Justice in the United States was truly a *qipa*, Robert told me sarcastically, a rare and beautiful flower. *Qipa* is one of those words that has come to connote the very opposite of its literal meaning. People typically use it to describe something weird and repugnant.

In the small visitation room at Butner, I asked Robert if he had any regrets. He said that if he could do everything over again, he would not have protested in the streets in 1989. The events of the preceding years had eroded his faith in democracy. Now more than ever, he was nagged by the feeling that he should have gone to work for DBN straightaway. This way he could have avoided his years in the United States. In this alternative vision of his life, he would have been a man firmly in one country. Instead, he became a pawn in an international struggle, pulled between two places.

The correctional officer opened the door to announce that our time was up. I scribbled a few last notes and closed my notebook, then filed out of the room behind Robert. We said an awkward good-bye, and then he was led back through the yard, to the other side.

In January 2019, Robert wrote me that his sentence was almost completed and he would soon be deported. In the weeks that followed, he sent me periodic updates. First, he was shuttled onto a bus to a federal prison in Atlanta. He stayed there for a week and was then taken to an institution in Tallahassee, Florida, closer to his family but still distant from the suburban comforts that had once characterized his life in America. He complained about the food. "Baloney almost a whole week long," read one email. But he seemed resigned. He told me that he used the time to refine his poems. One titled "Snow" read:

> Lonely flowers braided from rain
> A lofty heart loathes how low the firmament stoops.
> Where once were white petals, innocent and pure,
> Now wither and fall, ground into the mud.

That March, Secretary of State Mike Pompeo appeared at the World Food Prize building, flanked by Terry Branstad, to speak to members of the Iowa Farm Bureau. He talked of agricultural breakthroughs that had arisen out of American creativity, adding that China now threatened these innovations. "A few years ago," he said, "an Iowa farm security guard saw something suspicious in a field and stopped to investigate. He caught a Chinese national digging in the dirt." A few months later, Robert's wife, Carolyn, told me that he was awaiting deportation at an immigration detention facility in Folkston, Georgia, operated by the private corporation GEO Group. Carolyn said she had no idea how long he would be there or when he would be deported. His only task was to wait.

Maybe someday Robert will write me from the safety of Beijing. Once back in China, he told me, he planned to write a book about the *qipa* that was the U.S. justice system. The first time he was shackled to another inmate and transported across state lines, he was taken through an obscure section of Miami International Airport. In the distance, he glimpsed the terminal used by businesspeople and families, the one that he had flown out of so many times on his trips to Iowa and Beijing. He wanted to share with readers the way he felt on that day—the strange sensation that he was living in an underground world. He planned to call the book *Catch That Chinese Spy*.

ACKNOWLEDGMENTS

This book is built on the kindness and patient assistance of many people. First, I owe thanks to Robert Mo, Mark Betten, Jason Griess, and Kevin Montgomery for giving their time to answer questions about minute details. In addition to telling his own story, Kevin spent many hours explaining farming and corn breeding concepts to me. I also appreciate the assistance of the friends and family members of Robert and Kevin who spoke with me or otherwise assisted with the project, including Robert's wife, Carolyn Li.

I thank Ling Woo Liu, who early in my reporting shared her family's story and suggested seeking more information about the FBI's Chinese scientist program. The FBI's response to my Freedom of Information Act request was incomplete, and I am indebted to the team of attorneys at Arnold & Porter who took on my case pro bono and helped me appeal it: Murad Hussain, Amanda Sherwood, and Stuart Turner. I am hopeful that we may still obtain more documents.

Nelson Dong, Brian Sun, the Xi family, and Peter Zeidenberg helped me understand the issues at stake with prosecutorial overreach. I also thank Aryani Ong and Steven Pei for assistance in reporting on the NIH crackdown, and Peter Toren for help in understanding the history of the Economic Espionage Act. I spoke with many other attorneys on background, and I am grateful for their assistance.

A special thanks to the experts who assisted me with the technical aspects of the manuscript: Abigail Coplin with the Chinese seed industry and Forrest Sondahl with the Navier-Stokes equations. A stroke of good luck came early on when Julian Snelder mailed me from Hong Kong a thick file of newspaper clippings that he had collected over the years. I also appreciate his comments on an early draft. Peter Mattis's writing on economic espionage and Zuoyue Wang's scholarship on transnational science in the Cold War era were indispensable. Zuoyue kindly provided me with primary source material on Tsien Hsue-Shen and carefully reviewed a draft of the manuscript. Any lingering errors are mine.

Over the course of my reporting I spoke with many people whom I did not quote by name. These include a host of experts and businesspeople with invaluable China expertise: Greg Austin, Benjamin Bai, Huang Dafang, Cameron Johnson, Lu Chuanying, Jim MacGregor, Bill McCahill, Maxime Oliva, Caroline Pan, Carly Ramsey, Derek Scissors, and Shirley Zhao. I am grateful as well for the assistance of Ian Driscoll at the American Chamber of Commerce in Shanghai.

I thank New America for supporting me financially for two years of this project. Awista Ayub, Peter Bergen, Albert Ford, Clarke Reeves, and Ian Wallace: thank you. The other writers and scholars in the National Fellows program provided early guidance and astute commentary. Emily Hunt taught me how to obtain court documents in PACER, and Chris Leonard shared his expertise on agribusiness. The food and agriculture reporter Leah Douglas and others at the Open Markets Institute shaped my thinking on food and power. I'm also grateful to Konstantin Kakaes, at New America and later *Technology Review*, and to Martin Enserink, David Malakoff, and Richard Stone, my editors at *Science*, for carefully editing some of the material that ended up in this book.

Many friends, relatives, and experts reviewed chapters of the manuscript at various stages: Jason Albert, Mary Bergstrom, Frank Bures, Rebecca Catching, Mengfei Chen, Yangyang Cheng, V. V. Ganeshananthan, Candice Gillmore, Jason Good, Laurel Kilgour, Celina Li, Jessica Nordell, Megan Shank, Emily Sohn, William Souder, and Kim Todd. I am also grateful to Darwin Tsen and Lexi Yeh for help with early research, and to the writer and translator Jeannette Ng, who provided a lyrical translation of Robert Mo's prison poems on short notice.

I thank my agent, Gillian MacKenzie, for believing in this project long before people in Washington were warning of a "new cold war." My editor at Riverhead, Jake Morrissey, was indefatigably patient as the book evolved into something very different from what I initially proposed. I appreciate his flexibility and vision. I feel lucky to have worked with a stellar team at Riverhead: Molly Fessenden, Bruce Giffords, Kevin Murphy, and Shailyn Tavella.

My mother, Laura Danielson, has edited my work since the beginning. She has been a tireless advocate for this project, and her experiences as an immigration attorney helped shape my understanding of Robert Mo's case. Finally, I thank Aksel Çoruh and our two children, one of whom was born shortly after I conceived the idea for this book. I reported the project in snatches, sometimes with family members in tow, and Aksel never questioned why we were spending part of our summer vacation in an Iowa cornfield in ninety-degree heat. For the last year that I was working on it, our daughter regularly asked me, "Did you finish your book yet?" As a result of having Aksel at my side as my life partner, I can finally tell her yes.

A NOTE ON SOURCES AND NAMES

The following includes potential spoilers.

This book is based on interviews with participants and witnesses, firsthand reporting, and extensive court and government documents. These include police reports, FBI files, property records, business filings, and more than 800 court documents—692 of them from the case *United States v. Mo Hailong*.

I interviewed more than 150 people in the course of reporting this book. These include Justice Department officials, FBI agents, former CIA analysts, historians, scholars of innovation, seed breeders, activists, community organizers, cybersecurity experts, intellectual property attorneys, businesspeople, scientists, and farmers in both the United States and China. My interviews with Robert Mo were largely done by email, using the federal prison correspondence system Corr-Links, over a sixteen-month period beginning in 2017. I met with Robert in person on May 17, 2018, at Butner Low Federal Correctional Institution in Butner, North Carolina. I also reached out to friends, family, and former colleagues of both Robert and Kevin Montgomery. Including all of their names in the text would have bogged down the story. They nonetheless provided useful background information that enriched the narrative.

If a source is quoted directly, the remark comes from an interview I conducted, court documents, or publicly available news reports. When I did not personally interview the person, the source is provided in the notes. The government's translation of intercepted Chinese dialogue in the Robert Mo case was often stilted, and I aimed to avoid halting or inexpert translations wherever possible. Dialogue in italics is adapted from incomplete or awkward phrasing, with minor changes to punctuation or syntax.

In chapters told primarily from one subject's perspective, I largely remained faithful to that person's version of events. Whenever possible, I checked those accounts against documents and other external records or against the accounts of other sources. Kevin Montgomery, for example, provided me with copies of emails he exchanged with Robert Mo as well as an account he wrote of his initial FBI interview shortly after it occurred. The timing of events he related also lined up with other dates in the case. While there are inconsistencies in Robert Mo's larger story, his account of his arrest and of his experiences while in prison is broadly consistent with other defendants' accounts of similar situations. In places where two or more subjects disagree over what transpired, I have indicated the discrepancy either in the text or in the notes.

When the narrative follows subjects' thoughts, they were either related to me directly or conveyed in court hearings, transcripts, or documents. Despite being settled before it could go to trial, *United States v. Mo Hailong* involved lengthy pretrial hearings in which subjects took the witness stand to answer questions about their motivation and intentions. The court record also includes whole conversations and instant message chats that were intercepted by U.S. intelligence. I included several of these in the book.

For historical flashbacks, I relied on primary source documents and chronicles of specific periods, a selection of which are listed in the bibliography. In recounting FBI investigations of Chinese-American scientists from the 1950s through the 1970s, I was greatly aided by the work of historian Zuoyue Wang and the late writer Iris Chang. I also benefited from time spent perusing the archives of the Committee on Scholarly Communication with the People's Republic of China, housed at George Washington University.

Only two names were changed in the book: those of Lily Cheng and Michael Yao. While the FBI had suspicions about both individuals, neither was ultimately charged with a crime. Readers may notice some variation in the style used throughout the book for Chinese names. In China, a person's surname usually appears first, but overseas Chinese or people who take on English names sometimes list their surname last. Typically, two-syllable given names are written as one word, without a hyphen, but outside of mainland China, some individuals choose to add a hyphen or render each syllable as a separate word. Often courts and journalists mix up defendants' given names and surnames, adding to the confusion. In most cases, I have adhered to individuals' personal preferences. When those were not possible to ascertain, I used the names that appeared in court documents.

Robert Mo signed his messages to me "Hailong," but in his interactions with many contacts in the United States, including Kevin, he went by "Robert," so I have used that name throughout. Tsien Hsue-Shen spelled his name several different ways throughout his lifetime. I stuck with the version that he used in an application declaring his intent to file for U.S. citizenship, filed in 1949.

In notes referencing court cases, I have provided the document number from the case docket and the date of filing, not the date of the hearing. The principal case cited in this book is *United States v. Mo Hailong*, 4:13-cr-00147-RP-CFB (S.D. Iowa 2013–2016).

Additional cases cited include:

Bowman v. Monsanto Co., 569 U.S. 278 (2013)

Monsanto v. E.I. du Pont de Nemours & Co., 13-1349 (Fed. Cir., 2014)

Pioneer Hi-Bred v. Holden Foundation Seeds, 35 F.3d 1226
    (8th Cir., 1994)

United States v. Guoqing Cao and Shuyu Li, 1:14-mc-00071-WTL-
    TAB (S.D. Ind., 2013–2014)

United States v. Sherry Chen, 14-cr-00149 (S.D. Ohio, 2014)

United States v. Dongfan "Greg" Chung, 08-cr-00024 (C.D. Cal.,
    2008–2010)

United States v. Dongfan "Greg" Chung, 10-50074 (9th Cir., 2011)

United States v. Ji Li Huang, 4:12-cr-00296 (W.D. Mo., 2012–2013)

United States v. Kexue Huang, 3:15-cr-00234 (S.D. Ind., 2010–2011)

United States v. Liew et al., 4:11-cr-00573-JSW (N.D. Cal., 2011–
    2015)

United States v. Walter Liew, 14-10367 (9th Cir., 2017)

United States v. Hong Meng, 10-cr-00056 (D. Del., 2009–2010)

United States v. Gary Min aka Yonggang Min, 06-cr-00121 (D. Del.,
    2006–2007)

United States v. Michael David Mitchell, 09-cr-00425 (E.D. Va.,
    2009–2010)

United States v. Xiaoxing Xi, 15-cr-00204 (E.D. Pa., 2015)

Xiaoxing Xi v. FBI Special Agent Andrew Haugen and John Doe(s),
    2:17-cv-02132-RBS (E.D. Pa., 2017–present)

Readers looking for more information on specific industrial espionage
cases can find a detailed, searchable database at https://jeremy-wu.info
/fed-cases/. The database allows users to sort cases by date, company,
and status.

NOTES

CHAPTER ONE

1 AVOID ALL NEGATIVE TALK: A Dino's Storage employee told me that the company regularly updates the message, usually with quotes from the Book of Proverbs. When I visited Bondurant in July 2017, the marquee read RUN FROM EVIL THOUGHTS. At another moment, Google Street View showed it reading DO NOT SPEAK IMPULSIVELY.

1 toward the corn: Details about Cass Bollman's role are sourced from an interview with him in Bondurant, Iowa, on July 17, 2017. I also relied on testimony given by Bollman in court at *U.S. v. Mo Hailong*, Document 372 (May 19, 2015), and on the incident report that Bollman filed about the encounter. (Cass Bollman, "Field Interrogation Report," Polk County Sheriff's Office, September 6, 2011.)

1 *South of here walking*: Dale Petersen, "Calls for Service Report," Polk County Sheriff's Office, September 6, 2011.

2 doing his morning rounds: This account, and what follows, is based on interviews with Bollman and with the Monsanto contract farmer, who did not wish to be named because of concern for his family's privacy. The field in question is technically called a grower plot, meaning that it produced hybrids for production.

3 spliced with genes: Interview with the Monsanto contract farmer.

3 the Monsanto plot was unmarked: *U.S. v. Mo Hailong*, Documents 1 (December 11, 2013) and 6 (December 17, 2013).

3 detassel the female rows: Interview with the Monsanto contract farmer.

4 Bondurant, population 3,860: "Population & Housing Occupancy Status 2010: Bondurant, Iowa," United States Census Bureau American FactFinder, https://factfinder.census.gov/faces/tableservices/jsf/pages/productview.xhtml ?pid=DEC_10_PL_GCTPL2.ST13&prodType=table. Racial breakdown is drawn from "Race and Hispanic or Latino Origin in Iowa's Incorporated

Places: 2010," State Data Center of Iowa, http://www.iowadatacenter.org/archive /2011/02/cityrace.pdf.

4 **by a gray SUV:** Bollman, "Field Interrogation Report."

5 **90 percent of the starch:** "Corn Overview," Georgia Corn Growers Association, http://georgiacorngrowers.org/corn-overview/.

5 **percentage of a McDonald's:** Michael Pollan, *The Omnivore's Dilemma* (New York: Penguin, 2007), 117.

5 **grown in a corn by-product:** M. El-Marsafy et al., "Evaluation of Various Brands of Corn Steep Liquor for Penicillin Production," *Starch—Starke* 27, no. 3 (January 1975): 91–93.

5 **cosmetics contain corn:** F. A. Andersen et al., "Final Report of the Safety Assessment of Cosmetic Ingredients Derived from Zea Mays (Corn)," *International Journal of Toxicology* 30, no. 3 supplement (May 2011), https://journals.sagepub .com/doi/abs/10.1177/1091581811403832.

5 **ninety-three million acres:** "Charts and Maps, Field Crops: Corn," U.S. Department of Agriculture National Agricultural Statistics Service (USDA NASS), https://www.nass.usda.gov/Publications/Todays_Reports/reports/pspl0319.pdf.

5 **produces more corn:** "Charts and Maps, Field Crops: Corn: Acreage & Change from Previous Year by State," U.S. Department of Agriculture National Agricultural Statistics Service (USDA NASS), https://www.nass.usda .gov/Charts_and_Maps/Field_Crops/index.php.

5 **millions of dollars in grants:** "Monsanto Soybean Breeding Chair," Iowa State University Department of Agronomy, https://www.agron.iastate.edu /tags/monsanto. Also see "Monsanto," Iowa State University Foundation, https:// www.foundation.iastate.edu/s/1463/giving/interior.aspx?pgid=1027&gid =1&cid=3248.

6 **Type of Suspicious Activity:** Bollman, "Field Interrogation Report."

CHAPTER TWO

7 *Did we do anything wrong?:* Interview with Robert Mo.

7 **spotted him and Wang Lei:** A description of this encounter appears in *U.S. v. Mo Hailong*, Documents 1 (December 11, 2013) and 6 (December 17, 2013). Robert maintains that he was driving.

8 **more than $100,000:** The judge who heard Robert's case noted that at DBN, he "made easily three and almost four times" his previous salary of $40,000. *U.S. v. Mo Hailong*, Document 661 (November 1, 2016).

8 **the company's legitimate business:** Interview with Robert Mo. Investigators also acknowledge that much of his work for DBN was legal.

8 **Robert had complained:** *U.S. v. Mo Hailong*, Document 558 (December 22, 2015).

8 **waged bloody battles:** Jim Yardley, "For Visitors, Graveyard Holds Memories of a Bloody Era," *New York Times*, April 10, 2006, https://www.nytimes.com /2006/04/10/world/asia/for-visitors-graveyard-holds-memories-of-a-bloody -era.html. Other general background on Daichi during the Cultural Revolu-

tion is drawn from *Guangyuan wenshi zike,* ed. Cai Yuanzao (Guangyuan, Sichuan: Guangyuan City Government, n.d.).

9 **a world of jagged walls:** Details about mines from the era are drawn from Ren Zongjing, "Behind the Clouds," in *Exiled Pilgrim: Memoirs of Pre–Cultural Revolution Zhiqing,* ed. Peng Deng (Leiden: Brill, 2015).

9 **His mother, He Fangxun:** Interview with Robert Mo.

9 **raised chickens and rabbits:** Interview with Robert Mo.

11 **march to the mayor's office:** Ibid. I was not able to independently confirm Robert's participation in the protest, but his lawyers gave the claim enough credence that they mentioned it in court. *U.S. v. Mo Hailong,* Document 661.

11 **took refuge in the U.S. embassy:** Jim Mann, "Chinese Dissident Fang and Wife Fly to Britain," *Los Angeles Times,* June 26, 1990, https://www.latimes.com/archives/la-xpm-1990-06-26-mn-722-story.html. Fang eventually took a post at the University of Arizona in Tucson.

11 **started his first PhD:** Interview with Robert Mo; confirmed by sources close to the case.

11 **married in 1998:** The date of Carolyn's marriage to Robert, and information on her life before leaving China, appear in *U.S. v. Mo Hailong,* Document 12 (December 27, 2013).

12 **the organization that kept tabs:** Anne-Marie Brady, "Magic Weapons: China's Political Influence Activities Under Xi Jinping," conference paper presented in Arlington, Virginia, September 16–17, 2017.

12 **took an untenured research position:** A sampling of papers that Robert Mo published while affiliated with Florida International University can be found at https://www.researchgate.net/scientific-contributions/2057010675_H_L_Mo.

12 **around $40,000 a year:** *U.S. v. Mo Hailong,* Document 661.

12 **a visit from the police:** "Offense Incident Report," Miami-Dade Police Department, October 21, 2004. Also see *U.S. v. Mo Hailong,* Document 12.

12 **lined up the position:** Interviews with Robert Mo and other sources.

12 **Forbes China rich list:** "China's 400 Richest," *Forbes* (2011), https://www.forbes.com/lists/2011/74/china-billionaires-11_rank.html.

13 **enough for a down payment:** "Mortgage deed: Hailong Mo and Ping Li," prepared by Ariel Melendez, Sky Investments, November 24, 2009.

13 **PhD in veterinary science:** Information on Mo Yun's background appears at *U.S. v. Mo Hailong and Mo Yun,* Document 90 (July 21, 2014).

14 **three thousand dollars in capital:** Xiaoying Dong et al., *Zhongguancun Model: Driving the Dual Engines and Science and Technology and Capital* (Singapore: Springer, 2018), 218. Shao reportedly founded DBN with twenty thousand RMB. The company was officially incorporated in 1994.

14 **"modernize" people's diets:** Mindi Schneider, "Developing the Meat Grab," *Journal of Peasant Studies* 41, no. 4 (2014): 613–33, doi: http://dx.doi.org/10.1080/03066150.2014.918959.

14 **created a subsidiary:** "Beijing Kings Nower Seed Science & Technology," LinkedIn, https://www.linkedin.com/company/beijing-kings-nower-seed-science-&-technology-co-ltd.

14 by one count 8,700: "China Seeks to Develop Global Seed Power," *Wall Street Journal*, May 23, 2015, https://www.wsj.com/articles/china-seeks-to-develop -global-seed-power-1427049765.

15 swipe top-notch seeds: This shortcut is explained in various court documents, but particularly in *U.S. v. Mo Hailong*, Documents 559–2 through 559–5 (December 22, 2015).

15 he needed to be careful: *U.S. v. Mo Hailong*, Document 558 (December 22, 2015).

15 one hundred seed lines: *U.S. v. Mo Hailong*, Document 290–1 (April 27, 2015).

15 five thousand samples: Ibid.

15 lived in fear: In our interviews, Robert Mo maintained that he feared that the seeds would be intercepted by Chinese customs, because it is illegal to import seed into China without a permit. But his actions suggest that he also feared the haul might be intercepted by U.S. customs.

16 two thousand seeds: *U.S. v. Mo Hailong*, Document 559–3 (December 22, 2015). Robert asked Dr. Li in an online chat, "The seed quantity is still inadequate? There were more than 2000 pieces for each variety. Too heavy—I lived in fear for more than a week."

16 escorted back to China: Ibid.

16 followed by the Chinese press: See, for example, "*She jiandie an: Zhong Dongfan chong qiu jin 16 nian*," Sina.com, February 2, 2010, http://dailynews.sina .com/bg/news/int/singtao/20100209/04121185039.html.

16 fifteen years in federal prison: "Former Boeing Engineer Sentenced to Nearly 16 Years in Prison for Stealing Aerospace Secrets for China," Department of Justice, February 8, 2010, https://archives.fbi.gov/archives/losangeles /press-releases/2010/la020810.htm. Chung was seventy-three at the time of his conviction but seventy-four by his sentencing.

16 save money on flights: *U.S. v. Mo Hailong*, Document 558.

17 *Let Dr. Li come:* Ibid. In a chat with a co-worker, Robert described the DO NOT ENTER signs and the gun violence in America.

CHAPTER THREE

18 "an unusual and brazen scheme": John Eligon and Patrick Zuo, "Designer Seed Thought to Be Latest Target by Chinese," *New York Times*, February 4, 2014, https://www.nytimes.com/2014/02/05/us/chinese-implicated-in-agricultural -espionage-efforts.html?_r=0.

20 Stealing the color white: Del Quentin Wilber, "How a Corporate Spy Swiped Plans for DuPont's Billion-Dollar Color Formula," *Bloomberg Businessweek*, February 4, 2016, https://www.bloomberg.com/features/2016-stealing-dupont -white/.

20 allocated funding for spaceflight: Micah Springut, Stephen Schlaikjer, and David Chen, "China's Program for Science and Technology Modernization: Implications for American Competitiveness," report prepared for the U.S.- China Economic and Security Review Commission, January 2011, 28.

21 **Between 1991 and 2016:** "Is China a Global Leader in Research and Development?," CSIS ChinaPower, https://chinapower.csis.org/china-research-and-development-rnd/.

21 **number two in the world:** Geoff Dyer, "China Overtakes Japan on R&D," *Financial Times*, December 3, 2006, https://www.ft.com/content/da4ed9f2-82fa-11db-a38a-0000779e2340. The Organization for Economic Cooperation and Development estimates that China will outspend the United States in R&D by 2020.

21 **China ranks first in the world:** "Overview of the State of the U.S. S&E Enterprise in a Global Context," National Science Foundation, https://www.nsf.gov/statistics/2018/nsb20181/report/sections/overview/research-publications.

21 **second in international patent filings:** WIPO IP Statistics Data Center, World Intellectual Property Organization, https://www3.wipo.int/ipstats/index.htm?tab=patent (total patent applications by applicant's origin).

22 **eighty-four new pulsars:** "China's FAST Telescope Identifies 84 Pulsars," *China Daily*, July 3, 2019, http://www.chinadaily.com.cn/a/201907/03/WS5d1c5d19a3105895c2e7b754.html. Also see Mara Hvistendahl, "Radio Astronomers Go for High Gain with Mammoth Telescope," *Science*, June 19, 2009, https://science.sciencemag.org/content/324/5934/1508.full?rss=1.

22 **named it after me:** Jun Wang et al., "*Aphlebia hvistendahliae* sp. nov. from the Early Permian Wuda Tuff Flora, Inner Mongolia," *Review of Paleobotany and Palynology* 210 (November 2014), https://www.sciencedirect.com/science/article/pii/S0034666714001110.

22 **pocketed 30 percent:** "Research and Embezzlement," *Economist*, March 20, 2014, https://www.economist.com/analects/2014/03/20/research-and-embezzlement.

23 **"blueprint for technology theft":** James McGregor, "China's Drive for 'Indigenous Innovation': A Web of Industrial Policies," U.S. Chamber of Commerce, July 27, 2010, https://www.uschamber.com/report/china%E2%80%99s-drive-indigenous-innovation-web-industrial-policies.

23 **United Front Work Department:** Peter Mattis, "China's Digital Authoritarianism: Surveillance, Influence and Political Control," testimony before the House Permanent Select Committee on Intelligence, May 16, 2019. Other goals include stamping out dissident movements and maintaining political control. Anne-Marie Brady, "Magic Weapons: China's Political Influence Activities Under Xi Jinping," conference paper presented in Arlington, Virginia, September 16–17, 2017.

25 **filled with counterfeits:** "*Daoban, shanzhai manyan shichang 'taopai' lihai shanghai zhong ye chuangxin li*," QQ.com, December 16, 2010, https://finance.qq.com/a/20101216/004986.htm.

25 **putrid, black ears:** Meng Xingshi, "*30 duo wei nonghu huaiyi maidao jia xianyu 335: guanfang zhuoshou diaocha*," Shijiazhuang News Agency, September 12, 2014, http://www.chinaseed114.com/news/14/news_66415.html.

25 **GM sued in Chinese court:** Gong Zhengzheng, "GM Charges Chery for Alleged Mini Car Piracy," *China Daily*, December 18, 2004, http://www.chinadaily.com.cn/english/doc/2004-12/18/content_401235.htm.

25 **"difficulty in pursuing it":** In 2012, former GM engineer Du Shanshan and her husband, Qin Yu, were convicted of conspiring to steal trade secrets from her employer and pass them to Chery. In that case, however, the trade secrets in question concerned hybrid vehicles.

26 **KFC has nearly:** Daniel Shane, "Robot Waiters and Snail Pizza: What US Fast Food Brands Do to Please Chinese Diners," CNN, March 5, 2019, https://www.cnn.com/2019/03/05/business/kfc-fastfood-pizza-hut-china/index.html.

26 **Starbucks has more than:** "Starbucks Has an Eye-Popping New China Plan," *Fortune,* May 16, 2018, https://fortune.com/2018/05/16/starbucks-china-plan-store-15-hours/.

26 **claimed 12 percent:** Lynn Hicks, "Feeding China: Monsanto Not a Big Player in Corn—Yet," *Des Moines Register,* October 13, 2014, https://www.desmoines register.com/story/money/agriculture/2014/10/13/feeding-china-monsanto/17204813/.

26 **more cars in China:** While a slowing Chinese economy has affected sales, the country remains a critical market for auto manufacturers. "General Motors China Goes into Reverse as Market Stalls," Reuters, October 8, 2018, https://www.reuters.com/article/us-gm-china-sales/general-motors-china-sales-go-into-reverse-as-market-stalls-idUSKCN1MI1N3.

CHAPTER FOUR

28 **four federal trade secrets theft cases:** *U.S. v. Gary Min/aka Yonggang Min* (District of Delaware), *U.S. v. Hong Meng* (District of Delaware), *U.S. v. Michael David Mitchell* (Eastern District of Virginia), and *U.S. v. Walter Lian-Heen Liew* (Northern District of California).

31 **remembers the East India Company:** Such events nonetheless provoked outrage at the time. In the nineteenth century, the Germans dubbed Switzerland *der Räuber-Staat*—the nation of pirates—for neglecting to enforce patents. For more on these cases, see Sarah Rose, *For All the Tea in China: How England Stole the World's Favorite Drink and Changed History* (New York: Penguin, 2010) and Doren Ben-Atar, *Trade Secrets: Intellectual Piracy and the Origins of American Industrial Power* (New Haven, Conn.: Yale University Press, 2004). The Jesuit priest is François Xavier d'Entrecolles.

32 **No international treaty . . . just one federal statute did:** Hedieh Nasheri, *Economic Espionage and Industrial Spying* (Cambridge: Cambridge University Press, 2005), 131.

32 **particularly concerned about France:** News had recently broken that Air France had spied on passengers with hidden microphones installed throughout its first-class cabins. Concern mounted further when the French consul general in Houston was caught rooting through the trash outside a wealthy U.S. executive's home. William M. Carley, "Corporate Targets: As Cold War Fades, Some Nations' Spies Seek Industrial Secrets," *Wall Street Journal,* June 17, 1991, A1. Also see Peter Schweizer, "The Future of Spying Is Business: In the New World of High-Tech Trade Rivalry, There Are No Allies," *Baltimore Sun,* March 31, 1996, https://www.baltimoresun.com/news/bs-xpm-1996-03-31-1996091058-story.tml.

32 COLD WAR'S END: Paul Richter, "Cold War's End Brings Enemy Gap," *Los Angeles Times*, September 30, 1991, https://www.latimes.com/archives/la-xpm-1991 -09-30-mn-2212-story.html.

32 COSTLY, INEPT, ANACHRONISTIC: Roger Morris, "C.I.A.—Costly, Inept, Anachronistic," *New York Times*, June 10, 1990, http://www.nytimes.com/1990/06/10 /opinion/cia-costly-inept-anachronistic.html?pagewanted=all.

33 "New world out there": Tim Weiner, *Legacy of Ashes: The History of the CIA* (New York: Anchor Books, 2008), 500.

33 "new program of counterintelligence": George Lardner, Jr., "CIA Seeks to Define New Role; Economic Espionage Sparks Wide Debate," *Washington Post*, November 13, 1990, A1.

33 "The law gives the FBI": Robert Dreyfuss, "The New Espionage Scare: Spy vs. No-Spy," *New Republic*, December 23, 1996, 9–10.

33 the law's biggest backers: Sometimes there was overlap with the intelligence community. One particularly vocal enthusiast was Stansfield Turner, a former CIA director who in the early 1990s sat on the board of Monsanto.

33 spying on other countries' firms: Stansfield Turner, "Intelligence for a New World Order," *Foreign Affairs* 70, no. 4 (Fall 1991): 150–66. Also see John Hillkirk, "U.S. Move into Corporate Spying Gains Support," *USA Today*, June 20, 1990, 1B. Other supporters of this approach included CIA director Gates and Senator David Boren.

34 "the United States stole books": James A. Lewis, "China's Economic Espionage: Why It Worked in the Past but It Won't in the Future," *Foreign Affairs*, November 13, 2012, https://www.foreignaffairs.com/articles/china/2012-11-13 /chinas-economic-espionage. Lewis is now senior vice president of CSIS.

34 dedicated Economic Espionage Unit: Interview with FBI special agent Mark Betten and supervisory special agent John Hartnett, acting head of the FBI's Economic Espionage Unit, June 2017.

35 sentenced to seven years: "Chinese National Sentenced to 87 Months in Prison for Economic Espionage and Theft of Trade Secrets," Department of Justice Office of Public Affairs, December 21, 2011, https://www.justice.gov /opa/pr/chinese-national-sentenced-87-months-prison-economic-espionage -and-theft-trade-secrets.

35 emissaries of the Chinese government: The Economic Espionage Act divided crimes into two types: those that involved foreign government backing and those that did not. Defendants found guilty of stealing secrets with no clear government connection faced up to ten years in prison and a $250,000 fine. When a foreign government was involved, that rose to fifteen years and a $500,000 fine. A 2013 amendment to the Economic Espionage Act raised the maximum fine for individuals found guilty of spying on behalf of a foreign power to $5 million.

CHAPTER FIVE

40 "irritating or ineffective": This quote is from Ronald William Clark, *The Life of Bertrand Russell* (London: Bloomsbury, 2012), 279.

40 any other area of food production: Diana Moss, "Competition, Intellectual Property Rights, and Transgenic Seed," *South Dakota Law Review* 58, no. 3 (Fall 2013): 548.

40 spent on research and development: Research intensity increased from the 1990s to early 2000s, in the early years of genetically modified crops, but it has since dropped back to mid-1990s levels. Keith O. Fuglie et al., "Research Investments and Market Structure in the Food Processing, Agricultural Input, and Biofuel Industries Worldwide," USDA Economic Research Service (December 2011), 16. Also see Moss, "Competition, Intellectual Property Rights, and Transgenic Seed," 549–52.

41 "most troubling phases": Diana L. Moss and C. Robert Taylor, "Short Ends of the Stick," *Wisconsin Law Review* 337 (2014): 339.

41 to make up the difference: The high prices were passed on to consumers. Moss, "Competition, Intellectual Property Rights, and Transgenic Seed," 552.

CHAPTER SIX

45 Aztecs believed that the world: Arturo Warman, *Corn and Capitalism: How a Botanical Bastard Grew to Global Dominance*, trans. Nancy L. Westrate (Chapel Hill: University of North Carolina Press, 2003), 35.

45 "affixed by nature": Betty Harper Fussell, *The Story of Corn* (New York: Alfred A. Knopf, 1992), 17.

46 as rapidly as syphilis: C. Wayne Smith, Javier Bertrán, and E. C. A. Runge, eds. *Corn: Origin, History, Technology, and Production* (New York: Wiley, 2004), 152.

46 in a Des Moines basement: John C. Culver and John Hyde, *American Dreamer: A Life of Henry A. Wallace* (New York: W. W. Norton, 2001), 8.

47 "self-building food-factory": Fussell, *The Story of Corn*, 68.

47 "corn in the hands": Ibid., 67.

47 remainder for $7.7 billion: Steven Lipin, Scott Kilman, and Susan Warren, "DuPont Agrees to Purchase of Seed Firm for $7.7 Billion," *Wall Street Journal*, March 15, 1999, http://www.wsj.com/articles/SB921268716949898331.

48 a bubble diagram: This diagram originally appeared in Philip H. Howard, "Visualizing Consolidation in the Global Seed Industry: 1996–2008," *Sustainability* 1 (2009): 1266–87. An updated version reflecting recent mergers and acquisitions is available at https://philhoward.net/2018/12/31/global-seed-industry-changes-since-2013/.

48 nearly 90 percent: Jorge Fernandez-Cornejo et al., "Genetically Engineered Crops in the United States," U.S. Department of Agriculture (February 2014), 8, https://www.ers.usda.gov/webdocs/publications/45179/43668_err162.pdf.

48 controlled 80 percent: Gene Kronberg, "Overview of the Seed Industry," *AgriMarketing* 50, no. 8 (October 2012): 35–36.

48 Microsoft's licensing Windows: Testimony of Diana Moss, "Public Workshops Exploring Competition in Agriculture: Des Moines Area Community College," U.S. Department of Justice/U.S. Department of Agriculture, March 12, 2010, 158.

48 80 percent of all corn: Chris Leonard, "Monsanto Seed Business Role Revealed," December 13, 2009, http://archive.boston.com/business/articles/2009/12/13/ap_impact_monsanto_seed_business_role_revealed/?page=full.

49 "consumers are harmed": "Vigorous Antitrust Enforcement in This Challenging Era," speech by Christine A. Varney, May 12, 2009, https://www.justice.gov/atr/speech/vigorous-antitrust-enforcement-challenging-era.

49 "We must change course": Ibid.

49 "Monsanto investigation might have": Peter Whoriskey, "Monsanto's Dominance Draws Antitrust Inquiry," *Washington Post*, November 29, 2009, http://www.washingtonpost.com/wp-dyn/content/article/2009/11/28/AR2009112802471.html.

49 "When I started farming": Testimony of Fred Bower, "Public Workshops," 132.

49 "needed to feed the world": Testimony of Harvey Howington, "Public Workshops," 308.

CHAPTER SEVEN

52 clueless once they set foot: *U.S. v. Mo Hailong*, Document 559–1 (December 22, 2015).

53 Pekin High School's teams: Richard B. Stolley, "Pekin Choose," *Sports Illustrated*, November 23, 2015, https://www.si.com/vault/issue/1015972/15.

53 "If God wants you": Interview with Robert Mo. I was not able to confirm this with Wang Lei.

54 first came to China in 1896: "New 'Sherlock Holmes' Translation Gets a Classical Chinese Twist," *Global Times*, November 11, 2012.

54 Holmes fought the evils: Paul French, "Sherlock Holmes and the Curious Case of Several Million Chinese Fans," *Los Angeles Review of Books*, January 9, 2014, https://blog.lareviewofbooks.org/chinablog/sherlock-holmes-curious-case-several-million-chinese-fans/.

54 set aside funding: Cong Cao, *GMO China: How Global Debates Transformed China's Agricultural Biotechnology Policies* (New York: Columbia University Press, 2018), 44–46.

55 seeds were biological weapons: Ibid., 185.

55 a genetically modified product: Ibid., 152.

55 allowed it to fester uncensored: Ibid., 126–27.

55 included stealing seed: Chuin-Wei Yap with Li Jie, "Spat over 'Stolen' GMO Seeds Touches Nerves in China," *Wall Street Journal*, May 6, 2014, https://blogs.wsj.com/chinarealtime/2014/05/06/spat-over-stolen-gmo-seeds-touches-nerves-in-china/.

55 considered a state secret: Fred Gale, "China's Agricultural Policies: Trade, Investment, Safety, and Innovation," testimony before the U.S.-China Economic and Security Review Commission (April 26, 2018).

55 same number of acres: *U.S. v. Mo Hailong*, Document 501–2 (November 20, 2015).

56 **cut off China's supply:** The trade war started in 2018 effectively did cut off China's supply of American grain—a topic that is covered in chapter 39.

56 **critical to raising farmers' incomes:** Peter Wood, "Food Security and Chinese 'Comprehensive National Security,'" Jamestown China Brief, March 2, 2017, https://jamestown.org/program/food-security-chinese-comprehensive -national-security/.

56 **China's $16 billion:** "China Updates Seed Law to Encourage Innovation," Reuters, November 5, 2015, https://www.reuters.com/article/china-seeds/update -1-china-updates-seed-law-to-encourage-innovation-idUSL3N1301Y620151105 ?feedType=RSS&feedName=basicMaterialsSector.

56 **encouraging mergers and acquisitions:** Zhou Siyu, "Sowing the Seeds of Doubt," *China Daily*, August 3, 2011, http://www.chinadaily.com.cn/bizchina /2011-08/03/content_13040950_2.htm.

57 **dragon head enterprises:** Mindi Schneider, "Dragon Head Enterprises and the State of Agribusiness in China," *Journal of Agrarian Change* 17, no. 1 (March 2016): 3–21. Also see Thomas A. Hemphill and George O. White II, "China's National Champions: The Evolution of a National Industrial Policy—or a New Era of Economic Protectionism?," *Thunderbird International Business Review* 55, no. 22 (March/April 2013).

57 **need for a "national hero":** *U.S. v. Mo Hailong*, Documents 559–4 and 559–5 (December 22, 2015).

57 **use the foreigners' technology:** *U.S. v. Mo Hailong*, Document 559–4.

CHAPTER EIGHT

60 **tilted stone sundial:** A photo of this instrument can be found at William A. Joseph, "Sundial at the Forbidden City," https://library.ucsd.edu/dc/object /bb57372037.

63 *Pianzi Jie*, **or Crook Street:** Cong Cao, "Zhongguancun and China's High-Tech Parks in Transition," in *Key Papers on Chinese Economic History Since 1949*, ed. Michael Dillon (Leiden: Brill, 2016), 984. Also see Qi Zhong, "*Zhongguancun zhuanji zuoji de boke*," http://blog.sina.com.cn/s/blog_4b78794d0100hit3.html.

64 **killed insects found only:** Interview with Kevin Montgomery. This is Kevin's interpretation of DBN's work.

CHAPTER NINE

70 **"contributed my best knowledge":** Harry Sheng to Rep. Milton Robert Carr, September 20, 1975.

72 **member of the party:** Correspondence with Zuoyue Wang (a historian focused on transnational science in the mid- to late-twentieth century); also see interview with Li Yuchang in Weimin Xiong, *Duiyu lishi, kexuejia youhuashuo: 20 shiji zhongguo kexuejie de ren yu shi* (Beijing: Dongfang Press, 2017), 225–48.

72 **FBI file as "yellow":** "File No. 65-3265," FBI, June 6, 1949. (Obtained under the Freedom of Information Act from the FBI; requested as "copies of all documents related to the individual Hsue-Shen Tsien [Qian Xuesen]," September 2016; received December 2016.)

72 putting pressure on their relatives: Iris Chang, *Thread of the Silkworm* (New York: Perseus, 1995), 152.

72 SECRET and CONFIDENTIAL: Ibid., 156.

72 contained critical secrets: Ibid., 160–61.

73 near-constant FBI surveillance: Ibid., 173.

73 allowed him to leave: Ibid., 188–90, 199.

73 greeted him as a hero: Ibid., 199.

73 testing a nuclear-tipped missile: Tsien also spawned interest in China in systems engineering, an interdisciplinary field focused on controlling physical and societal systems. The field helped shape the one-child policy, the construction of the Three Gorges Dam, and the evolution of the modern surveillance state. For more on this, see Mara Hvistendahl, "How China's Smart Cities, Social Credit System and Mass Surveillance Were Sparked by Rocket Scientist," *South China Morning Post Magazine*, August 5, 2018, https://www.scmp.com /magazines/post-magazine/long-reads/article/2158142/how-chinas-smart -cities-social-credit-system-and.

73 "I grew up speaking": Email correspondence with the author.

74 "It was the stupidest thing": Chang, *Thread of the Silkworm*, 200.

74 "strong ties to the Orient": J. Edgar Hoover, "How Red China Spies on U.S.," *Nation's Business* 54, no. 6 (June 1966): 6.

74 "Western-trained scientists": Director's office, FBI, "Letter to SAC, Boston," June 28, 1967. (Obtained under the Freedom of Information Act from the FBI; requested as "copies of all documents related to the FBI program 'Chinese Communist Contacts with Scientists in the U.S.,' code-named 'IS-CH,'" in September 2016; received November 2018.)

74 cull names of ethnically Chinese researchers: The Department of Defense assembled a similar list in 1955, but the purpose was to address the question of whether ethnic Chinese scientists like Tsien could be allowed to return to China. The list included 5,000 people. The department determined that only 110 had technical knowledge that could endanger national security; 108 of the scientists were permitted to leave. One of the two who wasn't allowed to leave was Tsien. Chang, *Thread of the Silkworm*, 188.

74 estimated four thousand ethnically Chinese scientists: Further detail is given in R. D. Cotter, FBI, "Letter to Mr. W. C. Sullivan," September 28, 1967.

75 two hundred files: Special agent in charge, New York field office, FBI, "Letter to Director, FBI," September 18, 1967.

75 as many as seventy-five files: Special Agent in Charge, San Francisco Field Office, FBI, "Letter to Director, FBI," November 24, 1967.

75 seventeen years earlier: Director's office, FBI, "Letter to SAC, Boston," October 16, 1967.

75 two thousand ethnic Chinese students: Special agent in charge, New York field office, FBI, "Letter to Director, FBI," January 13, 1967.

75 file of Tsien Hsue-Shen was reopened: Special agent in charge, Los Angeles field office, FBI, "Letter to Director, FBI," August 2, 1967.

75 relatives of his friends: Special agent in charge, Los Angeles field office, "Letter to Director, FBI," November 29, 1967.

75 returned to visit long-lost friends: Many U.S.-based scientists who visited China at the time used their trips as a way to bring up nuclear arms control, an important strategic goal for the United States. See Zuoyue Wang, "Controlled Exchanges," in *How Knowledge Moves*, ed. John Krige (Chicago: University of Chicago Press, 2019).

76 with "some hostility": Jay Matthews, "China, Taiwan Woo Nobel Scientists of Chinese Descent," *Washington Post*, October 7, 1977, https://www.washington post.com/archive/politics/1977/10/07/china-taiwan-woo-nobel-scientists-of -chinese-descent/713994b6-ae1c-473f-a634-ca949eb3728e/.

76 renounced his American citizenship: "Nobel Laureate Courts Controversy over Decision to Come Back to China," *Global Times*, February 2, 2015, http:// www.globaltimes.cn/content/1034613.shtml.

76 monitored the phone numbers: Special agent in charge, Baltimore, "Letter to Director, FBI," December 5, 1973. (Obtained under the Freedom of Information Act from the FBI; requested as "copies of all documents related to the individual Chih-Kung Jen" in December 2016; received April 2019.)

76 Jen recalled that FBI and NSA: C. K. Jen, *Recollections of a Chinese Physicist* (Los Alamos, N.M.: Signition, 1990), 128–30.

76 FBI followed him: FBI, "San Francisco, California: Han T'ang Mural Exhibition in the United States," April 29, 1977, available at https://www.document cloud.org/documents/490414-chang-lin-tien-fbi-file.html. Also see Soumya Karlamangla, "Tracking UC Berkeley's Former Chancellor Chang-Lin Tien," *Daily Californian*, October 29, 2012, https://www.dailycal.org/2012/10/29 /tracking-uc-berkeleys-former-chancellor-chang-lin-tien/.

76 encompassed non-Russians: Michael Morisy and Robert Hovden, "The Feynman Files: The Professor's Invitation Past the Iron Curtain," *Muckrock*, June 6, 2012, https://www.muckrock.com/news/archives/2012/jun/06/feynman -files-professors-invitation-past-iron-curt/.

77 "harass Chinese academicians": FBI, "Chang-Lin Tien HQ 9252," March 10, 1980, available at https://www.documentcloud.org/documents/490414-chang -lin-tien-fbi-file.html.

CHAPTER TEN

78 "active and persistent perpetrators": Office of the National Counterintelligence Executive, "Foreign Spies Stealing U.S. Economic Secrets in Cyberspace: Report to Congress on Foreign Economic Collection and Industrial Espionage, 2009–2011" (October 2011), https://www.dni.gov/files/documents /Newsroom/Reports%20and%20Pubs/20111103_report_fecie.pdf.

81 James Bond Wannabes: "The Insider Threat: An Introduction to Detecting and Deterring an Insider Spy," FBI, https://www.fbi.gov/file-repository/insider _threat_brochure.pdf/view.

81 vulnerable to flattery: Ibid.

81 four thousand sensitive documents: "Chinese National Sentenced for Stealing Ford Trade Secrets," FBI, April 12, 2011, https://archives.fbi.gov/archives /detroit/press-releases/2011/de041211.htm.

81 **microprocessor design trade secrets:** Jordan Robertson, "Former Silicon Valley Engineers Sentenced to 1 Year for Chip-Design Theft," *Mercury News*, November 21, 2008, https://www.mercurynews.com/2008/11/21/former-silicon -valley-engineers-sentenced-to-1-year-for-chip-design-theft/.

81 **what she purported to be:** When I called Cheng after the conclusion of the case, she told me that she had no knowledge of any illegal activity. She recalled of Robert, "Whenever he talked to people, he strikes people as someone who is pretty sincere, and he's always wearing a smile. . . . But we just didn't know that they were doing all of these illegal activities as they were visiting the United States." After his arrest, she added, she and her colleagues "were all very shocked."

81 **secured a court:** *U.S. v. Mo Hailong*, Documents 224–1 (March 13, 2015) and 263–1 (April 9, 2015).

82 **mentioned in support of probable cause:** *U.S. v. Mo Hailong*, Document 524–1 (December 4, 2015).

CHAPTER ELEVEN

83 **their son's bedroom:** Kate Wells, "China's Heir Apparent Rekindles Early Ties to Iowa," NPR *Morning Edition*, February 7, 2012, https://www.npr.org /2012/02/07/146466598/chinas-heir-apparent-rekindles-early-ties-to-iowa.

83 **met a young governor:** Kyle Munson, "The Rise of the 'Iowa Mafia' in China, from a Governor to Xi's 'Old Friends,'" *Des Moines Register*, November 9, 2017, https://www.desmoinesregister.com/story/news/local/columnists/kyle -munson/2017/11/09/china-iowa-mafia-beijing-xi-jingping-branstad -dvorchak-old-friends/784205001/.

84 **as participants filed off the bus:** Interview with Robert Mo.

84 **$30 million overhaul:** "World Food Prize Receives $5 Million Pledge from Monsanto to Honor Norman Borlaug," Monsanto, February 15, 2008, https:// monsanto.com/news-releases/world-food-prize-receives-5-million-pledge -from-monsanto-to-honor-norman-borlaug/. The cost of the renovation is detailed at "The World Prize Hall of Laureates Awarded Prestigious LEED Platinum Certification," World Food Prize, March 2, 2013, https://www.world foodprize.org/index.cfm/87428/40180/the_world_food_prize_hall_of _laureates_awarded_prestigious_leed_platinum_certification.

85 **close ties with both industry:** DuPont Pioneer (now Corteva Agriscience) and Monsanto (now Bayer CropScience) both donate money to the World Food Prize. See "World Food Prize: Sponsors," World Food Prize, https://www .worldfoodprize.org/en/about_the_prize/sponsors/. In 2013, the prize was awarded to Monsanto's chief technology officer, along with two other recipients, sparking significant controversy.

85 **featured speakers at the conference:** "2011 Symposium and Side Event Agenda," World Food Prize, https://www.worldfoodprize.org/en/borlaug_dia logue/previous_years/2011_borlaug_dialogue/2011_symposium_agenda/.

85 **were joined by executives:** Ibid.

85 **jointly conducting research:** "Xi: China, US Should Deepen Agricultural

Ties," China.org.cn, February 17, 2012, http://www.china.org.cn/world/Xijin ping_visit/2012-02/17/content_24665387.htm.

85 **$4.3 billion worth:** Michael Scuse, "The United States Is China's Soybean Supplier of Choice," U.S. Department of Agriculture, https://www.usda.gov /media/blog/2012/02/22/united-states-chinas-soybean-supplier-choice.

85 **"momentous one for U.S.-China":** Ibid.

85 **"I will not stand by":** Barack Obama, "State of the Union 2012" speech, Washington, D.C., January 24, 2012, https://obamawhitehouse.archives.gov/the -press-office/2012/01/24/remarks-president-state-union-address.

86 **exported to China was corn:** William M. Blair, "China Buys Corn on U.S. Market," *New York Times*, October 28, 1972, https://www.nytimes.com/1972 /10/28/archives/china-buys-corn-on-us-market-nixon-discloses-18million -sale-in.html.

86 **Lily Cheng complimented him:** *U.S. v. Mo Hailong*, Document 559–1 (December 22, 2015).

87 **pulled aside for searches:** Interview with Robert Mo. I was not able to independently confirm this with Robert.

CHAPTER TWELVE

89 **No, Robert said:** Interview with Kevin Montgomery.

91 **"hanging on by their fingertips":** Michele Wolfson, "Farmers Meet Wall Street," personal site of Marcus Samuelsson, December 12, 2011, https://mar cussamuelsson.com/posts/news/farmers-meet-wall-street.

91 **"They have poisoned":** Jonathan Capehart, "What Occupy Wall Street Could Learn from the Tea Party," *Washington Post*, October 4, 2011, https://www .washingtonpost.com/blogs/post-partisan/post/what-occupy-wall-street-could -learn-from-the-tea-party/2011/03/04/gIQAxAz3KL_blog.html?noredirect =on&utm_term=.cbb135862abf.

92 **led to hyper-resistant superweeds:** Nick Carne, "Herbicide-Resistant 'Superweeds' on the Rise," *Cosmos*, June 14, 2019, https://cosmosmagazine.com /biology/herbicide-resistant-superweeds-on-the-rise. Also see Brandom Keim, "New GM Crops Could Make Superweeds Even Stronger," *Wired*, May 1, 2012, https://www.wired.com/2012/05/new-superweed-evolution/.

92 **resistance was one reason:** Interview with Diana Moss.

92 **In bringing an antitrust suit:** Kevin didn't fully agree with the action. He felt that focusing on licensing agreements was too obtuse.

92 **not DBN's first choice:** This is according to Kevin.

CHAPTER THIRTEEN

94 **Mark Betten received a tip:** Interview with Mark Betten.

94 **Mark tailed Wang Lei:** *U.S. v. Mo Hailong*, Document 1 (December 11, 2013).

94 **be on the lookout:** Interview with Mark Betten.

94 **using the name Wu Hougang:** *U.S. v. Mo Hailong*, Document 1.

95 **"Visitors are an obvious vector":** *IOSS Intelligence Threat Handbook*, Inter-

agency OPSEC Support Staff (June 2004), 45, https://fas.org/irp/threat/hand
book/index.html.

95 **dug through the trash:** *U.S. v. Mo Hailong*, Document 224–3 (March 13, 2015).

95 **They tailed Robert:** *U.S. v. Mo Hailong*, Document 1.

95 **watched from outside:** Interview with Mark Betten.

95 **obtained a warrant:** *U.S. v. Mo Hailong*, Document 560–1 (originally sealed as
252–16) (December 22, 2015).

95 **location of Robert's cell phone:** *U.S. v. Mo Hailong*, Document 224–3.

95 **CR-V showed it parked:** *U.S. v. Mo Hailong*, Document 560–3 (originally
sealed as 251–18) (December 22, 2015).

95 **determine the rough location:** This has since changed. See Adam Liptak, "In
Ruling on Cellphone Location Data, Supreme Court Makes Statement on Digital Privacy," *New York Times*, June 22, 2018, https://www.nytimes.com/2018
/06/22/us/politics/supreme-court-warrants-cell-phone-privacy.html.

95 **ten or more miles apart:** *U.S. v. Mo Hailong*, Document 560–3.

95 **Mark rushed to secure:** Ibid.

96 **"[T]here is probable cause":** Ibid.

96 **sometimes thought of passages:** Ibid.

96 **"The Surrounding Plains":** Meriwether Lewis and William Clark, *The De-
finitive Journals of Lewis & Clark*, vol. 3, *Up the Missouri to Fort Mandan* (Lin-
coln: University of Nebraska Press, 2002), 10–11.

97 **on asphalt roads:** Interview with Mark Betten.

97 **he would drive slowly:** *U.S. v. Mo Hailong*, Document 1.

97 **Mark was close behind:** Ibid.; interview with Mark Betten.

97 **Thomas filled him in:** *U.S. v. Mo Hailong*, Document 1.

97 **Robert asked for six bags:** Ibid.

97 **stuck to a single type:** Interview with Joel Thomas.

98 **struck by Robert's ethnicity:** *U.S. v. Mo Hailong*, Document 524–1 (December 4, 2015).

98 **tech agreement to sue:** *Bowman v. Monsanto Co.*, 569 U.S. 278 (2013).

98 **contained Monsanto traits:** Unlike hybrid corn seed, soybeans produce significant yield if saved and replanted.

98 **too busy to think straight:** Interview with Joel Thomas.

98 **total came to $1,533.72:** *U.S. v. Mo Hailong*, Document 1.

98 **six more bags of seed:** Ibid.

98 **A&M Mini Storage:** *U.S. v. Mo Hailong*, Document 57 (July 2, 2014).

99 PICK OUT YOUR UNI: I observed this in a visit to the storage space.

99 **sheds were transitional garages:** Interview with Mike Hills.

99 **he opened the padlock:** *U.S. v. Mo Hailong*, Document 1.

CHAPTER FOURTEEN

100 **"locusts in a swarm":** Jeff Stein, "May a Thousand Spies Bloom," *Newsweek*,
January 16, 2014, http://www.newsweek.com/2014/01/17/may-thousand-spies
-bloom-245082.html. Among other errors, Stein mixed up Robert Mo's first
and last names.

101 **intelligence conference in 1996:** Interview with Paul Moore.

101 Moore explained China's approach: Paul Douglas Moore, "Chinese Culture and the Practice of 'Actuarial' Intelligence," conference presentation, http://crimeandterrorism.org/sites/default/files/Actuarial_Intelligence_by_Paul _Moore.pdf.

102 Chinese as "blue ants": This term was coined by French writer Robert Guillain after he traveled to China in 1955 and described a population clad in drab grays and blues, stripped of all individuality. Robert Guillain, *The Blue Ants: 600 Million Chinese Under the Red Flag* (London: Secker & Warburg, 1957). Chinese leaders didn't always help dispel these ideas. During the Communist Revolution, Mao espoused the notion of a "people's war," in which villagers would overwhelm the more professional enemy through sheer numbers.

102 "human wave" of students, scientists: See, for example, "Espionage with Chinese Characteristics," Stratfor, April 24, 2010, https://worldview.stratfor.com /article/chinese-espionage-hacking-intelligence-mosaic.

102 seeks good people: Interview with Paul Moore.

102 to pursue small pieces: Moore, "Chinese Culture."

103 "always ethnic Chinese": Paul D. Moore, "How China Plays the Ethnic Card," *Los Angeles Times*, June 24, 1999, http://articles.latimes.com/1999/jun /24/local/me-49832.

103 "it does not work": Interview with Paul Moore.

104 "belong to their families": As quoted in William C. Hannas, James Mulvenon, and Anna B. Puglisi, *Chinese Industrial Espionage: Technology Acquisition and Military Modernization* (New York: Routledge, 2013), 166.

104 to "borrow brains": Ibid., 174.

104 Our foe was unsophisticated: There is a historical parallel in assumptions about American superiority prior to World War II. The belief that the Japanese were inept might have made U.S. policy makers blind to the very real threat that Japan posed. See Steve Twomey, *Countdown to Pearl Harbor: The Twelve Days to the Attack* (New York: Simon & Schuster, 2016).

104 China had some knowledge: Dan Stober and Ian Hoffman, *A Convenient Spy: Wen Ho Lee and the Politics of Nuclear Espionage* (New York: Simon & Schuster, 2001), 115.

104 code-named Kindred Spirit: Ibid., 122.

104 all ethnic Chinese researchers: Ibid., 113.

105 soon settled on Lee: Stober and Hoffman write that the FBI was "given a suspect to investigate, rather than a crime to solve," *A Convenient Spy*, 150.

105 cold-called a Taiwan-born: "Report on the Government's Handling of the Investigation and Prosecution of Dr. Wen Ho Lee," U.S. Senate Judiciary Committee Subcommittee on Department of Justice Oversight, December 20, 2001, https://fas.org/irp/congress/2001_rpt/whl.html.

105 failed to report contact: Stober and Hoffman, *A Convenient Spy*, 78, 124.

105 "virtually always target": Ibid., 214.

105 seeking the names of all students: Annie Nakao, "Wen Ho Lee Papers Shed Light on Case," *San Francisco Chronicle*, October 22, 2011, https://www.sfgate .com/bayarea/article/Wen-Ho-Lee-papers-shed-light-on-case-Rights -2867513.php.

105 **set fire to the home:** "China Gives Green Light to Embassy Protests, but Warns Against Violence," CNN, May 9, 1999, http://edition.cnn.com/WORLD /asiapcf/9905/09/china.protests.02/.

105 **maple leaf patches on our backpacks:** This was probably an excessive precaution in our case, but during World War II, when the U.S. government interned more than 120,000 Japanese Americans, many Chinese Americans wore badges that advertised their ethnicity.

106 **twenty-three hours a day:** "Report on the Government's Handling of the Investigation."

106 **called on researchers to boycott:** Sam McManis, "Ling-chi Wang: Activist Fights for Asian Americans at U.S. Labs," *San Francisco Chronicle*, March 27, 2002, https://www.sfgate.com/news/article/NEWSMAKER-PROFILE-Ling -chi-Wang-Activist-2861358.php.

106 **fifty-eight of the fifty-nine charges:** "Report on the Government's Handling of the Investigation."

106 **chastised the Justice Department:** "Statement by Judge in Los Alamos Case, with Apology for Abuse of Power," *New York Times*, September 14, 2000, https://www.nytimes.com/2000/09/14/us/statement-by-judge-in-los-alamos -case-with-apology-for-abuse-of-power.html.

106 **"Patient Zero of the unnerving present":** Lowen Liu, "Just the Wrong Amount of American," *Slate*, September 11, 2016, https://slate.com/news-and -politics/2016/09/the-case-of-scientist-wen-ho-lee-and-chinese-americans -under-suspicion-for-espionage.html.

106 **98 percent of its recruitment:** *IOSS Intelligence Threat Handbook*, Interagency OPSEC Support Staff (June 2004), 20–21, https://fas.org/irp/threat/handbook /index.html.

106 **culling *People* magazine:** Ibid., 22.

107 **"China has the largest population":** "Espionage with Chinese Characteristics."

107 **"rely on ethnic Chinese agents":** Sean Noonan, "Chinese Espionage and French Trade Secrets," Stratfor, January 20, 2011, https://worldview.stratfor .com/article/chinese-espionage-and-french-trade-secrets.

107 **a series of articles:** See, for example, Peter Mattis, "China's Amateur Spying Problem," *Diplomat*, December 11, 2011, https://thediplomat.com/2011/12/chi nas-amateur-spying-problem/; and Peter Mattis, "Beyond Spy vs. Spy: The Analytical Challenge of Understanding Chinese Intelligence Services," *Studies in Intelligence* 56, no. 3 (September 2012), https://www.cia.gov/library/center-for -the-study-of-intelligence/csi-publications/csi-studies/studies/vol.-56-no. -3/pdfs/Mattis-Understanding%20Chinese%20Intel.pdf.

107 **national security spying:** See, for example, the cases of Kevin Mallory and Glenn Shriver.

108 **sentenced to four years:** "Retired University Professor Sentenced to Four Years in Prison for Arms Export Violations Involving Citizen of China," Department of Justice Office of Public Affairs, July 1, 2009, https://www.jus tice.gov/opa/pr/retired-university-professor-sentenced-four-years-prison -arms-export-violations-involving.

108 **guilty of economic espionage:** Ed Marcum, "Engineers Convicted in Corporate Spy Case Sentenced to Probation," *Knoxville News Sentinel*, August 25, 2011, http://archive.knoxnews.com/business/engineers-convicted-in-corporate-spy -case-sentenced-to-probation-ep-403279137-357585231.html/.

108 **court in Austria convicted:** Erin Ailworth, "Chinese Firm Found Guilty of Stealing Wind Technology from U.S. Supplier," *Wall Street Journal*, January 24, 2018, https://www.wsj.com/articles/chinese-firm-found-guilty-of-stealing-wind -technology-from-u-s-supplier-1516829326.

109 **"All girls need money":** Ibid.

110 **a source was shot:** Mark Mazzetti et al., "Killing C.I.A. Informants, China Crippled U.S. Spying Operations," *New York Times*, May 20, 2017, https://www .nytimes.com/2017/05/20/world/asia/china-cia-spies-espionage.html.

110 **penetrated the CIA's covert:** Zach Dorfman and Jenna McLaughlin, "The CIA's Communications Suffered a Catastrophic Compromise. It Started in Iran," Yahoo News, January 2, 2018, https://news.yahoo.com/cias-communica tions-suffered-catastrophic-compromise-started-iran-090018710.html.

110 **21.5 million Americans:** Andy Greenberg, "OPM Now Admits 5.6M Feds' Fingerprints Were Stolen by Hackers," *Wired*, September 23, 2015, https:// www.wired.com/2015/09/opm-now-admits-5-6m-feds-fingerprints-stolen -hackers/.

110 **in some cases fingerprints:** Ibid.

CHAPTER FIFTEEN

111 **six different ways:** This is according to Kevin. Kevin provided his email correspondence with Robert, which confirmed his version of events.

112 **pink and yellow fiberglass insulation:** I visited the outbuildings.

113 **suggested Pioneer stock:** *Pioneer Hi-Bred v. Holden Foundation Seeds*, 35 F.3d 1226 (8th Cir. 1994). Holden was acquired by Monsanto in 1997.

113 **$46.7 million in damages:** Ibid.

113 **comply with a court order:** Ibid.

114 **published a smear page:** "Statement: Percy Schmeiser," Monsanto (now Bayer), April 11, 2017, https://monsanto.com/company/media/statements/percy -schmeiser/.

CHAPTER SIXTEEN

115 **At around 5:00 P.M.:** This account is based on testimony given in court by Angel Lorenzo and Alex Reina. See *U.S. v. Mo Hailong*, Document 372 (June 10, 2015). I also visited the area and retraced the route described by the officers.

116 **twenty-two-year veteran:** Ibid.

116 **everyone went home frustrated:** Ibid.

116 **decided it would do:** Ibid. Detective Lorenzo testified that the vehicle was "10 to 15 feet from the crosswalk" when the light changed from yellow to red.

117 **in the car was Lin Yong:** The passengers are identified in *U.S. v. Mo Hailong*, Document 298 (April 27, 2015). Their ages are drawn from birthdates appear-

ing on FBI WANTED posters; for example, "Lin, Yong," FBI, https://www.fbi
.gov/wanted/counterintelligence/lin-yong.

117 **Kings Nower had purchased a forty-acre:** "Trustee's Deed," *Will County
    [Illinois] Recorder*, April 11, 2012.

117 **Yao's mortgage brokerage:** I was not able to reach Yao, but his wife denied
    that either of them was involved in the conspiracy.

118 **"Take the money and RUN":** Interview with Bill and Ann Rab.

118 **check for the entire $600,000:** Ibid.

118 **a forgotten gravel road:** *U.S. v. Mo Hailong*, Document 89 (July 21, 2014).

118 **use the two farms:** Interview with Mark Betten.

119 **weighed in at 250 pounds:** *U.S. v. Mo Hailong*, Document 57 (July 2, 2014).

119 **unique four-digit code:** *U.S. v. Mo Hailong*, Document 1 (December 11, 2013).

119 **logistics company in Hong Kong:** *U.S. v. Mo Hailong*, Document 57.

119 **replace it with outdated seed:** The account that follows is based on an inter-
    view with Mark Betten.

119 **fake company names:** Jack Gillum, "FBI Behind Mysterious Surveillance Air-
    craft over US Cities," Associated Press, June 2, 2015, https://apnews.com
    /4b3f220e33b64123a3909c60845da045.

120 **surveilling Robert and others from the air:** *U.S. v. Mo Hailong*, Document
    263–1 (April 9, 2015); interview with Mark Betten.

120 **cell phone tracking technology:** Gillum, "FBI Behind Mysterious Surveil-
    lance."

120 **circle locations for hours:** Peter Aldhouse and Charles Seife, "See Maps
    Showing Where FBI Planes Are Watching from Above," *BuzzFeed News*, April 6,
    2016, https://www.buzzfeednews.com/article/peteraldhous/spies-in-the-skies.

120 **knew he could drop back:** Interview with Mark Betten.

120 **using a secret warrant:** *U.S. v. Mo Hailong*, Document 224–1 (March 13, 2015).

121 **intercepted a phone conversation:** *U.S. v. Mo Hailong*, Document 559–1 (De-
    cember 22, 2015). The exchange that follows is drawn from the FBI's transla-
    tion of the conversation.

121 **"map the roads":** The court record gives only the English translation of the
    conversation.

CHAPTER SEVENTEEN

124 **wearing dark sunglasses:** What follows is Kevin's version of events, based on
    an account that he wrote after the interview. Kevin's role in the investigation
    was confirmed by investigators and in court documents.

CHAPTER EIGHTEEN

128 **"Oh, my," Ye Jian said:** Unless otherwise noted, dialogue in this chapter is
    drawn from *U.S. v. Mo Hailong*, Document 57 (July 2, 2014); *U.S. v. Mo Hailong*,
    Document 290–1 (April 27, 2015); and *U.S. v. Mo Hailong*, Document 597 (Jan-
    uary 28, 2016).

129 **Arrowsmith, Foosland, Rantoul:** *U.S. v. Mo Hailong*, Document 57.

130 **collected whole ears of corn:** Ibid.; interview with Mark Betten and Jason Griess.

130 **slow things down:** *U.S. v. Mo Hailong*, Document 661 (November 1, 2016).

131 **highly publicized arrests:** At the time of the corn collection trip, Xue Feng, a U.S. citizen employed by a Houston-based petroleum research company, was languishing in Chinese prison on charges of stealing state secrets. Xue's defenders say he merely gathered information on Chinese oil wells that is commonly included in public databases. See Catherine Matacic, "Geologist Reflects on Life Behind Bars in China," *Science*, July 6, 2015, https://www.sciencemag.org/news /2015/07/geologist-reflects-life-behind-bars-china. Chinese-American scientists are in the unenviable position of falling under suspicion in both countries.

131 **the printing press:** Ezra Vogel, *Deng Xiaoping and the Transformation of China* (Cambridge, Mass.: Belknap, 2013), 671.

131 HEY CHINA! STOP STEALING OUR STUFF: *Bloomberg Businessweek*, March 19, 2012.

131 **"greatest transfer of wealth":** Keith Alexander, "Cybersecurity and American Power," speech presented at American Enterprise Institute (July 9, 2012), https:// www.aei.org/events/cybersecurity-and-american-power/. Alexander spoke generally about cyberespionage and intellectual property theft from all countries. He later narrowed the remark to apply specifically to China.

132 **Ye Jian sighed audibly:** The laughs and sighs are noted in the transcript of this conversation, which appears at *U.S. v. Mo Hailong*, Document 290–1.

CHAPTER NINETEEN

133 **replaced by a supervisory agent:** This is according to Kevin.

134 **hired someone to spray:** The weed problem, the remodeling project, and the vandalism are corroborated by Kevin's email correspondence with Robert. Photos of the house posted online when it was put up for sale after Robert's conviction show the effects of both the remodeling project and the vandalism.

135 **Mow the lawn:** Kevin Montgomery email to Robert Mo, July 21, 2012.

135 **"So when can you send the seed?":** This is Kevin's recollection of the conversation.

136 **"I would like to know how":** Kevin Montgomery email to Robert Mo, October 6, 2012.

CHAPTER TWENTY

137 **gave them forty-eight hours:** A visit from the FBI might have made the matter more urgent for the manager. *U.S. v. Mo Hailong*, Document 1 (December 11, 2013).

137 **rented the shed:** Ibid.

137 **a rented silver Dodge:** Ibid.

138 **exercising in the gym:** Interview with Robert Mo. Mark Betten confirmed some details surrounding his visit, but said that the FBI did not know what Robert did in his hotel.

138 *Ninety-five percent chance:* Ibid.

138 **bearing mooncakes:** Ibid.

138 **joined by Michael Yao:** *U.S. v. Mo Hailong,* Document 1.

138 **they coded these packets:** Ibid.

139 **broke for a meal:** Interview with Robert Mo.

139 **returned the Dodge Journey:** *U.S. v. Mo Hailong,* Document 1.

139 **send a set of seeds:** *U.S. v. Mo Hailong,* Document 558 (December 22, 2015). Robert disputes that he carried one of the sets to Florida.

139 **"Your Z-1 F-1 is a set?":** *U.S. v. Mo Hailong,* Document 599 (January 28, 2016).

140 **a federal jury:** "Former Employee of New Jersey Defense Contractor Convicted of Exporting Sensitive Military Technology to China," FBI, September 26, 2012, https://archives.fbi.gov/archives/newark/press-releases/2012/former -employee-of-new-jersey-defense-contractor-convicted-of-exporting-sensitive -military-technology-to-china.

140 **stealing hybrid car secrets:** "Two Convicted in Conspiracy to Steal GM Trade Secrets Sentenced to Prison," FBI, April 30, 2013, https://archives.fbi .gov/archives/detroit/press-releases/2013/two-convicted-in-conspiracy-to-steal -gm-trade-secrets-sentenced-to-prison.

140 *Remove any traceable marks:* *U.S. v. Mo Hailong,* Document 57 (July 2, 2014).

140 **"The car has been washed many times":** Ibid.

141 **included a plastic bag:** *U.S. v. Mo Hailong,* Document 1.

141 **loose kernels of corn:** Ibid.

CHAPTER TWENTY-ONE

142 **liberally used since September 11, 2001:** See, for example, Sophia Cope, "Law Enforcement Uses Border Search Exception as Fourth Amendment Loophole," Electronic Frontier Foundation, December 8, 2016, https://www .eff.org/deeplinks/2016/12/law-enforcement-uses-border-search-exception -fourth-amendment-loophole.

142 **Pop Weaver and Orville Redenbacher boxes:** The account that follows is primarily based on *U.S. v. Mo Hailong,* Document 57 (July 2, 2014).

143 **guise of U.S. agriculture regulations:** Email correspondence with Jason Griess.

143 **a thousand company documents:** Vikki Ortiz, "Woman Indicted in the Theft of Business Secrets," *Chicago Tribune,* April 3, 2008, https://www.chicagotribune .com/news/ct-xpm-2008-04-03-0804021072-story.html.

143 **in the rural Midwest:** Interview with Mark Betten and Jason Griess.

143 **hadn't yet been translated:** Interview with Jason Griess.

144 **let the men fly back:** Ibid.

144 **said he was traveling alone:** *U.S. v. Mo Hailong,* Document 57.

144 **from a man named Mo Hailong:** *U.S. v. Mo Hailong,* Document 558 (December 22, 2015).

144 **United flight to Burlington:** The account that follows is primarily based on *U.S. v. Mo Hailong,* Document 57.

CHAPTER TWENTY-TWO

146 Ye Jian called him: Interview with Robert Mo. Mark Betten confirmed that the various DBN employees were in touch with one another after the airport bust.

146 *It's normal for them to check:* Ibid.

147 opened a document: Interview with Mark Betten.

147 "The team led by Dr. Li": *U.S. v. Mo Hailong*, Document 558 (December 22, 2015). The FBI found this draft letter on Robert's devices when his house was searched following his arrest. It's unclear whether he sent it.

148 in a basketball game: Interview with Robert Mo.

CHAPTER TWENTY-THREE

149 conviction rate is 93 percent: "United States Attorneys' Annual Statistical Report for Fiscal Year 2012," Department of Justice, http://www.justice.gov /usao/reading_room/reports/asr2012/12statrpt.pdf.

150 news in his office: Interview with Haipei Shue.

150 charging her with four felonies: Nicole Perlroth, "Accused of Spying for China, Until She Wasn't," *New York Times*, May 9, 2015, https://www.nytimes .com/2015/05/10/business/accused-of-spying-for-china-until-she-wasnt .html. Also see Mara Hvistendahl, "Chinese-American Scientists in the Cross-hairs," *Science*, November 12, 2015, https://www.sciencemag.org/news/2015/11 /feature-chinese-american-scientists-crosshairs.

150 letter to Attorney General Loretta Lynch: Ted Lieu to Loretta E. Lynch, November 5, 2015.

151 "civil rights problem": Ted Lieu, "Statement on Xi Xiaoxing," September 14, 2015, https://lieu.house.gov/media-center/press-releases/representative-lieu-sta tement-xi-xiaoxing.

151 received a reply: Lieu to Lynch.

151 emigrated from China in 1989: Many of these details are drawn from report-ing I did. Hvistendahl, "Chinese-American Scientists."

152 fanned out through the house: This is Joyce Xi's account. The FBI declined to comment on the details of Xi's case.

152 a backstop charge: Interview with Nelson Dong.

152 "just completely misconceived": Hvistendahl, "Chinese-American Scien-tists."

152 "came to the attention": Ibid.

153 "emailing while Chinese-American": Clif Burns, "US Drops Charges Against Prof Accused of Emailing While Chinese-American," *Export Law Blog*, September 13, 2015, https://www.exportlawblog.com/archives/7187.

153 "America I thought I knew": Joyce Xi, "To Get My Father, Xiaoxing Xi, FBI Twisted America's Ideals," *USA Today*, September 20, 2015.

153 three other ethnically Chinese: Charges were dismissed against a sixth de-fendant, former Michigan State University professor Ning Xi, in July 2019.

153 his job responsibilities: *U.S. v. Guoqing Cao and Shuyu Li*, Document 195 (No-vember 21, 2014).

153 **published papers years earlier:** Hvistendahl, "Chinese-American Scientists."
153 **"The word is not treason":** "Indictment: Ex-Lilly Workers Stole Trade Secrets," Associated Press, October 8, 2013, https://www.apnews.com/70a17950 c12342b9805fd091cd8acbaf.
154 **"two and two together":** Hvistendahl, "Chinese-American Scientists."
154 **"As a former prosecutor":** Interview with Peter Zeidenberg.
154 **legal defense fund:** "Sherry Chen Legal Defense Fund," https://www.sherry chendefensefund.org/.
154 **"Fifteen years had passed":** Interview with Aryani Ong.
155 **governing trade secrets theft:** Interviews with Nelson Dong and Peter Zeidenberg (two of the presenters); PowerPoint presentation prepared by Peter Zeidenberg.
155 **"The indictments have instilled":** Hvistendahl, "Chinese-American Scientists."
155 **21 percent of defendants:** Andrew Chongseh Kim, "Prosecuting Chinese 'Spies': An Empirical Analysis of the Economic Espionage Act," *Cardozo Law Review* 40, no. 2 (February 2019), http://cardozolawreview.com/prosecuting -chinese-spies-an-empirical-analysis-of-the-economic-espionage-act/.
     Kim also found that defendants with Chinese surnames received longer sentences than those with Western names—twenty-five months versus eleven months. A separate study analyzing 137 trade secrets theft cases using a different methodology found a similar gap: Defendants with Chinese surnames received an average sentence of thirty-two months. Those without Chinese surnames received only fifteen months. Thomas Nolan, "Trends in Trade Secrets Prosecutions," White Paper, http://jeremy-wu.info/wp-content/uploads /2016/01/Trends-in-Trade-Secret-Prosecutions.pdf.
155 **"findings raise the possibility":** Andrew Kim, "Prosecuting Chinese 'Spies,'" White Paper for Committee of 100, May 2017, https://committee100.org/wp -content/uploads/2017/05/2017-Kim-White-Paper-online.pdf.
155 **"an ethnic cast":** Noah Feldman, "Prosecutors' Misplaced Fear of Scientists," Bloomberg, September 17, 2015, https://www.bloomberg.com/opinion/articles /2015-09-17/prosecutors-misplaced-fear-of-scientists.
156 **10 percent of all science:** "Doctorate Recipients from U.S. Universities 2017," National Science Foundation, December 4, 2018, https://ncses.nsf.gov/pubs /nsf19301/data.
156 **Los Alamos club:** "America's Hidden Role in Chinese Weapons Research," *South China Morning Post*, March 29, 2017, https://www.scmp.com/news/china /diplomacy-defence/article/2082738/americas-hidden-role-chinese-weapons -research.
156 *60 Minutes* **aired a segment:** "Collateral Damage," *60 Minutes*, May 15, 2016, https://www.cbsnews.com/news/collateral-damage-60-minutes-bill-whitaker/.
156 **"acted with reckless haste":** "The Rush to Find China's Moles," *New York Times*, September 15, 2015, https://www.nytimes.com/2015/09/15/opinion/the -rush-to-find-chinas-moles.html.
156 **instituted a rule change:** Matt Apuzzo, "After Missteps, U.S. Tightens Rules for Espionage Cases," *New York Times*, April 26, 2016, https://www.nytimes

.com/2016/04/27/us/after-missteps-us-tightens-rules-for-national-security
-cases.html.

156 **"patently racist accusation"**: "Ohio Scientist Accused of Spying Sues Government After Charges Dropped," 9 WCPO Cincinnati, January 22, 2019, https://
www.wcpo.com/news/state/state-ohio/ohio-scientist-accused-of-spying-sues
-after-charges-dropped.

156 **brought a suit against:** *Xiaoxing Xi v. FBI Special Agent Andrew Haugen and
John Doe(s)*.

157 WASHINGTON'S SPY CHARGES . . . **"history of indulging":** *Global Times*, May 21,
2015, http://www.globaltimes.cn/content/922773.shtml.

CHAPTER TWENTY-FOUR

158 **obtained a warrant:** Interview with Mark Betten. The FBI had court authori-
zation to seize the seed but needed a secondary warrant to test it.

158 **twenty-five thousand seeds:** *U.S. v. Mo Hailong*, Document 506 (November
24, 2015).

159 **on both sides of the road:** Interview with Jason Griess.

159 **harsher on companies:** Lina Khan, "How Monsanto Outfoxed the Obama
Administration," *Salon*, March 15, 2013, https://www.salon.com/2013/03/15/how
_did_monsanto_outfox_the_obama_administration/.

159 **only a short note:** "Monsanto Notified That U.S. Department of Justice Has
Concluded Its Inquiry," Monsanto, November 16, 2012, available through Internet Archive at https://web.archive.org/web/20170309095207/http://www.monsan
to.com/newsviews/pages/monsanto-notified-that-us-department-of-justice-has
-concluded-its-inquiry.aspx.

159 **it was noteworthy:** Jason Griess maintained there is no connection between
the two cases.

160 **$6 million a year:** Russ Choma, "Monsanto's Deep Roots in Washington,"
OpenSecrets.org, May 9, 2012, https://www.opensecrets.org/news/2012/05/mon
santos-deep-roots-in-washington/.

160 **Monsanto's counsel feared:** Interview with Mark Betten.

161 **followed the FBI's investigation:** Interview with Jason Griess.

161 **$1 billion jury verdict:** Carey Gillian, "Monsanto, DuPont Strike $1.75 Billion Licensing Deal, End Lawsuits," Reuters, March 26, 2013, https://www
.reuters.com/article/us-monsanto-dupont-gmo/monsanto-dupont-strike
-1-75-billion-licensing-deal-end-lawsuits-idUSBRE92P0IK20130326.

161 **tend to be anticompetitive:** Interview with Diana Moss.

161 **sent out 652 seed samples:** *U.S. v. Mo Hailong*, Document 506.

162 **bus with tinted windows:** "*Xi Jinping: shishi chuangxin qudong bu neng dengdai
guanwang xiedai*," Xinhua, October 1, 2013, http://news.sina.com.cn/c/2013-10
-01/152428347406.shtml.

162 **first ever held off-site:** Richard P. Applebaum et al., *Innovation in China* (Cambridge, U.K.: Polity Press, 2018), 53.

162 **"We must seize the opportunities":** "*Xi Jinping: shishi chuangxin.*"

163 **a bust would squander:** Interview with Jason Griess.

163 **to attend the World Pork Expo:** Interview with Mark Betten.
163 **improve its negotiating position:** Ibid.
164 **sold at the end of the season:** Ibid.
164 **changed somewhere along the way:** Ibid. Kevin Montgomery believes DBN employees gave no indication of a desire to chase the self on the Monee property. Unless they were to purchase a specialized research planter—which, as far as Kevin knows, they did not—such an activity would have required hand-planting and other difficult farm labor. The existence of a nursery also would have been obvious to Kevin and any others who visited the property.
164 **have enough information to start:** *U.S. v. Mo Hailong*, Document 506.

CHAPTER TWENTY-FIVE

166 **lacked a command:** Interview with Kevin Montgomery.
167 *Seed Today* **and** *Seed World:* Details on the conference are available at ASTA Seed Expo 2012, https://www.betterseed.org/pdfs/events/asta-css-seed-expo/CSS2012-guide.pdf.
167 **"Nutrient Accumulation Patterns":** Ibid.
167 **"the CEO's brother-in-law":** Interview with Kevin Montgomery.
167 **telling Kevin that he was:** Ibid. The account that follows is as recalled by Kevin.
169 **create new super seeds:** *U.S. v. Mo Hailong*, Document 661 (November 1, 2016).
169 **the Keystone Kops:** Kevin was not the only person to make this comparison.

CHAPTER TWENTY-SIX

171 **6:00 A.M. on December 11:** Interview with Robert Mo. Mark Betten could not confirm the time, but he noted that raids often happen at 6:00 A.M. because that is the earliest hour permitted by most federal warrants.
171 **arrange the arrest date:** Interview with Mark Betten.
171 **spook and flee:** Ibid.
172 **Robert's wife, Carolyn:** Interview with Robert Mo.
172 **past a Christmas tree:** Interview with Valentin Rodriguez (the attorney who represented Robert Mo at his bail hearing).
172 **flash drives, external hard drives:** *U.S. v. Mo Hailong*, Document 224-3 (March 13, 2015).
172 **More than twenty devices in total:** *U.S. v. Mo Hailong*, Document 92 (August 1, 2014).
172 **seized tax records:** *U.S. v. Mo Hailong*, Document 153-2 (December 15, 2014).
172 **Robert and Carolyn's two children:** Interview with Robert Mo.
172 **sketch artist pulled out:** *U.S. v. Mo Hailong*, Document 224-3.
173 **$250,000 initiation fee:** Charles M. Sennott, "In Palm Beach, Donald Trump's Exclusive Golf Resort Sits Next to County Jail," *GlobalPost*, April 8, 2013, https://www.pri.org/stories/2013-04-08/palm-beach-donald-trumps-exclusive-golf-resort-sits-next-county-jail.

CHAPTER TWENTY-SEVEN

174 fifteen hundred inmates: Charles M. Sennott, "In Palm Beach, Donald Trump's Exclusive Golf Resort Sits Next to County Jail," *GlobalPost*, April 8, 2013, https://www.pri.org/stories/2013-04-08/palm-beach-donald-trumps-exclusive-golf-resort-sits-next-county-jail.

174 put on proper clothes: This is Robert's account of his arrest.

175 *The more famous:* Interview with Robert Mo.

175 recommended removing it: Interview with Robert Mo.

176 private wing of the jail: Julie K. Brown, "Even from Jail, Sex Abuser Manipulated the System. His Victims Were Kept in the Dark," *Miami Herald*, November 28, 2018, https://www.miamiherald.com/news/local/article219494920.html.

176 FBI's extensive bugging: *U.S. v. Mo Hailong*, Document 1 (December 11, 2013).

177 denying his request: *U.S. v. Mo Hailong*, Document 19–9 (January 23, 2014).

177 shackled his hands and feet: This is Robert's version of events. His description is roughly consistent with other accounts of prisoner transportation. Jason Griess confirmed that Oklahoma City is used as a transport hub.

177 the diesel treatment: Interview with Robert Mo.

CHAPTER TWENTY-EIGHT

178 the Chinese Press: Chen Jia, "Seeds Becoming a Mysterious—and Dangerous—Business," *China Daily*, December 18, 2013, http://usa.chinadaily.com.cn/epaper/2013-12/18/content_17182452.htm.

178 China-U.S. Friendship Farm: Kyle Munson, "China Is Recreating an Iowa Farm Near Beijing. And There's a Lot at Stake for Both Countries," *Des Moines Register*, September 23, 2017, https://www.desmoinesregister.com/story/news/local/columnists/kyle-munson/2017/09/23/china-rolls-out-red-carpet-begin-building-its-first-iowa-farm/696214001/; also see *"Zhongmei youyi shifan nong chang gainian xing guihua,"* http://www.jyuwliu.com/html/shouyegh42018-06-27901.html.

178 $1 billion worth of goods: "Iowa Companies Sign $1 Billion Trade Deals with Chinese Province," KCCI Des Moines, October 23, 2013, http://www.kcci.com/article/iowa-companies-sign-1-billion-trade-deals-with-chinese-province/6885083.

179 "this is a particular incident": Jason Noble, "Seed Theft Tests Relationship," *Des Moines Register*, December 17, 2013, B1.

179 filching hundreds of these: Matt Campbell, "Chinese National Tried to Steal a Valuable U.S. Trade Secret: Kansas Rice Seeds," *Kansas City Star*, April 5, 2018, https://www.kansascity.com/news/state/kansas/article208009774.html.

CHAPTER TWENTY-NINE

182 "greatest theft in the history": Nick Gass, "Trump: 'We Can't Continue to Allow China to Rape Our Country,'" *Politico*, May 2, 2016, https://www.politico.com/blogs/2016-gop-primary-live-updates-and-results/2016/05

/trump-china-rape-america-222689. Trump borrowed this remark from General Keith Alexander, who first said something similar in 2012.

183 **took office amid protests:** Karen J. Greenberg, *Rogue Justice* (New York: Broadway Books, 2017), 143–44.

183 **he could use email:** John P. Carlin with Garrett M. Graff, *Dawn of the Code War* (New York: PublicAffairs, 2018), 73.

183 **"Three Little Pigs":** Sari Horwitz, "9/11 Attacks Helped Shape New Leader of Justice's National Security Division," *Washington Post*, April 28, 2014, https://www.washingtonpost.com/world/national-security/911-attacks-helped-shape-new-leader-of-justices-national-security-division/2014/04/28/875cfafe-cee6-11e3-937f-d3026234b51c_story.html?.

184 **FBI WANTED posters:** "Five Chinese Military Hackers Charged," FBI (May 19, 2014), https://www.fbi.gov/news/stories/five-chinese-military-hackers-charged-with-cyber-espionage-against-us.

184 **"a very sophisticated form":** John Carlin with Benjamin Wittes, "Tackling Emerging National Security Threats Through Law Enforcement," event at Brookings Institution, Washington, D.C., May 22, 2014, https://www.brookings.edu/events/tackling-emerging-national-security-threats-through-law-enforcement.

184 **carve out a new mission:** Interview with Greg Austin (a professorial fellow at EastWest Institute and an expert on Chinese cyberpolicy).

184 **"a giant 'no trespass' sign":** Chinese cyberattacks did in fact noticeably decline after the indictment, but exactly why is unclear. The drop in activity coincided with a reorganization of the People's Liberation Army and a crackdown on corruption within the Communist Party. Hacking from China targeting U.S. companies later picked back up again—it just became more professional. "Cyber's Role in America's Security Arsenal," transcript, 2016 Aspen Security Forum.

185 **"You and the FBI":** "Agricultural Economic Espionage: A Growing Threat," FBI, https://ucr.fbi.gov/investigate/counterintelligence/agricultural-economic-espionage-brochure.

185 **"Just say no to the Chinese!":** *The Company Man: Protecting America's Secrets*, https://www.fbi.gov/video-repository/newss-the-company-man-protecting-americas-secrets/view. The case on which the film is based is *U.S. v. Ji Li Huang* (Western District of Missouri), 4:12-cr-00296.

186 **"brazenly stole inbred corn seeds":** Laurie Bedord, "Midwest Is a Prime Target for Theft of Intellectual Property and Cyber Attacks," *Successful Farming*, April 5, 2016, https://www.agriculture.com/content/cybersecurity-is-not-just-a-big-city-problem.

186 **"What the government should do":** Interview with John Cline.

186 **"We didn't help Boeing":** Carlin, *Dawn of the Code War*, 146.

187 **"targeting our private companies":** Lesley Stahl, "The Great Brain Robbery," *60 Minutes*, January 17, 2016, https://www.cbsnews.com/news/60-minutes-great-brain-robbery-china-cyber-espionage/.

187 **talented employees to break off:** Omri Ben-Shahar, "California Got It Right: Ban the Non-Compete Agreements," *Forbes*, October 27, 2016, https://www

.forbes.com/sites/omribenshahar/2016/10/27/california-got-it-right-ban-the
-non-compete-agreements/#7e1fe2b03538.

188 **survey of private companies:** Jack Nelson, "Spies Took $300-Billion Toll on
U.S. Firms in '97," *Los Angeles Times*, January 12, 1998, http://articles.latimes
.com/1998/jan/12/news/mn-7575.

188 **domestic theft as the bigger threat:** Robert Dreyfuss, "The New Espionage
Scare: Spy vs. No-Spy," *New Republic*, December 23, 1996, 9–10.

188 **methodology was considered:** Rich Bell et al., "Estimating the Economic
Costs of Espionage," prepared for CENTRA Technology, May 3, 2010, 8.

188 **"laden with company bias":** Bell et al., "Estimating the Economic Costs," 7–8.

188 **Report to Congress on Foreign Economic Collection:** "Annual Report to
Congress on Foreign Economic Collection and Industrial Espionage—2002,"
Office of the National Counterintelligence Executive, 9–10, https://archive.org
/details/DTIC_ADA469059/page/n7.

188 **report from the IP Commission:** Dennis C. Blair et al., "The IP Commission
Report: The Report of the Commission on Theft of American Intellectual
Property," May 22, 2013, http://www.ipcommission.org/report/IP_Commission
_Report_052213.pdf.

188 **"anecdotes, extrapolation, and bad math":** James A. Lewis, "China's Economic
Espionage: Why It Worked in the Past but It Won't Work in the Future," *Foreign
Affairs*, November 13, 2012, https://www.foreignaffairs.com/articles/china/2012
-11-13/chinas-economic-espionage.

188 **cyberattacks at $250 billion:** Peter Maass and Megha Rajagopalan, "Does Cy-
bercrime Really Cost $1 Trillion?," ProPublica, August 1, 2012, https://www
.propublica.org/article/does-cybercrime-really-cost-1-trillion.

188 **estimate as "below abysmal":** Ibid.

188 **"so compromised and biased":** Ibid.

189 **in the profit it generates:** Interview with Derek Scissors (fellow, American
Enterprise Institute). Scissors believes that while spending on research is a poor
way of calculating value, sales figures can be a decent substitute. In some economic espionage cases, judges circumvent this issue by considering intended
loss, or how much defendants believe a technology is worth.

189 NOW WORKING FOR MONSANTO: J. D. Heyes, "The FBI Is Now Working for
Monsanto," *Natural News*, April 30, 2015, https://www.naturalnews.com/049544
_Monsanto_FBI_GMO_seeds.html.

CHAPTER THIRTY

190 **this improvised routine:** This is according to Robert Mo.

190 **$1,000 in charges:** Ibid.

191 **sensors that surrounded:** *U.S. v. Mo Hailong*, Document 44 (April 22, 2014)
and Document 47 (April 22, 2014).

191 **contact with the outside world:** The circumstances in which Robert could
leave the house are described in *U.S. v. Mo Hailong*, Document 47.

191 **$500 for transportation:** This is according to Robert.

192 **thousands of pages of documents:** *U.S. v. Mo Hailong*, Document 201 (February 18, 2015).

192 **painfully aware of the debt:** Interview with Robert Mo.

192 **vampires perched on his shoulders:** Ibid.

192 **resume his work for DBN:** Ibid.

193 *catch a big fish:* Ibid.

194 **suffered from high blood pressure:** *U.S. v. Mo Hailong*, Document 98–3 (August 28, 2014).

194 **home until eight:** Ibid.

194 **he tried to warn her:** Interview with Robert Mo.

CHAPTER THIRTY-ONE

195 **gathered law enforcement officers:** *U.S. v. Mo Hailong*, Document 372 (June 10, 2015).

195 **triggered an alert:** Interview with Mark Betten.

195 **images of Robert's devices:** Ibid.

195 **DBN's Boca Raton office:** *U.S. v. Mo Hailong*, Document 558 (December 22, 2015).

196 **"in charge of the specifics":** *U.S. v. Mo Hailong*, Document 57 (July 2, 2014).

196 **work through the CBP:** Betten testified to this at *U.S. v. Mo Hailong*, Document 372.

196 **bags of souvenirs:** *U.S. v. Mo Hailong*, Document 372.

196 **every chair was occupied:** Ibid.

196 **a bland Hudson News:** Ibid.

197 **"ask you some questions":** The dialogue that follows is drawn from a verbatim transcript of the encounter, which appears at *U.S. v. Mo Hailong*, Document 98–2 (August 28, 2014). Further details, such as what the various participants wore and where they stood while conversing, appear in testimony recorded at *U.S. v. Mo Hailong*, Document 372.

197 **daughter, who was five . . . twelve-year-old son:** *U.S. v. Mo Hailong*, Document 372.

198 **he still felt awkward:** Ibid.

199 **statement from Mo Yun:** Ibid.

201 **pulled the girl from her:** *U.S. v. Mo Hailong*, Document 83–1 (July 15, 2014).

201 **laying out her Miranda rights:** *U.S. v. Mo Hailong*, Document 373 (June 10, 2015).

CHAPTER THIRTY-TWO

202 **she chafed under the restrictions:** This is according to Robert Mo.

202 **Robert lay on a table:** Interview with Robert Mo. His cancer is also detailed at *U.S. v. Mo Hailong*, Document 660 (November 1, 2016).

203 **a million such cases:** "Cancer Statistics," National Cancer Institute, http://www.cancer.gov/about-cancer/understandingstatistics.

203 fewer than one thousand . . . never encountered the condition: *U.S. v. Mo Hailong*, Document 660.

203 move from Des Moines: *U.S. v. Mo Hailong*, Document 159 (December 22, 2014).

204 Toddlers trudged the grounds: These are details that I observed on a trip to MD Anderson's campus.

204 all-inclusive packages: Alice Yan, "A Cut Above: Chinese Agencies Offer Overseas Medical Treatment—for a Price," *South China Morning Post*, June 2, 2015, https://www.scmp.com/news/china/money-wealth/article/1814711/cut-above -chinese-agencies-offer-overseas-medical-treatment.

204 sixteen stories of rooms: Adolfo Pesquera, "Blossom Hotel Project Transforms, Expands; Reaches Build Phase," Virtual Builders Exchange, https://www .virtuandersonalbx.com/construction-preview/blossom-hotel-project-trans forms-expands-reaches-build-phase/.

204 doctor in the country: *U.S. v. Mo Hailong*, Document 660.

204 six cycles of chemo: Ibid.; interview with Robert Mo.

204 recurring within two years: *U.S. v. Mo Hailong*, Document 660.

CHAPTER THIRTY-THREE

205 first economic espionage case: Interview with Jason Griess.

206 seventeen thousand intercepted emails: *U.S. v. Mo Hailong*, Document 254–1 (March 30, 2015).

206 samples appeared to match: *U.S. v. Mo Hailong*, Document 506 (November 24, 2015). Of the 652 samples submitted by the government, 115 matched seeds from Pioneer or Monsanto.

207 rejected only 12 requests: "Foreign Intelligence Surveillance Act Court Orders, 1979–2017," Electronic Privacy Information Center, https://epic.org /privacy/surveillance/fisa/stats/.

207 to collect bulk data: Spencer Ackerman, "FISA Court Order That Allowed NSA Surveillance Is Revealed for First Time," *Guardian*, November 19, 2013, https://www.theguardian.com/world/2013/nov/19/court-order-that-allowed -nsa-surveillance-is-revealed-for-first-time.

207 first time in U.S. history: *U.S. v. Mo Hailong*, Document 224–1 (March 13, 2015). Even in the Wen Ho Lee case, which involved allegations of traditional espionage, the FBI's application for a FISA warrant was denied. Robert's case might have been a turning point. FISA was later used in the Xiaoxing Xi case.

208 assistance from the NSA: *U.S. v. Mo Hailong*, Document 347 (May 13, 2015).

208 "We don't know": *U.S. v. Mo Hailong*, Document 305 (May 1, 2015).

208 affidavit from U.S. Attorney General: *U.S. v. Mo Hailong*, Document 376 (June 11, 2015).

209 "no 'significant need'": *U.S. v. Mo Hailong*, Document 224–1.

209 "an accepted practice": Interview with Kening Li.

209 Pioneer Chair in Agribusiness: *U.S. v. Mo Hailong*, Document 501–2 (November 20, 2015).

209 subpoenaed Pioneer and Monsanto: Recapped in *U.S. v. Mo Hailong*, Document 506 (November 24, 2015).

210 *"confidential and sensitive information"*: *U.S. v. Mo Hailong*, Document 207 (March 4, 2015).

210 **"Since this is a conspiracy"**: *U.S. v. Mo Hailong*, Document 506.

210 **"the emperor's new clothes"**: Interview with Robert Mo.

210 **"Monsanto is a victim"**: *U.S. v. Mo Hailong*, Document 358 (May 17, 2015).

210 **"Let me be straight"**: Ibid.

CHAPTER THIRTY-FOUR

211 **"You can be seated"**: Unless otherwise noted, details of the hearing are drawn from the transcript at *U.S. v. Mo Hailong*, Documents 372 (June 10, 2015) and 373 (June 10, 2015), and from a visit that I made to the courtroom.

211 **held on a cattle fairground**: Julia Preston, "Immigrants' Speedy Trials After Raid Become Issue," *New York Times*, August 8, 2008, https://www.nytimes .com/2008/08/09/us/09immig.html?em.

212 **invited a public rebuke**: Julia Preston, "Life Sentence Is Debated for Meat Plant Ex-Chief," *New York Times*, April 28, 2010, https://www.nytimes.com/2010 /04/29/us/29postville.html.

212 **"lesson in there"**: "After Long Sentence, US Judge Stephanie Rose Calls Herself 'Hulk,'" Associated Press, June 5, 2013, https://globegazette.com/news /iowa/after-long-sentence-us-judge-stephanie-rose-calls-herself-hulk/article _85254a16-ce10-11e2-a159-0019bb2963f4.html.

212 **splashed across the pages**: Clark Kauffman, "Prosecutor Who Got Judge's 'Hulk' E-mail Leaves Job," *Des Moines Register/USA Today*, June 6, 2013, https:// www.usatoday.com/story/news/nation/2013/06/06/iowa-judge-hulk-email -prosecutor-leaves-job/2397039/.

214 **threw out the MSN chats**: *U.S. v. Mo Hailong*, Document 420 (July 17, 2015).

214 **U.S. attorney's office dropped charges**: *U.S. v. Mo Hailong*, Document 435 (July 28, 2015).

CHAPTER THIRTY-FIVE

216 **on the deflections**: Interview with Kevin Montgomery.

218 **"unlike any other environment in the world"**: "William Niebur: Interview with Seed World Media President Shawn Brook," Issues Ink Media, July 9, 2014, https://www.youtube.com/watch?v=8PvuqJL-F-A. Niebur declined to comment on the seed investigation.

218 **brokered a licensing deal**: "DuPont Pioneer and Origin Agritech to Jointly Develop New Seed Technology for China's Farmers," DuPont Pioneer, April 4, 2016, https://www.pioneer.com/homesite/about/news-media/news-releases/tem plate.CONTENT/guid.63523AAD-9014-6DE9-A040-BBBB7A6F9A37.

218 **first branch outside China**: "Origin Agritech Establishes North American Operations in Des Moines," PR Newswire, October 3, 2016, https://www .prnewswire.com/news-releases/origin-agritech-establishes-north-american -operations-in-des-moines-300337769.html.

CHAPTER THIRTY-SIX

219 Robert looked on: Unless otherwise noted, details of the hearing are drawn from *U.S. v. Mo Hailong*, Document 597 (January 28, 2016), and from a visit that I made to the courtroom.

219 spread to his lungs: *U.S. v. Mo Hailong*, Documents 660 (November 1, 2016) and 661 (November 1, 2016).

219 Orville Redenbacher boxes: *U.S. v. Mo Hailong*, Document 263–2 (April 9, 2015).

219 twenty-two congresspeople's inquiry: *U.S. v. Mo Hailong*, Document 524–1 (December 4, 2015).

220 offhand comment from Joel Thomas: Ibid.

220 marred by racism and xenophobia: Ibid.

220 forbade unnecessary mention: *U.S. v. Mo Hailong*, Document 588 (January 12, 2016).

221 belted out a cover of "Teen Angel": "Professor Sha Na Na for Founder of the '60s Group, After Woodstock Came Forensic Linguistics," *Washington Post*, May 8, 2006, https://www.washingtonpost.com/archive/lifestyle/2006/05/08/professor-sha-na-na-span-classbankheadfor-founder-of-the-60s-group-after-woodstock-came-forensic-linguisticsspan/1b564795-7241-41cc-b828-116996db5193/?utm_term=.bd2de1bf997e. Also see Sha Na Na, "Teen Angel," https://www.youtube.com/watch?v=pqN9n2FbuJE.

221 judge threw out: *U.S. v. Mo Hailong*, Document 597.

222 there was "some weirdness": *U.S. v. Mo Hailong*, Document 506 (November 24, 2015).

222 agents of the U.S. government: *U.S. v. Mo Hailong*, Document 597.

223 thought that . . . was dubious: Interview with Robert Mo.

224 fifteen years in prison: Bob Egelko, "Spy Conviction Upheld for Bay Area Businessman," *SFGate*, May 5, 2017, https://www.sfgate.com/business/article/Spy-conviction-upheld-for-Bay-Area-businessman-11125307.php. The Ninth U.S. Circuit Court of Appeals later overturned one portion of the ruling.

224 another business transaction: Interview with Robert Mo.

224 laid out his rights: A transcript of the plea hearing is at *U.S. v. Mo Hailong*, Document 604 (February 23, 2016). The plea agreement is at *U.S. v. Mo Hailong*, Document 596 (January 27, 2016).

CHAPTER THIRTY-SEVEN

226 kept to their respective sides: Unless otherwise noted, details from the sentencing are drawn from my attendance and from transcripts appearing at *U.S. v. Mo Hailong*, Documents 659–661 (November 1, 2016).

227 keep the kids away: Interview with Robert Mo.

228 stopped the drain of resources: Interview with Jason Griess.

228 Griess found highly specious: In an interview, Griess called the idea that the Tahoe conversations were scripted "one of the most unusual notions I've seen in my career."

228 the abrupt conclusion: Ibid.

229 locking up drug runners: I first heard this analogy in an interview with Derek Scissors.

229 liberalize green card requirements: In "Assessing and Responding to China's Innovation Initiative," John Deutsch writes: "It is futile to maintain US competitiveness and its lead in early-stage innovation by trying to keep others out or, for that matter, our ideas in. The only effective response to China's growing capability is to master the new intellectual frontiers and continue to recruit the most talented workforce able to rapidly translate new ideas into practice." Deutsch, "Assessing and Responding to China's Innovation Initiative," in *Technology and National Security: Maintaining America's Edge*, eds. Leah Bitounis and Jonathon Price (Washington, D.C.: Aspen Institute, 2019), 162.

232 he learned about Robert's sentence: Interview with Kevin Montgomery.

CHAPTER THIRTY-EIGHT

233 some former FBI agents: "Senate Should Rename J. Edgar Hoover Building After Champion of Civil Liberties Don Edwards," Defending Rights & Dissent, August 1, 2017, https://rightsanddissent.org/news/senate-rename-j-edgar-hoover -building-strident-champion-civil-liberties-don-edwards/. Also see Allan Lengel, "Hoover Who? The Battle over the New $1.8B FBI Headquarters and a Name," ABC News, June 7, 2016, https://abcnews.go.com/US/hoover-battle -18b-fbi-headquarters/story?id=39640360.

233 build a new headquarters: At the time this book went to press, the location of a planned new headquarters was still being hotly debated.

235 FBI's Most Wanted list: "Most Wanted: Counterintelligence," FBI, https:// www.fbi.gov/wanted/counterintelligence.

236 hyping its own foreign espionage: *"Nanzi tou mai 90 xiang guojia jiemi qingbao; huoli 70 wan meiyuan bei pan sixing,"* Beijing Times, April 19, 2016, https:// new.qq.com/cmsn/20160419/20160419004086.

236 titled "Dangerous Love": "Dangerous Love on National Security Education Day," China Law Translate, April 16, 2016, https://www.chinalawtranslate.com /nsed/.

236 unveiled a hotline: DD Wu, "Anti-Espionage: A New Mass Line Campaign in China?," *The Diplomat*, April 17, 2017, https://thediplomat.com/2017/04/anti-espionage-a-new-mass-line-campaign-in-china/.

237 "innovation demonstration" labs: *"Dabeinong cheng shou pi guojia nongye; keji chuangxin yu zhenghe shifan jidi,"* Science and Technology Daily, December 28, 2014, http://big5.china.com.cn/gate/big5/finance.china.com.cn/roll/20141228 /2875843.shtml.

238 more than doubled: The company's operating revenue also increased from $1.7 trillion in 2012 to $2.5 trillion in 2015.

238 $43 billion bid for Syngenta: Details on this deal are drawn from reporting I did for *Science*, "China Aims to Sow a Revolution with GM Seed Takeover," April 7, 2017, https://science.sciencemag.org/content/356/6333/16.summary.

238 flashy fifteen-year anniversary bash: Details on this event are drawn from *"15 zai rongyao jidian; yangfan gong qi xin cheng,"* Kings Nower, http://www.jsnh

.com.cn/archives/324.html; and *"Dabeinong zuowu keji chanye Jinse Nonghua chuangye shiwu zhounian jinian dahui longzhong juxing,"* Dabeinong Group, August 16, 2018, http://www.dbn.com.cn/html/20160816/44925.html.

239 **"a major battleground":** *"Dabeinong zuowu keji changye . . . ,"* Dabeinong Group, August 16, 2018.

239 **DBN would become:** *"Shao Genhuo: Cong 20,000 yuan dao bai yi shenjia,"* Sina .com, April 12, 2010, http://finance.sina.com.cn/stock/newstock/zxdt/20100412 /16237733850.shtml.

239 **in all fifty states:** "A Chat with the Director of the FBI," Aspen Security Forum, July 18, 2018, https://aspensecurityforum.org/wp-content/uploads/2018/07/ASF -2018-A-Chat-with-Christopher-Wray.pdf.

239 **"The volume of it":** Ibid.

239 **"a whole-of-society threat":** Christopher Wray, testimony before the U.S. Senate Select Committee on Intelligence, February 13, 2018, https://www .intelligence.senate.gov/hearings/open-hearing-worldwide-threats-hearing-1. [No longer available. Archived version at https://web.archive.org/web/2019 0121160723/https://www.intelligence.senate.gov/hearings/open-hearing -worldwide-threats-hearing-1.]

239 **national intelligence law:** Murray Scot Tanner, "Beijing's New National Intelligence Law: From Defense to Offense," *Lawfare,* July 20, 2017, https://www .lawfareblog.com/beijings-new-national-intelligence-law-defense-offense.

240 **never got a reply:** Interview with Haipei Shue.

241 **arresting nearly 1,300 Japanese Americans:** Toshio Whelchel, *From Pearl Harbor to Saigon: Japanese American Soldiers and the Vietnam War* (London: Verso, 1999), 197.

241 **reported the Chinese grants:** Other advantages to working part-time in China include a more permissive biomedical ethics environment and access to abundant graduate students.

241 **took technologies back to China:** There is no evidence that this happened in the MD Anderson cases.

241 **set up "shadow labs":** Jocelyn Kaiser and David Malakoff, "NIH Investigating Whether U.S. Scientists Are Sharing Ideas with Foreign Governments," *Science,* August 27, 2018, https://www.sciencemag.org/news/2018/08/nih-inves tigating-whether-us-scientists-are-sharing-ideas-foreign-governments.

241 **accounts of twenty-three employees:** The account that follows is based on reporting I did for *Science.* See: "Exclusive: Major U.S. Cancer Center Ousts 'Asian' Researchers After NIH Flags Their Foreign Ties," April 19, 2019, https://www.sciencemag.org/news/2019/04/exclusive-major-us-cancer-center -ousts-asian-researchers-after-nih-flags-their-foreign; and "Concerns About Ties to China Prompt Firings," April 26, 2019, https://science.sciencemag.org /content/364/6438/314.

242 **the charges were dropped:** Rachel Leingang, "Keping Xie, Former U. of Arizona Prof, Cleared of Child Porn Charge in Texas," *Arizona Republic,* November 29, 2018, https://www.azcentral.com/story/news/local/arizona-education/2018 /11/29/keping-xie-former-university-arizona-medical-school-professor -cleared-child-pornography/2151078002/.

243 **audio recording of the event:** Details from this recording appear in my article "After Ousters, MD Anderson Officials Try to Calm Fears of Racial Profiling," *Science*, April 23, 2019, https://www.sciencemag.org/news/2019/04/after-firings -md-anderson-officials-try-calm-fears-racial-profiling.

243 **"How can you":** Ibid.

243 **urging U.S. universities:** Emily Feng, "FBI Urges Universities to Monitor Some Chinese Students and Scholars in the U.S.," NPR, June 28, 2019, https:// www.npr.org/2019/06/28/728659124/fbi-urges-universities-to-monitor-some -chinese-students-and-scholars-in-the-u-s.

243 **Americans on study-abroad:** Emily Feng, "American Graduates of China's Yenching Academy Are Being Questioned by the FBI," NPR, August 1, 2019, https://www.npr.org/2019/08/01/746355146/american-graduates-of-chinas -yenching-academy-are-being-questioned-by-the-fbi.

244 **"These are the top talents":** Interview with Steven Pei.

244 **Science and Technology Cooperation Award:** "MD Anderson Receives Top Chinese Science and Technology Award," MD Anderson, January 16, 2015, https://www.mdanderson.org/newsroom/md-anderson-receives-top-chinese -science-and-technology-award.h00-158984289.html.

244 **vice president flew to Beijing:** This was reported on the State Administration of Foreign Experts Affairs website, http://www.safea.gov.cn, on August 28, 2017. The site has since been shut down following government reorganization.

CHAPTER THIRTY-NINE

248 **call it Club Fed:** Asher Hawkins, "In Pictures: America's 10 Cushiest Prisons," *Forbes*, July 13, 2009, https://www.forbes.com/2009/07/13/best-prisons-cushiest -madoff-personal-finance-lockups_slide.html#598e985d3fb6.

248 **oncologists from Wake Forest:** *U.S. v. Mo Hailong*, Document 660 (November 1, 2016).

249 **"old friend of the Chinese people":** "'Old Friend' Branstad Is Welcome as Next Ambassador, Says Beijing," *China Daily*, December 9, 2016, http://usa .chinadaily.com.cn/world/2016-12/09/content_27623451.htm.

250 **Branstad faced off with Miller:** "US Considered Ban on Student Visas for Chinese Nationals," *Financial Times*, October 2, 2018, https://www.ft.com /content/fc413158-c5f1-11e8-82bf-ab93d0a9b321.

250 **"is a spy":** Annie Karni, "Trump Rants Behind Closed Doors with CEOs," *Politico*, August 8, 2018, https://www.politico.com/story/2018/08/08/trump-execu tive-dinner-bedminster-china-766609.

250 **"easy to win":** Donald Trump, Twitter post, March 2, 2018, 2:50 A.M., https:// twitter.com/realDonaldTrump/status/969525362580484098.

250 CHINA IS NOT AFRAID: *Da maoyizhan? Zhongguo bu pa shi*," Xinhua, March 26, 2018, http://www.xinhuanet.com/politics/2018-03/26/c_1122588181.htm.

250 **hundreds of millions in revenue:** Edward Balistreri et al., "The Impact of the 2018 Trade Disruptions on the Iowa Economy," Iowa State University Center for Agricultural and Rural Development, September 2018, https://www.card .iastate.edu/products/publications/synopsis/?p=1281.

250 urging farmers to take: Rod Boshart, "Branstad Urges Farmers to 'Take the Long View' in U.S.-China Trade Dispute," *Gazette*, July 14, 2018, https://www .thegazette.com/subject/news/government/branstad-urges-us-farmers-to-take -the-long-view-as-trade-dispute-between-china-and-united-states-continues -20180714.

251 $2 billion decline: Balistreri et al., "Impact of the 2018 Trade Disruptions."

251 got less than $5 . . . large agricultural companies: Donnelle Eller, "Dozens of Iowa Farmers Get Less Than $25 from Trump Tariff Assistance, Data Show," *Des Moines Register*, November 25, 2018, https://www.desmoinesregis ter.com/story/money/agriculture/2018/11/25/federal-trade-assistance-trickles -iowa-farmers-hurt-trade-war/2065652002/.

251 "Many Iowans remember": Terry Branstad, "Responding to China's Ad in the Des Moines Register, Trump's Ambassador Calls Out China," *Des Moines Register*, September 30, 2018, https://www.desmoinesregister.com/story/money /agriculture/2018/09/30/ambassador-terry-branstad-says-china-uses-us-free -press-bully-farmers-over-trade-war-tariffs/1454749002/.

252 argue against regulating them: In April 2018, for example, Facebook CEO Mark Zuckerberg told the U.S. Senate Commerce and Judiciary Committees that the United States should strike a balance between the need to obtain "special consent for sensitive features like facial recognition" and the risk that "we're going to fall behind Chinese competitors and others around the world who have different regimes for different, new features like that." Natasha Lomas, "Zuckerberg Urges Privacy Carve Outs to Compete with China," *TechCrunch*, April 10, 2018, https://techcrunch.com/2018/04/10/zuckerberg-urges -privacy-carve-outs-to-compete-with-china/.

252 a former Dow executive: Marc Heller, "Trump Picks Entomologist to Lead U.S. Farm Research Programs," *E&E News*, July 17, 2018, https://www.sci encemag.org/news/2018/07/trump-picks-entomologist-lead-us-farm-research -programs.

252 a probable carcinogen: Other regulatory agencies have arrived at different conclusions.

252 A new name: It wasn't the first time Monsanto executives proposed changing it.

252 "all of the efforts": Charla Lord, email correspondence with author, July 29, 2019.

253 "great building's tottering crash": Cao Xueqin, *The Story of the Stone*, vol. 1, *The Golden Days*, trans. David Hawkes (London: Penguin, 1973), 143.

253 an "evil mastermind": Interview with Robert Mo.

254 "No consequence for law": Ibid.

254 "competitor that is not Caucasian": Tara Francis Chan, "State Department Official on China Threat," *Newsweek*, May 2, 2019, https://www.newsweek.com /china-threat-state-department-race-caucasian-1413202. Skinner was later fired.

254 "control, domination and exploitation": "Guiding Principles of the Committee," Committee on the Present Danger: China, https://presentdangerchina.org /guiding-principles/.

254 a "stealth jihad": "Terror from Within: A Panel Discussion on 'Stealth Jihad,'" Center for Security Policy, February 11, 2019, https://www.centerforsecurity

policy.org/2009/02/11/terror-from-within-a-panel-discussion-on-stealth
-jihad-2/. Frank Gaffney has also advanced the falsehood that President Obama
might be a closet Muslim.

255 **"He caught a Chinese national":** Michael R. Pompeo, "Remarks to the Iowa
Farm Bureau," March 4, 2019, https://www.state.gov/remarks-to-the-iowa-farm
-bureau/.

BIBLIOGRAPHY

Alford, William P. *To Steal a Book Is an Elegant Offense: Intellectual Property Law in Chinese Civilization.* Stanford, Calif.: Stanford University Press, 1995.

Andreas, Peter. *Smuggler Nation: How Illicit Trade Made America.* New York: Oxford University Press, 2013.

Applebaum, Richard P., Cong Cao, Xueying Han, Rachel Parker, and Denis Simon. *Innovation in China.* Cambridge, U.K.: Polity Press, 2018.

Austin, Greg. *Cyber Policy in China.* Cambridge, U.K.: Polity Press, 2014.

Ben-Atar, Doron S. *Trade Secrets: Intellectual Piracy and the Origins of American Industrial Power.* New Haven, Conn.: Yale University Press, 2004.

Bitounis, Leah, and Jonathon Price, eds. *Technology and National Security: Maintaining America's Edge.* Washington, D.C.: Aspen Institute, 2019.

Cai Yuanzao, ed. *Guangyuanshi wenshi zike.* Guangyuan, Sichuan: Guangyuan City Government, n.d.

Cao, Cong. *GMO China: How Global Debates Transformed China's Agricultural Biotechnology Policies.* New York: Columbia University Press, 2018.

Cao Xueqin. *The Story of the Stone,* vol. 1, *The Golden Days.* Translated by David Hawkes. London: Penguin, 1973.

Carlin, John P., with Garrett M. Graff. *Dawn of the Code War.* New York: PublicAffairs, 2018.

Chang, Iris. *The Chinese in America.* New York: Penguin, 2004.

———. *Thread of the Silkworm.* New York: Perseus, 1995.

Chinese Exclusion Act, The. Directed by Ric Burns and Li-Shin Yu. San Francisco: Steeplechase Films and the Center for Asian American Media, 2017.

Clampitt, Claudia. *Midwest Maize: How Corn Shaped the Heartland.* Urbana: University of Illinois Press, 2015.

Culver, John C., and John Hyde. *American Dreamer: A Life of Henry A. Wallace.* New York: W. W. Norton, 2001.

Deng, Peng, ed. *Exiled Pilgrims: Memoirs of Pre–Cultural Revolution Zhiqing.* Leiden: Brill, 2015.

Dikötter, Frank. *The Cultural Revolution: A People's History, 1962–1976*. New York: Bloomsbury, 2016.

Dillon, Michael, ed. *Key Papers in Chinese Economic History Since 1949*. Leiden: Brill, 2016.

Dong, Xiaoying, et al. *Zhongguancun Model: Driving the Dual Engines and Science and Technology and Capital*. Singapore: Springer, 2018.

Eftimiades, Nicholas. *Chinese Intelligence Operations*. Scott Valley, Calif.: CreateSpace, 1994.

Fialka, John J. *War by Other Means: Economic Espionage in America*. New York: W. W. Norton, 1997.

Fink, Steven. *Sticky Fingers: Managing the Global Risk of Economic Espionage*. Chicago: Dearborn Trade, 2002.

Fussell, Betty Harper. *The Story of Corn*. New York: Alfred A. Knopf, 1992.

Golden, Daniel. *Spy Schools: How the CIA, FBI, and Foreign Intelligence Secretly Exploit America's Universities*. New York: Henry Holt, 2017.

Greenberg, Karen J. *Rogue Justice*. New York: Broadway Books, 2017.

Hamilton, Peter. *Espionage and Subversion in an Industrial Society: An Examination and Philosophy of Defence for Management*. London: Hutchinson, 1967.

Hannas, William C., James Mulvenon, and Anna B. Puglisi. *Chinese Industrial Espionage: Technology Acquisition and Military Modernization*. New York: Routledge, 2013.

Harris, Shane. *@War: The Rise of the Military-Internet Complex*. New York: Houghton Mifflin Harcourt, 2014.

Jen, C. K. *Recollections of a Chinese Physicist*. Los Alamos, N.M.: Signition, 1990.

Johns, Adrian. *Piracy: Intellectual Property Wars from Gutenberg to Gates*. Chicago: University of Chicago Press, 2009.

Koehn, Peter, and Xiao-huang Yin, eds. *The Expanding Roles of Chinese Americans in U.S.-China Relations: Transnational Networks and Trans-Pacific Interactions*. Armonk, N.Y.: M. E. Sharpe, 2002.

Krige, John, ed. *How Knowledge Moves*. Chicago: University of Chicago Press, 2019.

———, ed. *Writing the Transnational History of Science and Technology*. Chicago: University of Chicago Press, 2018.

Lee, Wen Ho, with Helen Zia. *My Country Versus Me: The First-Hand Account by the Los Alamos Scientist Who Was Falsely Accused of Being a Spy*. New York: Hyperion, 2001.

Lewis, John Wilson, and Xue Litai. *China Builds the Bomb*. Palo Alto, Calif.: Stanford University Press, 1988.

Lindsay, Jon R., Tai Ming Cheung, and Derek R. Reveron. *China and Cybersecurity: Espionage, Strategy, and Politics in the Digital Domain*. New York: Oxford University Press, 2015.

Mattis, Peter, and Matthew Brazil. *Chinese Communist Espionage: An Intelligence Primer*. Annapolis, Md.: Naval Institute Press, 2019.

Mendell, Ronald L. *The Quiet Threat: Fighting Industrial Espionage in America*. Springfield, Ill.: Charles C. Thomas, 2003.

Mertha, Andrew. *The Politics of Piracy: Intellectual Property in Contemporary China*. Ithaca, N.Y.: Cornell University Press, 2005.

Nasheri, Hedieh. *Economic Espionage and Industrial Spying*. Cambridge, U.K.: Cambridge University Press, 2005.

Pollan, Michael. *The Omnivore's Dilemma*. New York: Penguin, 2007.

Potter, Evan H., ed. *Economic Intelligence and National Security*. Ottawa, Canada: Carleton University Press, 1998.

Rose, Sarah. *For All the Tea in China: How England Stole the World's Favorite Drink and Changed History*. New York: Penguin, 2010.

Schweizer, Peter. *Friendly Spies: How America's Allies Are Using Economic Espionage to Steal Our Secrets*. New York: Atlantic Monthly Press, 1993.

Sibley, Katherine A. *Red Spies in America: Stolen Secrets and the Dawn of the Cold War*. Lawrence: University Press of Kansas, 2004.

Smith, C. Wayne, Javier Bertrán, and E. C. A. Runge, eds. *Corn: Origin, History, Technology, and Production*. New York: Wiley, 2004.

Stober, Dan, and Ian Hoffman. *A Convenient Spy: Wen Ho Lee and the Politics of Nuclear Espionage*. New York: Simon & Schuster, 2001.

Sulick, Michael J. *American Spies: Espionage Against the United States from the Cold War to the Present*. Washington, D.C.: Georgetown University Press, 2013.

Tchen, John Kuo Wei, and Dylan Yeats. *Yellow Peril! An Archive of Anti-Asian Fear*. New York: Verso, 2014.

Thrall, A. Trevor, and Jane K. Cramer. *American Foreign Policy and the Politics of Fear: Threat Inflation Since 9/11*. New York: Routledge, 2009.

Twomey, Steve. *Countdown to Pearl Harbor: The Twelve Days to the Attack*. New York: Simon & Schuster, 2016.

Vogel, Ezra. *Deng Xiaoping and the Transformation of China*. Cambridge, Mass.: Belknap, 2013.

Warman, Arturo. *Corn and Capitalism: How a Botanical Bastard Grew to Global Dominance*. Translated by Nancy L. Westrate. Chapel Hill: University of North Carolina Press, 2003.

Weiner, Tim. *Enemies: A History of the FBI*. New York: Random House, 2013.

———. *Legacy of Ashes: The History of the CIA*. New York: Anchor Books, 2008.

Whelchel, Toshio. *From Pearl Harbor to Saigon: Japanese American Soldiers and the Vietnam War*. London: Verso, 1999.

Winkler, Ira. *Corporate Espionage: What It Is, Why It's Happening in Your Company, What You Must Do About It*. Rocklin, Calif.: Prima Publishing, 1997.

Wise, David. *Tiger Trap: America's Secret Spy War with China*. Boston: Houghton Mifflin Harcourt, 2011.

Xiong, Weimin. *Duiyu lishi, kexuejia youhuashuo: 20 shiji zhongguo kexuejie de ren yu shi*. [*Scientists Have Something to Say About History: People and Events in the Circle of Science in 20th Century China*]. Beijing: Dongfang Press, 2017.

Yung, Judy, Gordon H. Chang, and Him Mark Lai, eds. *Chinese American Voices: From the Gold Rush to the Present*. Berkeley: University of California Press, 2006.

INDEX

See also ethnic Chinese, profiling
of; Mo case
Federal Bureau of Investigation (FBI)
corporate relationships, 27–28,
33, 185
headquarters of, 233
and Japanese-American
internment, 240–41
Joint Terrorism Task Force, 116
Most Wanted list, 235
U.S. universities' and research
institutions' monitoring, 243
See also Betten, Mark; ethnic
Chinese, profiling of; FBI
industrial espionage focus;
Mo case
Feldman, Noah, 155
Feynman, Richard, 76
Field of Dreams, 52
FISA warrants, 120–22, 206–9
flashlight seed breeding, 112–13, 232
Florida International University, 12
Foreign Intelligence Surveillance Act
(FISA), 120–22, 206–9
Foreign Intelligence Surveillance
Court, 206
Fourth Amendment, 142
Freedom of Information Act (FOIA),
71, 74

Gaffney, Frank, 254
Gates, Robert, 32
General Motors, 25, 26
genetically modified corn
and agribusiness consolidation,
47–48
Chinese ban on, 55, 56, 64,
68, 114
Chinese reactions to, 54–55
environmental opposition to, 50,
55, 91, 189
Monsanto, 2–3, 47–49, 54–55, 56
patents on, 48–49

and pesticide-resistant weeds,
91–92
stacking of traits, 92,
160, 161
and Syngenta takeover, 238
Global Times, 157
glyphosate. *See* Roundup; Roundup
Ready seed
GMOs. *See* genetically modified corn
Grant, Hugh, 85
Greenpeace, 55
Green Revolution, 85
Griess, Jason
and case theories, 163–64
and FISA warrant, 206, 207–9
Mo case role, 205–6
and Mo indictment, 176
and Mo pretrial hearing, 220
and Mo's defense attorneys, 192
and Mo sentencing, 226–27, 228,
229–30
and Mo Yun case dismissal,
214–15
and Mo Yun pretrial
hearing, 213
and seized seed analysis,
161, 206

Hartnett, John, 234
Heartland Co-op, 68
He Fangxun, 9
Hi-Bred Corn Company, 46–47
See also DuPont Pioneer
Holden flashlight breeding case,
112–13, 232
Holden Foundation Seeds, 112
Hoover, J. Edgar, 71, 74, 233
Houston Chronicle, 242
Howley, Sean, 108
"How Red China Spies"
(Hoover), 74
Huang, Kexue, 35
Huntsman, Jon, Jr., 188